ALEXANDER

His most valued possession was a copy of the *Iliad*—whole sections of which he memorized by night. By day, he moved his men to the very edge of the world—and perhaps a step beyond.

An ascetic who indulged in the excesses of massacre, he was inflexible in tracking down his enemies and yet lacked exultation in his victories.

He was a constant dichotomy—the perfect enigma. A man without a formal title, he is remembered by the world as Alexander the Great. Here is both the *man* and the *conqueror* in all his complexity.

ALEXANDER OF MACEDON

by Harold Lamb

PINNACLE BOOKS   NEW YORK CITY

ALEXANDER OF MACEDON

Copyright © 1946 by Harold Lamb

A Pinnacle Books edition, published by special arrangement with Doubleday and Company, Inc.

ISBN: 0-523-00877-5

First printing, July 1976

Cover illustration by Ken Kelly

Printed in the United States of America

PINNACLE BOOKS, INC.
275 Madison Avenue
New York, N. Y. 10016

He lifted the civilised world out of one groove and set it in another; he started a new epoch; nothing could again be as it had been.

W. W. TARN, *Cambridge Ancient History* (Vol. VI)

CONTENTS

Alexander
of
Macedon

ONE

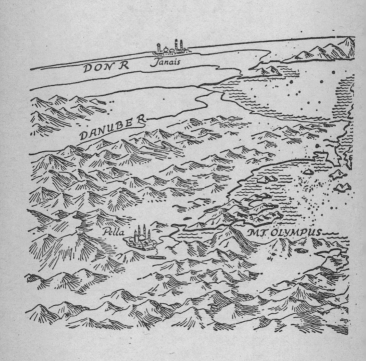

I. THE PASSAGE OF THE
CHARIOT OF THE SUN

When we hear of him first he was alone. Not that he was left to himself, because people always kept near him. He was alone in what he wanted most to do, and alone in his thoughts.

The thing he valued most was a copy of the *Iliad*, or *Troy Tale*, which he read at night until he knew much of it by heart. After reading it, he put it under his wooden headrest for the remainder of the night. So he thought a lot about Achilles, and one of the tutors nicknamed him Achilles. In the time just before sleep, when the lamp was taken away, the boy traveled with the heroes of the book across the sea and landed upon a strange coast in the east. That parchment book was something that belonged to himself, that he did not need to share with Kinsmen, Companions, tutors, or even the Theban veteran.

The tutors who drilled him in Greek and such things as rhetoric and logic had been selected by his mother. Rigid Leonidas, the governor of the tutors, was Kinsman on his mother's side. They filled the hours of the day for him, calling him before the first light, to run with the foot slave over a measured course before he tasted food.

"A run before daybreak," chanted the tutor at the starting point, "gives you a good breakfast. A light breakfast gives you a good dinner."

The boy ran a thousand paces, with knees bent in the lope of the mountain folk, out to the cemetery. At the turning point he could see the white marble of the shrine upon which had been carved the words: *I am an immortal god, mortal no more.* They used the pillar as a marker and started back on the other side of it, racing uphill to the city. The boy went eagerly, because the streak of sunrise along the mountain ridge meant that the chariot of the sun was rising out of its stable in the distant Ocean and starting on its course across the sky. When clouds moved over the mountains he thought he could see the heads of the horses uptossed. At the finish line by the first trees of the palace he lengthened his stride and drove ahead of the slave runner. He would not let himself be beaten, nor did the slave dare to outdistance the boy.

When he went in and anointed his hands by the embers of the altar fire he felt as if he were still greeting the racing sun. There in the east it was soaring through the heights of the gods who knew no darkness and never slept.

He took incense from the casket, scattering it recklessly over the embers, waiting for the vapor to rise and the glow to warm his cold face, muttering, *"To the God-Father, to his son born of the horned serpent— may they watch over us, and protect us."* Spoken in the darkness, these words would have been empty patter; now, in the growing light, they were spoken to those far-off benefactors, those mighty souls, patient and watchful.

That was how he thought of the shining fellowship of the gods, of Zeus and fleet-flying Aphrodite, who had whispered counsel to Achilles.

When he heaped incense too plentifully on the glowing altar Kinsman Leonidas touched his arm, speaking in a dry voice: "Powdered myrrh is not sand, to be thrown away by the handful."

At such times the boy felt choked, with a tightness pressing around his brain, and he could not speak. Frankincense and myrrh came a long way, it was true, from Araby; they had little enough of incense in the house. But they had appointed him to make sacrifice. How could he take a pinch of the precious stuff, to make a gesture of offering, in order to make the incense last a proper number of days? It seemed to him that he had to offer all of it, or nothing. Yet he could not explain his feeling about that to the Kinsmen.

It was not easy to talk with his mother's Kinsmen. They told him what he must do, and he did it. The boy understood why Leonidas would not allow him to run with his father's race horses on the new track, saying that mountain folk like the Macedonians had to climb mountains. Leonidas would not let him eat corn that was finely ground and softened with milk, explaining that the entrails of bear and the marrow of boar would give him courage, which he lacked.

Every day after the morning sacrifice Leonidas searched the cupboards in the boy's room to see if his mother had smuggled in honey cakes or bowls of milk wine—as she often did. The Kinsmen were doing their duty by him and training him like a Spartan because, they said, he would need courage to perform the duties of a king.

He was not sure that they believed in the gods. They said the earth was hung like a flat bowl, beneath its covering sky, within the immensity of Night. There had been no life upon this earth until Light came. Only old Chronos—Time—had been at work before that.

And now Light dwelt in the east, with Zeus the God-Father. From that height in the east where the chariot of the sun gained light in its course Prometheus had stolen with the first fire. Prometheus had been chained to those mountains of the barrier range in the east by way of punishment.

To the west, the boy knew, existed only the shadows of a twilight over Ocean. There the light of the sun's chariot was quenched in Ocean. And thither went the souls of men after death, to become slaves of the shadows, seeing no light.

He heard Leonidas say once to Lysimachus, the Greek tutor, that he, Alexander, was a devourer of books, an acolyte of sacrifice, who tried to escape reality and would never be a man of action like his father Philip. Alexander clung to the books because when he was immersed in them no one stood over his shoulder to

7

tell him what he must do or hear next; the friends within the parchment rolls went nimbly at his side, laughing and joyous, telling him all their secrets—they went as if on wings out of the city, to islands in the far seas.

"Has my father any friends?" he asked Leonidas once, abruptly.

The Kinsman seemed surprised. "Your father is King——" he began, and checked himself. He knew well what the boy meant. Had Philip, King of Macedon, any companions who were more than wine companions, who shared his thoughts and loved him in spite of his failings? Leonidas considered and answered honestly but carefully. "He has Parmenio and Antipater. Yes, and Demades the Athenian."

He had named two generals of the army and a politician.

"And who have I?" the boy persisted. "Name three."

This time Leonidas answered without thought. "Ptolemy, Nearchus, Harpalus—although I could name a dozen as easily."

A dozen, Alexander reflected, was the number of boys about his own age—from twelve to fourteen years—selected by his mother to share his classes with the tutors. Ptolemy, a year older than he, was quicker to learn and quicker to jest. *His* mother had been Arsinoë, a Greek prostitute-companion who dyed her hair in the eastern fashion. Although she never confessed it, Ptolemy believed that Philip himself had sired him by Arsinoë. So Ptolemy secretly thought himself equal if not superior to Alexander, yet placed beneath Alexander because his mother was not acknowledged.

Nearchus, on the other hand, had been born away from the mountains, in Crete. He had voyaged on ships from island to island, although he did not talk about it. Just now he was kept in the city as a hostage, and Alexander did not know what he thought about that. In fact Nearchus seldom said anything, he followed the

8

boys about, his brown face expressionless, and agreed to what they wanted to do. Alexander liked Nearchus, who never quarreled: but there was a gulf of silence between them. In the same way he shared nothing with Harpalus, who was a peasant's son and often too sick to study. His mother had selected Harpalus because she said Alexander must come to know all types.

"I asked the names of three friends," Alexander exclaimed angrily. "Not companions."

The Kinsman looked at him curiously. "A man's friends must be of his own making," he said after a moment. "You should know that by now."

Next to the loneliness was the fear. Alexander did not talk about that. When he thought of it he thought of the Theban veteran. The soldier from Thebes had a scar running down from one eye that made his face like a twisted quince. He had been brought from Thebes by Philip, who had spent his boyhood years there as a hostage and had learned the Theban phalanx drill in that time. Alexander remembered well what Philip had said when he brought the Theban to the boy. "If ever you wage war you must first learn how from those who are supreme in the making of war." And he had winked his good eye confidentially toward the boy, so it was not clear whether his words had been meant for the silent Theban or the equally silent boy.

This Theban was no giant of a man, but his muscles interlocked like twisted chains. He could take the twelve-foot *sarissa* spear in the fingers of one scarred hand and whirl it around his head. He could throw the heavy weapon thirty paces ahead of him.

Yet he trained Alexander not with the sarissa but with the sword. These swords were light, bright-polished iron that sang when the edge struck against metal. The Theban polished them after every exercise. If you kept a sword always in your hand, he said, like a walking staff or hunting knife, you would grow ac-

9

customed to one and could really use it. You could strike without thinking what you had to do.

Alexander resented the heavy words of the old man. Such talk of war by a phalanxman was as if a barley farmer discoursed on philosophy. He wondered if the Theban suspected he was afraid of weapons. Especially when he faced Ptolemy in a sword duel. When he fitted the clumsy wooden practice shield on his left arm sweat dampened his palms. He felt a paralysis of cold settle on his stomach—something quite different from the warm eagerness of headlong hunting or the sport of throwing javelins at a mark.

Ptolemy was slighter in body and cleverer than he. Running and training and riding had made Alexander hard. Straight he stood, with his head held on one side a little, his level blue eyes fixed on his opponent, the tangled red-gold curls bound back from his eyes. He had his mother's delicate skin that reddened over his face and body rather than darkened to brown under the sun. Like her, he had beauty.

But Ptolemy fought viciously, carefully, easily managing to keep ahead of Alexander in the count of blows scored on the wooden shield. Clearly, he showed that he was superior in skill. Then, at times, he hurt Alexander on the side away from the watching Theban—flicking the sword blade suddenly against his thigh or the side of his head, to draw blood and induce the Theban to stop the fight. Then Ptolemy would smile, as if tired of playing with such toys.

Once the Theban had not stopped the sword fight between the boys, and Alexander found himself limping so that he could barely shift his weight from one foot to the other, and blood running into his eyes half blinded him. He tried to shake the blood clear of his eyes; instead Ptolemy's face shone through a red haze, and suddenly the coldness went out of Alexander. His sword felt light, his arm moved free, and his legs drove him forward. Behind the red veil Ptolemy's shield was breaking, and his sword wavered helplessly.

Alexander felt the fierce warmth of a headlong hunt,

when he pressed close upon a weakened deer. Then he heard the Theban shouting, "Rest!" and the Theban's spear knocked the swords apart. Ptolemy was sobbing and staggering about, badly hurt.

The Theban held fast to Alexander's right arm and walked him away, until he quieted. "If you can't master that temper," he growled, "you won't live long."

To Philip the veteran made a different report. "He is incredibly fast, and he is much more dangerous than the others. But he sweats like a racing horse at the touch of chariot harness, and he loses his head. I doubt if he will ever learn to use weapons as he should."

"If so," Philip said, "he can thank his mother for it."

The same cold fear seized on Alexander when he tried to swim the river during the spring flood. Nearchus did not mind the flood. He went into water and worked his way through it methodically, as if it were a wheat field to be crossed. He drifted down the swift current but he got across. Alexander fought the water, and his breath failed him, until he had to turn back. It seemed to him that the Cretan boy had some skill or power that he could not have. However, the good-natured Nearchus did not boast of any such skill. "A water rat can do it much better." He grinned.

And Ptolemy got in one of his gibes at Alexander. "You are a marvelous runner. Why don't you enter for the Pythian games next year—if you're too young for the Marathon?"

Alexander thought of the crowds watching the great games, the athletes straining over the grass course, the chosen runners of the world. He shook his head.

"You're afraid of not coming in first," Ptolemy jeered. "A king's son shouldn't lose, should he?"

"I would enter," Alexander burst out, "if the others were kings' sons."

Ptolemy smiled.

The servants said that water would always be dangerous to Alexander. The spirit that resided in deep water was hostile to him, and no sacrifice could alter

11

that. Nearchus, who had been brought up on the blue sea, said that here in the mountains the torrents were dangerous enough, spirits or no spirits.

Why Alexander hated the city, his father's city of Pella, is not clear. It had no wall, because Philip declared it needed no wall; it was small and gray, with houses of granite blocks built like barracks. It had no gardens, and its streets were winding alleys with stairs leading up and down the hillside. Perhaps, because he was confined to it, the boy felt that it served as a prison for him; perhaps the constant building made the place as unsettled as if it were recovering from an earthquake. The new houses had pillared porticoes in the Greek style, yet Pella was ugly and dwarfed compared to the great Greek cities in the south.

Philip had insisted on moving down from their old home at Aegae in the hills to this lake near the seashore. "If we have no ships," he grumbled, "at least we can move the city nearer the highway." And for once his wife made no objection.

The handsomest place in their new capital was the hippodrome. Philip had designed with care for his race horses, down by the lake. ("We do have good stables," Alexander's mother had remarked when she first saw the racecourse laid out.)

His mother, who journeyed constantly to the Mysteries at Delphi and the markets at Corinth, belittled Pella to him. The city, she reiterated, was being made according to Philip's plan; he would leave nothing for his son to build after his death. And he had no more sense of design than a horse herder.

Perhaps Alexander hated Pella because of the pent-up antagonisms within it. Although Philip was absent most of the time with the armies, he domineered over Pella, not liking anything to be done in the city except on his advice.

Then Pella in its narrow upland valley was close to the great highway. From the ridge over the cemetery you could see the dark glint of the Great Sea; you could trace out the white line of the distant King's Way along the coast. Philip had nothing to do with that. It had been built by the Great King Xerxes, who came out of Asia to subdue Greece a century before, and it was still the best highway to the east.

Along that highway one day came a procession of men from the east. The procession wound up the dirt road to Pella in a haze of dust of its own making, and through the dust shone bright purple coats and cloth-of-gold tunics. Never had the boys seen such splendor.

"From Asia," said Nearchus, cupping his hands to shut out the sun glare. "They would be Magi wearing those tiaras."

"Showy," muttered Ptolemy enviously.

Alexander watched the horses, fascinated. Some of them were the largest he had ever seen, moving with a thrust of the haunches as if spurning the hillside down from them. Others moved nimbly, their small, delicate heads constantly upturned. Alexander had not seen such breeds as these before. They were finer than the best of the Thessalians.

It did not take the boys long to learn that the strangers were ambassadors from the King of Asia—Persians, the Greeks called them. Alexander hung around the entrance steps, staring, wanting to examine the equipment of the easterners but afraid to attract their attention.

"Philip being away as usual," Ptolemy muttered, "with all the Companions, there is no one above the rank of captain to do the honors for these folk."

In fact the envoys had dismounted and were standing in the shade while their baggage came up, looking around with amusement at the rambling streets of Pella. Then a woman house slave hurried to Alexander, saying all in a breath: "The Lady Olympias, your mother, greets you, bidding you salute the ambassadors and find quarters for them."

Alexander edged forward, his throat dry, unable to think of words. His mother had this way of forcing him to do things. She was more imperious than Philip, who

13

contented himself with watching the boy quizzically as if he were a foal of dubious breed. The visitors paid no attention to the boy, who wore an old wool shirt and loose riding trousers. When he had wine brought out for them, they refused it carelessly. It seemed they preferred water

The Magians among them wore white silk; their dark faces were thin and intent. They spoke in low, quick voices, as they inspected trays of gold objects and lengths of silk, pearl-sewn, that must have been gifts. Alexander heard Ptolemy laughing. But he was fascinated by a Persian horse that had a square of padded leather strapped behind its shoulders, with a cord dangling down on each side. The cord ended in twin loops.

"Footrests," explained one of the visitors who could speak Greek.

Immediately Alexander swung himself to the back of the horse, which reared, startled. The boy caught the rein, clung close to the great, arched neck, pleased. He got his feet into the loops, and the horse quieted. A servant tried to pull the presumptous boy off the horse, but an interpreter who had sighted Alexander above the crowd warned the visitors, low-voiced: "This is the only son of the king of the Macedonians; the others are idiots or bastards."

The ambassadors, sipping their water, studied Alexander calmly and answered his questions about the horses. His fear and shivering had left him, once he had to grapple with the great horse.

On such horses, the visitors explained, they could ride five hundred stadia—sixty thousand paces—in a day between sunset and sunrise. Because of the heat of their lands, they often rode in this fashion during the hours of darkness. The roads of Asia were wider than three streets of Pella, and relays of horses were kept at stations along the routes, so that by changing horses they could go without stopping.

This fired Alexander's curiosity. His questions tumbled out, one after the other. How far had they come—how had the crossing of the Great Sea [the Mediterranean] been made? How was their king called?

"Artaxerxes the Great King, the King of the Lands of the Earth."

Those lands, what were they, and how far did they stretch toward the place of the sun's rising? And this the ambassadors could not tell him. Not one of them had journeyed the breadth of the Great King's lands. They only knew that twenty-three nations inhabited those lands. One of them had heard it said that if a rider were to journey along the post roads without stopping, from west to east, he might come to the far end of the empire in a hundred days.

"And how many days have you spent in crossing Macedon?"

"Three."

Alexander had forgotten about welcoming these ambassadors and ushering them to quarters. The Asiatics were sitting around the steps helplessly and the boy was deep in his questions, when a silence fell, as abruptly as a cloud passes over the sun.

His mother Olympias appeared on the terrace above them, escorted by Kinsman Leonidas and a few guards. And no priestess coming before the curtain of the Mysteries could have attracted more attention. Indeed she looked like the priestess-princess she was, with myrtle twisted into her dark curling hair, her girdle shaped like a silver snake, her voice chiming melodious as a golden bell. "Greeting to the envoys of the Great King of Asia. Olympias of Macedon bids them enter her home."

The ambassadors neither answered nor moved at once. They were startled. Olympias, no more than thirty years of age, was the most striking woman of the northern mountains, and she knew well how to frame herself against a background. The gray monotone of granite walls and gnarled oaks brought out the coloring of her flesh, the challenge of her eyes. In silence the ambassadors began to climb the stairs, picking up the trays.

"What nice gifts." She smiled. "Shall I accept them for Philip?"

Alexander thought: She is very angry with my blundering. Ptolemy thought: How well she places herself in the center of the stage! Aloud he asked the boy, "You questioned them about everything except the girls of Asia."

"Women in the east," Alexander defended absently, "are secluded and veiled; they live apart from men who do not talk about them. At least so Herodotus says."

"Well, if you are content to learn about girls from books! Achilles!" Suddenly Ptolemy laughed. "If that's so, I wonder what they think about Olympias?"

What the Persians thought about Olympias was not easy to discover. They hid their thoughts and uttered only complimentary speeches. Yet the Magians among them kept their eyes turned away from the lovely queen of the Macedonians as if the sight of her might do them injury. Ptolemy noticed this, hopefully. His mother, Arsinoë, had the superior education of a Greek prostitute, and she had warned him that Olympias was a dominant woman intent on ruling, yet not intelligent enough to do so wisely. The dark-browned Olympias, Arsinoë confided to him, was still at heart what she had been before marriage, a girl devotee of the wild rites of Dionysos. She had never matured into a wife; she would never escape the slavery of her own ungovernable temper. Besides, even though a princess by birth, the *Despoina* Olympias was stupid. She had been brought up an orphan in the forests of Epirus and had given herself with passion to orgiastic worship of the hidden gods.

So the intelligent Arsinoë enlightened her son, warning him that he must never offend Olympias in a personal matter. That would be as dangerous as stepping upon one of her tame snakes.

That evening, after Olympias had received with her own hands all the gifts of the ambassadors from Asia intended for Philip, she sent for Alexander, and—as he had anticipated—tongue-lashed him with fury. "What

16

a dumb calf you are—what a bookworm, burrowing into dusty rolls of writing! Arrhidaeus could have greeted the ambassadors more fittingly!"

She had taken the myrtle out of her thick hair and was combing it savagely, paying no attention to the slave girl who tried to help her. And her words had barbs upon them, because Arrhidaeus was Alexander's bastard half brother who went around stealing food and stuffing his mouth so he always slavered and stammered when he tried to speak. The Kinsmen knew and Alexander suspected that because Arrhidaeus had been born of a Thessalian dancing girl Olympias could not tolerate the sight of him and had fed him as a child enough poison to numb his mind without killing him.

Alexander said nothing, knowing that his mother would get over her rage quickly.

"Feeding your mind with dreams about Achilles," she muttered, wrenching at a coil of hair, "when you have no more passion than a monk."

Alexander waited.

"Of course the tutors call you Achilles. And do you know why? To please me. Although"—and she relaxed a little—"you do have a splendid body for a stripling. But why did you have to seize upon a pad on the back of a horse to argue about with the envoys? Hadn't you seen a thing like that before?"

"No," Alexander began to explain eagerly, "and that thing they call a saddle makes it much easier to keep your seat when the horse——"

"Yes, the horse. Precisely, the horse! There speaks the Macedonian farmer. There speaks the breathing, living image of Philip, the son of Amyntas the horse breeder. Do you wonder, child"—Olympias now addressed the little slave—"that the Greeks say the forebears of the Macedonians were centaurs—men above and horses beneath? Even now you can't separate a Macedonian from his horse."

"Perhaps that's why," the boy laughed, "our cavalry can ride around the Greeks."

This pleased Olympias, who longed to see in her

17

backward Alexander some instinct of leadership such as the boy Ptolemy displayed. Unfortunately Alexander was not really interested in cavalry—only in horses. That was a Macedonian trait. They were all farmers at heart. Even the phalanxmen who were being drilled in a new way by Philip insisted on returning home for the spring planting and the fall harvesting.

"That is one of Philip's pet ideas," she answered her own thought rather than Alexander's word. "A military aristocracy of the soil—a nation that is an army, an army that is a moving nation, farming and fighting. The Greeks found out long ago that a soldier can't be a proper citizen, and the other way around."

Sometimes Olympias probed shrewdly at the truth. An accomplished actress, she could recognize pretense in others, and she had very few illusions. Moreover, her ancestors had ruled over folk who came to the Princess of Epirus [Albania] to have sickness healed or omens explained. The orphan girl Olympias had been in truth the youthful princess and priestess of a people. Now upon her son Alexander centered her jealousies, her passion, and her longing to create a second dominant self. She fought in Alexander everything that might belong to Philip.

Particularly she impressed upon the boy the inferiority of his father's people, the Macedonians. They had lived, she pointed out, too long in their mountains, keeping to the old ways of clan life. They had no true nobility; even the Companions who accompanied and advised Philip were no more than the owners of the biggest horse herds. Their songs were herders' chants, their dances bucolic stampings and whirlings when they stacked up the last of the harvests. They were still afraid of omens, and of drought and pestilence among the animals. Among these Macedonians had there ever been one orator, one philosopher or general or monarch equal in fame to a second-rate Athenian?

Alexander knew well the ignoble part his people had played in great events. Macedonian foresters had hewn the timber that, floated down to the sea, had built

Athenian warships. Macedonian horse breeders had supplied the Greek cities with animals. Their farms had produced the barley, grapes, and meat requisitioned—and paid for—by the invading armies of the great Kings, Darius and Xerxes. The highly educated Greeks had a right to call the Macedonians barbarians and peasants.

Until his father's time the only wars fought by Macedonians had been to beat off inroads of the forest folk from along the Danube or raids of the equally wild Scythian horsemen. Not until Philip possessed himself of the gold and silver mines around Mount Pangaeus had the Macedonian kings had a currency of their own. Until then they had used the fine silver coinage of Athens. Now the Pangaeus mines brought in a thousand talents a year; but this did not satisfy Olympias. "So we have become miners as well! Again we draw wealth out of the holy soil, and what wealth? It would not have hired General Xenophon's division of ten thousand Greek mercenaries—not that your father will consent to hire mercenaries, even when the Pharaohs of Egypt pay for a guard of Spartans."

In the eyes of Olympias all that Philip contrived was ignoble and wrong. She fought against Philip's will and she surrounded Alexander with the Kinsmen of her house. She made the palace slaves report to her all that Alexander did. She made the boy feel that she had no one except him to depend on, and Alexander did feel that he and his mother stood alone and disliked by Philip, who kept away from them on various pretexts.

Philip spoke to the boy of that estrangement only once. "I won't keep on sharing your mother's bed with the snakes," he muttered, closing his bad eye. He made a joke even of this.

The large snakes did have a way of emerging suddenly from the ivy hung about Olympias's sleeping room and the fans she used in the sacred dances. But the boy wondered why Philip should be bothered by ordinary serpents. Certainly it was no secret that Philip had been passionately bound, body and spirit, to his

19

bride at their marriage. He had craved her from the moment of their meeting that night during the Dionysian festival on the sacred island of Samothrace, when he had seen her in wavering torchlight, running, tearing at her garment, and crying out, possessed by the spirit of the god. From that moment, people said, until a year after their marriage bed, he had not left the side of the splendid orphan girl. Even when she had been delivered of the boy, Philip had been her devoted lover.

That birthnight old Aristander the Telemessan, the diviner, had come to Olympias's couch and had told her that at sunset he had seen a vision of flames rising from the eastern sky. And in time this omen was verified, because on that birthnight the temple of Aphrodite at Ephesus had burned on the Asian shore.

"And that night," Philip added, "one of my horses had won a course at the Olympic games."

Now Philip avoided Olympias, who was more beautiful than in her madcap girlhood. Philip drank of nights with his soldier cronies. And Philip drunk was a different man from Philip sober. When he was hot with wine he might throw his arm around any handsome woman he met in the corridors and force her to his room. Many of the women took care to keep out of his way, while others did not. Yet it does not seem that Philip loved any woman after Olympias.

Much as Alexander hated Pella and feared his father, he found that in some way when Philip came to Pella—which he rarely did now—the city changed its aspect. Visitors hurried in—job hunters, agents of the rich Delphic oracle, merchants, pilots, horse traders, mathematicians from Syracuse, bits of all the Mediterranean world, bringing information to Philip and trying to get a word from him. Pack horses moved faster through the alleys, and the hammers of carpenters rang louder on timbers, because Philip of Macedon was in Pella.

"Through the dust and uproar Philip limped, refus-

20

ing to ride a war horse to ease his lame leg. His brown, bearded face shone with sweat, and he kept wiping at the eye that had been blinded by a shield point. One arm hung stiff and useless. He boasted that he still had one good limb and organ of every kind, and two good testicles.

Never, apparently, did Philip read a book. His letters he dictated to a secretary who followed him around, parchment and marker in hand. Alexander used to steal off to the racecourse and watch the horse tryouts, keeping on Philip's blind side as much as he could. At such times he felt relaxed. Near the limping, cursing Philip he felt more secure than in the silence of his rooms by the women's quarter, where his books were piled.

He was down at the hippodrome early in the morning of the day when Philip sent all the teachers and tutors out of the palace.

Philip was watching the test of a new machine called a *gastraphete,* a catapult that shot a six-foot dart farther than a bowman could send an arrow. When Deiades, the conceited engineer-designer from Syracuse, released the catch, the twisted ropes snapped, the wooden machine thudded violently, and the heavy dart flashed away. Philip grunted. "Now take it down," he ordered.

To Alexander's surprise, two workmen flung themselves on the machine and began to wrench out pegs and cast off ropes. The thing came apart like a wheat stack when the blinding cord is slipped. "Now let's see you load it," Philip added mildly.

With some effort four of the men shouldered the various parts of the catapult and began to walk around as if on a march. Alexander had heard some talk of the new portable artillery Philip and Deiades were designing, to be carried with the field army. This, apparently, was one of the new type of engines. Stoop-shouldered Deiades watched the exhibition exultantly, saying loud enough for Philip to hear that so light a

21

catapult, with such power, had never been fashioned before.

Philip's good eye fastened on Deiades. "The power is sufficient; the weight is still too much by half. No four men could carry all that stuff uphill——"

"Two horses could."

"Two horses could do it nicely. Only, Deiades, in your magnificent self-adulation, you have forgotten that this catapult has to shoot something. Twenty of those heavy darts will load two more men, or another horse. No, you'll have to really scratch around and find a tougher seasoned wood and lighter hemp strands for the ropes."

Shaking his fists in the air, the machine designer howled, enraged. "Find, you say! Just *find*—a bit of Hermes' staff, or witchwood! Scratch around, for a rope lighter than this ten-ply Byzantine hemp!" Thrusting his heavy head at Philip he spluttered. "Shall I clip the tresses off your golden-haired curls, Philip, to make ropes fine enough to suit your fancy——"

"No," Philip shouted. "A woman's head of hair is heaviest of all—I've tested it. As far as I'm concerned your contrivance is lumber, as long as it takes six men to transport it."

"You think so?" Deiades ground his teeth to show his disdain. "It could make dogs' meat of any six men you pick."

Philip turned to Antigonus the One-Eyed. "Have this dart shooter set up again and send for five Cretan archers. Then clear the mid-field and I'll prove to this ivory-headed designer how wrong he is. Find out from him how he would like to be buried."

Deiades glared and called to his workmen to set up the catapult. Antigonus studied Philip uncertainly. Because Philip prized the engine designer more than the staff generals like Antigonus, he had a way of quarreling with Deiades's work, pretending it was faulty in order to drive the engineer to think of something better. So also did Philip mock at Antigonus, to make him exceed his efforts. There was no telling what was at the back of Philip's agile mind. Antigonus knew well enough that here in the open field Philip and his five archers would make short work of Deiades and his workmen and the catapult.

"These catapults are only fortification, pieces," he growled. "So if you're really minded to test it, let Deiades set it up on a housetop and let the archers assault it."

Instead of calming down Philip exploded. "Hell's cisterns and fish-eyes in the soup! How many years have I told all of you, in good plain Macedonian that even you can understand, One-Eyed, that I *do not want* to hear anything more about siege engines. And that I have no slightest intention of being pent like a sheep behind a wall; nor do I have the slightest desire ever to assault men who are fortified behind a wall and engines. The Spartans are the dumbest humans whelped out of women, but even they have learned to keep away from walls, out in the open."

Antigonus grinned. "Well, if you want a machine that can march with men, why don't you hitch a horse to it? One horse call pull this dart dingus."

Immediately Philip's shouting ceased. "Yes, if we put wheels on the shooter. We've done that. This piecemeal takedown is for mountain work. But suppose one horse pulls the machine—you need a man to drive the horse. Well, is it worth a single cavalry-man, in the field?"

The others were accustomed to following Philip's lightning—quick change of ideas. "Yes," said Antigonus, "no horseman could ride against the javelin of a catapult."

But Deiades was still smarting under the king's jeers. "Why didn't you say it could be put on wheels? In that case I can give you a discharge of six javelins instead of one."

Philip spun around. "Six—at once?"

"Certainly, with a bar projector. It won't have the range of this beauty, and," he added hastily, "you'll have to allow for a horse-drawn cart in addition, to carry the weapons for such a multiple machine."

Wiping at his blind eye, Philip pondered, visibly pleased. He began to pat Deiades's heavy shoulder. "Even if this one-shot machine is a bastard, never mind. It will bother a phalanx badly enough. But put your mind, Deiades my genius, on the six-shaft apparatus. Ask for anything you need. I'll give you its weight in g— in silver, Deiades, if it passes its test."

Deiades breathed deep and lifted his head with pride. "I can meet any stinking test," he shouted for all to hear, "if you'll simply tell Deiades *what* you have in mind."

And he waved to his workmen to carry away the pieces of the new-model catapult.

"If you make him angry," Philip muttered to Antigonus, "he often produces something really useful." He nodded, twisting his thin head on his stiff neck. "Six javelins at one discharge! From a hundred machines, six hundred missiles—held until the range is close . . ." His lips moved inaudibly. "But I'm afraid, I'm afraid. By the time Deiades is finished with this invention it will be heavy enough to need a team of horses to pull it over a day's march. That means still another pack horse to carry fodder for the other two. And that means at least three men . . ." His good eye roved around until it rested on Alexander, ten paces away. "That's the trouble with engineers. They always want to make machines bigger and heavier, without thinking once how we're going to find transport for them. If Deiades had his way we'd all be hauling moving towers, flying bridges, mine hoists, and fire projectors. Yes, he'd expect to turn the cavalry into teamsters and draft horses."

Philip scrutinized Alexander to discover if the boy gave his words any attention. But Alexander, perched on a course marker, was wholly intent on a string of colts from Thessaly that were being put through their paces in mid-field by Philip's inspectors, who picked out the best of the animals.

24

One of these yearlings gave constant trouble by trying to break away from its holders. Its smooth black coat shone in the morning sun glare; its nervous head, tossing and pulling at the halter, was marked by a single white blaze. Alexander could not take his eyes off this black colt with the gigantic limbs and massive head. He went over to it, as close as he dared approach the busy inspectors.

When they turned to examine the black horse it backed away, making a swirl among the men as it circled and kicked out. It's handlers, losing patience, tried to throw a cape over its head. When one jumped to its back the colt reared, and he was thrown heavily. It seemed to Alexander that this colt with the white marking of an ox on his great black head was almost human in feeling such distress and excitement when the men crowded around, shouting at it. One of the inspectors said it must have some internal strain to make it so savage. And Alexander felt a longing for this defiant colt. It was superior to all the other horses he had seen.

He ran over to the officers around Philip when he heard the inspectors reject Oxhead—Bucephalus—as he christened the black colt. He shoved in beside Antigonus. "It's a shame to lose that horse," he cried. He was quivering with suspense, knowing that no one paid attention to him. "Look," he blundered, "you mustn't—that colt——"

Antigonus only glanced at the colt, now being led away. And Alexander felt his body grow hot with rage. "Listen," he shouted, "or it will be too late."

They stopped their talk then, and Philip stared, blinking, at his son. Antigonus the One-Eyed explained about the rejected colt. An inspector added that, besides being unmanageable, the black yearling was held at a price of thirteen talents by its owner. Alexander felt the sting of tears in his eyes and choked. Philip began to talk about a transport train again, without heeding him.

25

"It's the finest horse," the boy cried, "and they don't know how to manage him!"

This time Philip paid attention to him. "Are you trying to tell me that the inspectors can't handle a colt?"

Alexander saw his mistake but he felt desperate. "I can manage this horse. I can bring him under my hand."

Philip did not smile. "And ride him around the course, and hold him to the rein?" he asked.

When Alexander nodded Antigonus put in, "And if you can't, what will you pay up for your foolishness?"

"Thirteen talents, which is the price of Bucephalus."

The men laughed, all except Philip, who asked if Alexander had thirteen talents. The boy said no, but he could get the money. Philip said, "You have made a wager. Now go through with it. By the same token, if you gentle this—this Oxhead, he is yours."

Alexander started to run out toward the black horse and for a moment he felt the paralyzing chill that seized him when he faced Ptolemy with a sword. Remembering that Bucephalus had struggled against a blinding cloth, the boy loosed the cape from his own shoulders, letting it fall as he came up to the horse at a walk. When he took the rein and motioned the handlers away the cold feeling left him. Talking to Bucephalus, he saw the muscles quivering under the smooth hide, the restless flickering of the ears, and he loved the colt. Gently he turned its head around into the sun, still talking.

Not until the horse thrust its muzzle down toward the grass did the boy jump to its bare back, without tightening the rein. Bucephalus tensed, leaped forward, and Alexander bent down to keep its head into the sun by pressure on a rein. He did not strike or kick the horse but when it galloped free, coming into the racecourse, he hauled in on the rein, turning it into the runway. For a moment the black horse strained forward, then yielded to the rein, rounding the course at an even canter and slowing when the boy checked him. Not until then did Alexander notice that all the

26

staff officers and his father were watching him. Antigonus called out that it was neatly done; but Philip only gave command to pay for the colt out of his private account. Then he motioned for Alexander to come with him and limped over to a deserted tier of stone seats.

When they were out of hearing of the others Philip grunted, "Lovely to look at, but how was it done? Did you bribe the handlers to make the horse cut up?"

This stung the boy. He almost shouted, "What are you trying to make out?" Thinking about it, he explained curtly that he had watched the men inspecting the colt, and at that early hour the long shadows of the horse and restless men had twisted along the ground in front of Bucephalus and must have frightened the colt. Alexander had only turned its head into the sunlight and had treated it quietly. There was nothing the matter with the splendid colt.

"Umm," Philip grunted, and asked what Greek stuff the boy was reading now. Philip himself spoke only the harsh Macedonian dialect, which made his utterances sound abrupt, but Alexander suspected that he understood eloquent, polished Greek well enough.

Excited over Bucephalus, grateful to his limping, swearing father, the boy poured out in words his newest delight—he had been searching out all the tales of Heracles, the son of Zeus, the mighty archer, the slayer of beasts who wore the mask of a lion's hide on his head and journeyed without fear into the regions of outer darkness, killing the witch Hippolyte and taking her girdle, then crossing the stream of Ocean itself——

The boy had mastered every variation of the *Heracles Tale,* and he confided in his father his discovery of the hero.

Restlessly Philip listened and then exploded: "Hell's sweet sewers! You've been grazing on hero tales. First Achilles and his white armor—now Heracles in a lion's pelt." Philip coughed and spat irritably, because he could not think of the right words to use with Alexander. "Ptolemy has a head for politics, Amyntas, your cousin, knows a deal more mathematics. Yes, Arrhidaeus would know better than to chant a hymn to Heraclse! Now let's hear you read."

When anything bothered Philip he worried at it, like a hungry panther getting marrow out of bones. Taking Alexander off to his littered study, he made the boy read loud the whole of an oration of a young Athenian, Demosthenes. Alexander felt stirred by the majestic sentences that rang out like choral tones, invoking the citizens of Athens to take up arms and die rather than surrender their rights to a tyrant. *I hold him to be our enemy, for everything that he has done until now has been a gain to him and a harm to us.*

It bothered Alexander, although it did not seem to trouble Philip, when he discovered that the tyrant against whom Demosthenes stormed was Philip of Macedon, his father.

Indeed, while the boy read with feeling Philip lolled on a bench chewing at a bunch of grapes, listening not the less intently. At the end, when the boy laid down the scroll, thrilled by the power of the peroration, Philip nodded—it had been well read—and asked if he liked it.

"All but the attack on you, Father," Alexander said honestly.

"It *is* an attack on me—one of Demosthenes' Philippics. He is a modern Heracles, laboring for an ideal good—yes, trying to cure the weakness of a city-state by a fine ideal." Philip fell utterly silent, rubbing his injured arm, his thoughts going far away from them, as often happened with him. "You might call it the rule of the people, that ideal, that democracy of his. He is a magnificent speaker-to-the-people—demagogue, the Greeks call it—and I'd judge that speech to be worth a brigade. Now read this—here."

Fishing among a pile of letters, the lame man tossed Alexander a thin strip of parchment. "A copy of course." And the boy read: *"Philip to Demosthenes the Athenian: Greeting, and welcome at any time to speak before me at Pella and return safe."*

This, even if written by a scribe, pleased the boy, because it was generous to invite an enemy in this manner. It showed that Philip could be magnanimous as well as cunning and avaricious. But when he said that, Philip fell into silence again, seemingly not pleased. (And not until years afterward did Alexander learn how Demosthenes had come, to be received with ostentation and to be made so nervous by Philip's ceremonious preparations for his speech that the high-strung orator broke down and made such a labored effort, people thought he could find nothing to say before Philip. For Demosthenes stammered at times.)

"By the way," observed Philip suddenly, "this great Athenian says that you are a bookish, sacerdotal worm. What do you think, eh?"

Alexander laughed. "Perhaps he is right."

Philip swore softly. "Your tutors agree that you can do anything you have a mind to, in the way of study. Here you are, stinking of incense, golden-haired, girl-eyed, I don't know what! Building stairways to Parnassus in imagination. Faugh!" Abruptly his voice roared at the boy. "Why can't I put iron in your milky flesh? How else are you going to meet danger, eh? Do you think milk calves will live, when the herd starts to run?" He glared helplessly, angered at himself. "Never mind, you, never mind. Don't look like a stricken moon calf. We soldiers ever use words like tools, to shape acts. I'm afraid—it irks me to see you buried alive in books, a suppliant at a shrine, mocked by a Demosthenes. Eh, you make me think of Astyanax, killed by conquerors——" And Philip cried out in Greek words: *"A poor, dear child: uncrowned by manhood or by marriage: or by kingship that makes of man a god: in service of his country*—why don't you read Euripides instead of those Homeric legends? Or if you want to meddle with sick souls learn to be a doctor." Philip stopped abruptly. "A physician. No physician or blacksmith was ever murdered."

Something in this thought pleased Philip, "Go, boy, hunt up all your preceptors, tutors, and what nots. Tell them Philip has a word to say to them. Don't forget to stable Oxhead. He's a fine beast. I'd like him myself for the ten-stadia course, but he's yours."

And Philip kissed his son over one ear, pressing him hard with his good arm. "What else did they say about Astyanax? I forget—no—*and thou, if nothing else of his, shalt have thy father's shield there with thee!* So you shall. This is a day of good omens, this day of Bucephalus. Tell the gate guard to fetch me some good red Thessalonican wine, no more of that thin Chian syrup. Hail!"

Alexander shouted the message to the guard as he ran out to find the black colt. That night when he curled up on his pallet by the flickering lamp and opened his manuscript of Homer he could still hear the echo of his father's complaining, even when his mind drifted out upon a long galley speeding with straining sail toward his beloved Troy. When his mother came in to kiss him her scent was like the smoke of incense and her low voice chimed, "Philip was drunk again this evening, dear. He sent all your teachers, even Leonidas, out of Pella. He swears he is sending you off on some black colt to school away from Pella in a deserted temple sacred to the nymphs. And what's more, if you can imagine all that, he condemns you to study under one man from Stagyra, a physician named Aristotle. I think his father used to be your grandfather's physician. As if you could be exiled, to study medicine!"

But Aristotle the Stagyrite came. The deserted temple was made over into Aristotle's private academy. It proved to be not far from Pella, and Philip allowed the other boys—Ptolemy and Nearchus and the rest—to go along with Alexander.

Mounted on Bucephalus, Alexander could ride back to Pella in a few hours. And Olympias pretended to be content, because in this matter of schooling Philip refused, in his sober intervals, to change his mind.

II. THE RIDDLE OF THE
EARTH'S SHAPE

Olympias could change her mind as quickly as she moved her eyes. And since she could not get rid of the Stagyrite philosopher and his *academia* for the boys, she determined to profit by him. From her spies she learned that Aristotle taught more than medicine and had a flair for politics—that his closest friend was Antipater, the most reliable general on the staff, and that Philip himself often rode in to consult the eccentric philosopher.

In fact Philip had been so eager to get Aristotle near to Pella that he had agreed to pay a great price: to rebuild all the homes of Stagyra which had been devastated by a war. Olympias could appreciate influence.

"You are old enough to have a mind of your own," she told Alexander. "Don't waste yourself on medicine. This Stagyrite can reveal the scerets of politics and government to you. You ought to be given some authority of your own—especially when Philip's away hunting or marching most of the time. You *should* be regent when he's away.

Authority given to Alexander would mean more power in the queen's deft hands.

Before venturing to visit the new school at Mieza, Olympias, who bothered to read few books, read the tragedies of Euripides carefully, especially the Medea. It seemed to her that Medea had stood, like herself, unaided except by sorcery against the strength of men. And she appeared like a living goddess within the Temple of the Nymphs. When she dismounted from her chariot, her supple body draped in sheer silk, whipped about her by the wind, the boys stared. Few married women ventured out of doors with face and body so exposed. Alexander did not notice but Ptolemy observed that the queen brought with her two handsome slave girls who laughed at the gray stone figures of the nymphs standing along the entrance terrace. To Aristotle, who came out perforce to greet her, she deferred prettily, saying that she was old-fashioned as this deserted shrine, being brought up in the Mysteries, without a notion of science. And she quoted Andromache's lines: *"The only joy of a woman's heart is to have her sorrows ever on her tongue."*

She left behind her at Mieza the impression that this fascinating woman trusted Aristotle with the future of her only son.

To Aristander the diviner she confided that this new-world philosopher named Aristotle lisped and had nothing really to offer in the way of creative ideas. Probably he owed his reputation, such as it was, to being one of Plato's favored pupils and to his habit of denying the powers of the gods.

The boys at Mieza found the temple and the gardens filled with strange *apparata*. Piles of variegated rocks, collection boxes of shellfish, stuffed birds, insects, occupied all the corners, along with furnaces, basins of living fish, books of butterflies and pressed leaves—as if specimens of all living and growing things had been gathered in. They began the study of medicine by examining the blood stream in animals and drawing sand charts of human anatomy. Moreover the Stagyrite himself had little to say to them; a staff of assistants worked with them through the endless experimentation that began with the first daylight after Alexander had finished his sacrifice to Zeus.

The assistants explained that Aristotle worked like that. He would not reason—not at first, anyway. He would only examine and experiment to determine natural causes, answering the *what* before the *why* and avoiding wondering about the *wherefore*. In this strange method of taking nothing for granted it was necessary to learn the causes of sickness before being taught the cures. Not until the noble young Macedonians had advanced beyond the study of natural things could they gain knowledge of phenomena, of the Mysteries. Aristotle had a way of dodging talk about the Mysteries by saying that life was enough of a mystery of one man's mind.

"He's a phenomenon himself," Ptolemy complained. "He doesn't preach, he doesn't teach, he tells us not to believe what we read but to ask questions. And when we ask questions he says he doesn't know the answers.'

This assistants said no, Aristotle had plenty of Mysteries tucked away in his head, of which he had worked out the solutions. He simply didn't believe it to be as important to hit on an answer as to be able to work it out. "It's like that Gordium knot in the shrine over in Asia. Aristotle would say you couldn't untie it without knowing how it was tied. After finding that out any galley slave could undo it."

"And did this mean, Ptolemy reported, that they were expected to work like galley slaves? It seemed so. They might be royal Kinsmen but they were set to sorting out and classifying all the varied species of *things*, from coral to the constellations of the stars. Until they had finished measuring and identifying things they would not be ready to cope with *ideas*.

Into this enormous task Alexander threw himself as if it had been a challenge. It seemed to him that the Greek assistants expected him to fail and that Aristotle himself was secretly amused by his pupil's clumsy efforts. Alexander resented the silence of the philosopher who would never reveal the Mysteries he had ascertained for himself.

Only at the end of the day, in the sunset hour, would the Stagyrite emerge from his study to walk through the gardens with the boys, glancing at the work they were finishing up, his lined head outthrust, his thoughts seemingly off somewhere in the cloudy horizon. And the first direct question he asked them set off Alexander's quick temper. He wanted to know what

33

they would do if they were caught in a small sailing craft offshore with a storm coming up.

Harpalus, the canny peasant's son, said he would knot the sail ropes fast and sail before the wind, holding to the steering oar; Ptolemy would make a quick sacrifice of anything valuable he had, to the Powers of the sea, to secure his life: while Nearchus thought he would unship the mast, wrap the sail around it, secured by the ropes, and let the boat ride behind this sea anchor until the sudden storm blew itself out. Aristotle turned at last to Alexander.

"How can I tell you?" the boy burst out. "How can I know until the thing happens?"

The Stagyrite eyed him thoughtfully for a moment, as if taking notice of him for the first time. "That is well said. It's honest, at least." And he was walking on, dismissing the matter, when Alexander stepped in front of him, angered.

"Well, who is right—Ptolemy or Nearchus?"

"Who?" Aristotle shook his head. "Why, it would depend on the storm, and only a ship's master could tell you about that." His eyes narrowed, forcusing on something. "I can only tell you it would be wrong for this—this Cretan to pray, and for Ptolemy, son of Lagus, to try his luck with a sea anchor."

"That's begging the question. You're being paid to teach us, not to quibble with words. What is the truth? Does the god Poseidon control the force of the waves or does the wind blow of its own accord? Either one or the other must be the truth. You can't divide truth, like a number, into smaller parts!"

Without anger Aristotle continued to inspect the sunset. "When you speak of truth you mean an idea. An idea can be divided again and again, and down and down until you reach what is indivisible."

When you arrived at the indivisible, Aristotle maintained, you knew that you had come face to face with reality. Until then you could not be sure.

Stubbornly Alexander stood his ground, certain that truth couldn't be divided up like a silver drachma. Instead of arguing, the philosopher reached into the nearest specimen case and took out something that proved to be a dried-up crawfish with a tag on it. "What is this?" he asked.

"A small crawfish."

"Yes." Aristotle glanced at the tag. "But it happens to be one of the small varieties from the Cyclades Islands. Yet it may be small only because it is half grown, and it may also be found as far away as the Euxine Sea. It's a crustacean, and also prototype of land shell animals, a vestige of the earliest life that existed in the waters before land had formed. Then again, it is food for a castaway, a rare seasoned dish for a gourmet, related to a lobster, and in miniature forms the kind of sea life that gave rise to legends of sea serpents and monsters of the deep seas. Still, as you say, it is indeed a smallish crawfish." He tossed it back and continued his walk along the path in the glow of sunset.

When he was out of hearing Ptolemy laughed. "And for this we work like galley slaves!" He considered his friend speculatively. "What are you, lad? Come now, let's divide the truth. You're Alexander certainly, and I think nearly full grown. You're the only child of Olympias' womb. Also the only sane and legitimate offspring of Philip. You're human, judging by the blood that runs out of you—it isn't ichor by any means—yet you seem to have a divine spark, bequeathed to you by Heracles or Achilles. Or at least that's what you think. Tell me, do you breathe ordinary air or heavenly ether? Let's see what else. You're a barbarian youth trying to master the wisdom of the Greeks——" He broke off quickly, aware that Alexander stood rigid and silent, holding in his anger. Since the day when he had nearly died in the sword fight Ptolemy had been careful not to irritate the single-minded Alexander too far. "Look, if you want to find out what this Stagyrite believes, pin him down to something. Experiment on him: show him a verse about Medea safeguarding her lover Jason by magic." For a second Ptolemy contemplated Olympias in the role of Medea and added hastily, "You're quite right about one thing—either the gods exist or they don't.

That night Alexander ventured alone into the laboratory, where the students were not allowed after lamp-lighting. Under his arm he carried the roll of a manuscript, worn with much use. And he found Aristotle busied with the assistants over a furnace into which a copper caldron had been set, filled with water. They were observing the hot vapor that rushed from the narrow outlet pipe of the caldron when the water was heated to a high temperature. This vapor jet generated force enough to turn a heavy wooden wheel; yet the philosophers did not concern themselves with the force within the vapor—they watched it fly up against a cold metal plate hung from the roof. On this plate the vapor distilled into drops of water that dripped down like rain. In fact they were making within the laboratory a miniature rainfall.

To the action of this vapor Aristotle paid close attention. He believed, as the boys knew, that beside the four familiar elements—earth, air, fire, and water—there existed a fifth elementary force in vapor.

Aristotle believed that the sun's heat drew vapor from the bodies of water upon the earth's surface and that this vapor encountered a cold stratum of upper air and condensed into rain or snow which fell in turn upon mountain summits, feeding the streams that ran into rivers discharging into the smaller, earthbound seas. From these seas water flowed out through gates like the Pillars of Heracles in the west to the vast enveloping body of water embracing the land mass and known as Ocean. So, as the flow of blood within the arteries sustained life in man, this incessant circulation of water sustained all life throughout the firmament. If this fifth element, vapor, should cease to aid the water flow, rivers and lakes would dry up and life in its manifold forms—insect, plant, animal—would cease, in time.

If rain came in this manner from the circulation of moisture it could not come from the flight of the sons of the North Wind across the sky vault, aided by the Cyclopean giants who struck thunder from the clouds.

For some time the boy watched the drip of artificial rain before Aristotle noticed him. Flushed and holding himself tense against a rebuke, Alexander handed over his manuscript. "Will you note for me," he asked abruptly, "what is wrong in this?"

Opening it, the philosopher found it to be a much-worn copy of Homer's *Tale of Troy*. Without comment the Stagyrite said, "Ask for it again in three days—but not in the night study hour."

To Alexander's surprise, when he examined Aristotle's annotations upon his prized copy of Homer, he found no questioning of the powers of the gods who aided mortals. Only correction of some wording and explanation of many puzzling points, so that the lines were easier to read than before. When the boy demanded why he had merely revised the reading instead of getting at the truth of the *Iliad*, the Stagyrite explained that it was rhetoric, and not a history such as the books of Herodotus. "It is fine work, as a poem. And that is far from being a history of natural things."

"If it were that!"

For once a smile crossed the lined face of the philosopher. "That book has not been written yet."

So at Mieza the boy worked alone, fearful of failing, feeling that the older men had condemned him as stupid. They had no sympathy for his imagining, as he plowed his way through rhetoric, logic, and endless experimentation in their new natural science. He drove himself at this work, determined to find out for himself the truth of the Mysteries in which he believed and concerning which Aristotle would not speak. Apparently Aristotle paid no attention to him and, because he himself worked sixteen hours in the day and night, did not realize that his pupil was overtaxing both eyes and mind.

Carefully Olympias egged him on, saying that Heracles, his ancestor, had achieved greatness by supernatural labors. When she returned from one of her visits to the Delphic shrine she was full of gossip that she had heard at the hostel. "Fancy—the people were saying how fortunate are the Macedonians to have a Philip for their general and Alexander for their king. How strange that they should mention my darling as king—although you *are* sixteen and past the age when many boys serve as regent. Aristotle must know that. In truth he is doing more for you in teaching you to live wisely than Philip, who has done nothing for you except to claim you as his son, and I doubt if that is a blessing."

Imperceptibly she changed toward her son. When he rode the black horse Bucephalus into the grounds at Pella, where Olympias had put the finishing touches to the palace buildings, her servants greeted him with ceremony. She made a point of asking his opinion and showing her dependence on him. Then when he stayed the night she took pains to have young, Greek-trained prostitutes display themselves where he could not help but notice them in the halls. Alexander, she thought, was old enough to need such girls. and Olympias much preferred that he should avail himself of the handmaids she could keep under observation. But the girls reported to her that he noticed them no more than other household servants, as if they were merely slaves to do Olympias's hair or anoint her after a bath.

It troubled Olympias that she could not bind her son closer to her by one of these girls. She scolded them, telling them to use other oils and scents than hers. And then she heard of the fantastic happening with the naiad in the garden.

A gardener's wife related it, frightened, as she had heard it from her man, who had been at the wheat. It had been unbelievable, as if it were a sending from the Powers.

At the end of the day Alexander had been seen riding headlong as usual from the residence across the gardens toward Mieza. He had leaped the black horse over a stone wall and had almost run down a strange girl who was carrying grapes in a woven basket on her head. She had her skirt wrapped around her waist, leaving her legs bare, and she was singing. With the grapes flying and crushing, the young lord had bent down to pick the falling girl in his arm and had swung her up. Her hair spread over him like spun gold threads, waving in the wind. So had he held fast to her, and she had not cried out.

Out in the mown wheat the young lord had stopped the horse and set this yellow-haired naiad down. But he had got down himself with his arm around her and had stayed there with her, pulling his cloak over them, in the wheat field until the sunset had dimmed, so that the gardener could see no more.

When Alexander had gone off this unknown girl had wandered back to look for her basket. And when the gardener spoke to her to ask her name she had not been able to answer in either Macedonian dialect or Greek. So the gardener believed she had been a naiad of the forest, appearing in that hour of the night's beginning and then returning to her forest haunt.

But Olympias, who did not believe in forest spirits who picked a basket of grapes in the out-gardens, had inquiries made at first among the servants and then in the slaves' quarters for a barbarian girl with ruddy hair. And a Scythian was brought to her, who had been bought recently in the Delian market and set to picking wine grapes. When Olympias discovered that the girl had a shapely body and nice eyes and hair even seen by daylight, she ordered the slave to be taken from Pella at once and sold in Thebes. She had no intention of sharing Alexander with a mistress who was not one of her own slaves. She was careful to have the Scythian searched before being hurried off. And as she half expected a token was found on the barbarian—a silver belt clasp ornamented with a lion's head that Olympias herself had given to Alexander. When she threw the clasp into the fire the girl wept.

After the Scythian had been sent off in a closed cart Olympias summoned the gardener and the various slaves who had seen the girl and ordered them to say no word about the presence of the barbarian. If it became known that such a girl had been in Pella even for a night they would all be tied to stones and thrown into the lake. On the other hand, Olympias declared, they need make no secret of the fact that an elfin girl had been seen emerging from the forest the previous evening.

At the end of that day, as she had anticipated, Alexander reappeared with Bucephalus and roamed the outer gardens, going restlessly from wheat field to forest edge. Until full starlight he kept his rendezvous and then sought out the gardeners and slaves, to question them awkwardly about the young Scythian. They all agreed that they had seen only a naiad stealing from the wood to pick grapes.

Alexander asked no more questions. For a while he lingered in the wheat field alone, then instead of entering the palace he rode back toward Miez. It bothered Olympias that he did not come to her then nor speak to her afterward about the vanished girl.

When he stayed to supper next Olympias was careful to order fruits and whipped milk served, with other delicacies. She dressed with some pains in the loose garment of the *threskeuein* devotees of the forest gods, twisting some ivy into the dark mass of her hair. Lying so clad across the table from him, seen between gleaming lamps, Olympias appeared lovelier than any priestess. The Greek prostitutes she had sent away. But she arranged for the music of flute and pipes to be heard at the table, although the musicians remained invisible. Upon this stage so set she hoped to draw confidences from the youth who had always confided in her before.

This evening Alexander would not taste the luxurious dishes, saying that Leonidas had long ago accustomed him to a Spartan meal. Nor did he look full into Olympias's dark eyes. When she questioned him about his studies he said he was working at the shape of the habitable world. At last the queen herself had to mention the servants' talk about seeing a forest girl in the grounds. A naiad, the servants declared. Olympias was skeptical, quite skeptical, about such appearances of the divine so close to human habitations.

It appeared that Alexander was also skeptical. "Naiads don't usually have names," he said curtly.

This startled his mother, who refrained with difficulty from demanding what the girl's name had been. She wondered how the boy, who spoke no Scythian, had learned it. If he knew the slave's name he had a tangible clue to her identity. Briefly Olympias pondered the possibility that she might have a child by him.

Carefully she suggested that this half-human sprite of the woods might have an ordinary name. Such as——

"She called herself," Alexander broke in impatiently, "the daughter of the Sun."

Again Olympias felt a shock of surprise. The children of the Sun were indeed immortals, easily to be recognized by the brightness of their eyes—evidence of their descent from the God of the Sun who drove his chariot of fire across the vault of the sky. She felt relieved that accident had aided her own deceit. For she had satisfied herself that the Scythian was entirely mortal.

That night Alexander went quickly away from Pella, riding headlong down the road, being careful to avoid the gardens. What hurt he felt at the disappearance of the strange girl he had known for the beginning of a night he concealed. He withdrew into one of his moody silences, working through much of the night at a plan of the star constellations, because he found it hard to sleep.

Then Olympias demonstrated that she was shrewd but not wise. Thinking only of herself, she had a way of acting upon instinct. Now something like fear disturbed her. Deeply superstitious, she wondered if the strange appearance of the barbarian girl had not been, in reality, an omen intended for her. If so, what did the sending portend? Olympias worried about that and also about Alexander. She felt that he was no longer obedi-

41

ent to her will; something had changed him, setting him apart from her.

At that time Olympias had no hatred for Philip; she could not endure him because he seemed to be indifferent to her, only speaking to her when they met after absence, when he saluted her in his clownlike fashion as queen mother, not as his proper wife.

Olympias hardly knew the meaning of fear. Now, undecided and having no one to confide in, she sent for Aristander of Telemess, the diviner who could not be bribed like the Greeks. Olympias understood very well that it would take more than money to enlist Aristander in her service. To him she poured out her troubles.

The soothsayer took his time about answering her. "The stars in their courses," he muttered absently, "arbitrate human fate. What were the omens at the birth of *your* son?"

Olympias moved impatiently. Aristander remembered as well as she how the temple at Ephesus in Asia had burned that same night. Still wrapped in thought, Aristander murmured that since then two things had been made clear: certainly she had had no other child, and plainly Alexander was peculiar. "The omen," he continued, "was one of fire. It descended from the heavens. And does not Philip now call you queen *mother?*"

Drawing the dark hair like a veil across her mouth, Olympias studied him. Pride stabbed at her like a goad. "And if fire did descend from the sky that night, and if Philip were not the boy's father?"

"That," declared Aristander, "is something you would know best."

When it came to a question of exalting herself Olympias never hesitated. Moreover Aristander had no more than hinted at what was already in her thoughts. Before the diviner left her the priestess of Samothrace had made up her mind.

Only gradually and by the older servants was it spoken about at the palace, and only then during Philip's absence. It was no more than rumor arising out of the

42

omens at first, whispered in the women's quarters—
that Alexander might not be Philip's son. That an unknown had impregnated the priestess that night, when
a snake had been seen coming from the marriage bed.
Some of the servants pointed out that Philip had seen
the snake and had become blind in one eye soon
thereafter.

Arsinoë, who had belonged to Philip before his marriage, heard the gossip with dread. Now happily installed as mistress of Lagus's house, she understood the
wayward Philip and the explosive Olympias better than
they knew each other. In her fright Arsinoë sent word
to Mieza, to Ptolemy. Her son's future was bound up
with Philip's whims. And the astute Ptolemy found
food for thought in the message.

"Instead of trying to find out what the morning stars
are singing," he warned Alexander, "you'd better lend
an ear to what is said in the market place of Pella."

"What?" Alexander demanded, surprised.

"Nobody can tell you *what*. You have to hear things
with your own ears and see them with your eyes, personally, before you believe anything. Eh, if the vault of
the sky were cracking open you'd go on poring over
map projections until it all came down on your head."

The last thing Alexander cared to do, at that time,
was to visit the market where peasants' wives cackled
over their onions and lentils. If he had not kept himself
buried in his cell with his drawings and notes he might
have been aware of the talk in Macedon, and he might
have avoided both humiliation and exile.

But it seems certain that in those years he never
freed his mind from study. He had labored through the
elementary work, and now he was mastering both politics and cosmography. Now he kept notebooks of his
own and raced through all the manuscripts. Aristotle
would lend him. From this labor in his cell he broke
off only to sacrifice and to walk through the hills in the
night hours. Although still at odds with Aristotle, he
had ceased to rebel at the teaching and was even on
the track of a discovery of his own.

Alexander had discovered, to his own satisfaction, the blank space, the unknown terrain, of the east. There had been in his imagination the place of the sun's rising, now he was learning that there might actually exist unvisited lands at the far end of the terrestrial globe, bordering upon Ocean.

The Stagyrite and his assistant philosophers no longer wasted thought on the early Milesian concept of the cosmos: that of primeval night extending through a void except where the points of light of the sun and moon illumined the earth and the planets revolved around it upon their orbits, harmoniously, creating the music of the spheres.

By now the philosophers had arrived at another concept. The earth they thought to be a sphere hung immovably in the center of the universe. (Aristotle believed this to be proved by the fact that during an eclipse the earth cast a round shadow against either sun or moon. And explorers had testified that in the far north the southernmost constellations of stars were no longer visible.)

About this terrestrial globe revolved the sun and moon, alternating light and darkness on the halves of the globe.

Upon this globe land had risen from the waters throughout the millenniums and this land mass was still extending, still rising, in spite of the corrosive action of the moving waters. But only a portion of this land remained habitable to man. This habitable portion, called the *Oikoumene*, stretched perceptibly farther along the course of the sun from east to west—in its *longitude*—than in breadth from north to south—in its *latitude*.

Above the Oikoumene lay the region of hyperborean cold, of perpetual snow and drifting ice. Aristotle had talked with Cimmerians [inhabitants of what is now Russia] who had ascended frozen rivers to the edge of this polar region. They were hunters, and they reported that there at the borderland of the habitable zone many animals had white pelts—evidence of existence in snow countries.

Below the Oikoumene extended of course the belt of tropical heat where human beings could not survive, and the land tended to become sand, burned by the sun's concentrated heat. Due south of Pella lay the fertile Libyan coast, whereas travelers who had penetrated inland reported that they had been surrounded by illimitable deserts, hostile to man. In those deserts only thornbush grew in the earth and poisonous vipers crawled upon it, while water dug from the ground had been salty and undrinkable. Evidently at this southern frontier of the Oikoumene existed forces that destroyed human life in the same manner as the bleak cold, the frost-bitten earth, the devastating winds, and the great white monsters of the hyperborean north sapped the life from men.

Certainly it seemed apparent that the north-south limits of the Oikoumene lay at no great distance apart and had already been reached by adventurous men such as the Argonauts—the crew of the ship *Argos*.

Aristotle, however, raised a question about these limits of latitude. He asked who had been known to visit the sources of the greatest rivers. Such rivers, if the theory of the global circulation of the waters was correct, must take their rise in distant mountains, where a myriad streams formed the watercourses. Where then lay the source of the mighty Nile that appeared in full girth within the otherwise dry valley land of Egypt? And where were the headwaters of the Danube, almost as huge as the Nile, that flowed through the forests north of Macedon, down to the far Euxine Sea [the modern Black Sea]?

Animal and plant life must exist, Aristotle argued, along such water sources. And if so, men could survive there. Yet no Greeks had penetrated to the sources of the Nile or Danube.

Alexander had his mind fixed on the far eastern limit of the Oikoumene. The western limit, whither the sun vanished, offered no attraction. In the Mieza laboratory he could study notes of the voyages of those rival traders, Phoenicians and merchants of Carthage who had seen and even passed through the western water gate of the Interior [Mediterranean] Sea. Between rocky heights called the Pillars of Heracles, or the Mount of the giant Atlas, water flowed out from the Mediterranean to the encircling Ocean. In that strait of water herds of strange dolphins had been encountered that played around the galleys, beyond the thresh of the oars. Farther out stretched the dark surface of the Ocean itself, subjected to the buffeting of the winged sons of the North Wind, and the screaming furies who were emissaries of the God-Father, Zeus.

Thus in the west the limit of human advance was fixed not only by the impassable Ocean but by the hostile leviathans of the deep salt waters, which could crush sailing galleys as easily as a man could break apart a wasp's nest. So said the venturesome mariners.

Even Aristotle had slight interest in the far western latitudes. He did not believe, as Plato had, that out upon this Atlantic portion of outer Ocean extended islands known in legends as the Blessed Isles, or sometimes as the lost island of Atlantis. He did not believe it for the simple reason that he had come across no evidence of it. Nor would he waste thought upon a lost Atlantic civilization—pointing out that civilization seemed to have advanced from east to west, not the other way around. At least the sciences had been known in Asia before they were known in Crete; apparently the Greeks had learned from Asia also, especially from Egypt.

This only set Alexander more firmly on the path of his discovery.

By now he felt certain—and Aristotle did not deny it—that the eastern limits of the Oikoumene were not known at all. True, the *Iliad* mentioned the threshold of Asia, the water gate of the Dardanelles where Troy stood. Troy had been there without a doubt. Yet the Argonauts had passed beyond, along the chain of waterways, through the Dardanelles, into the far Euxine. Somewhere around the Euxine factual knowledge ended and myth began. Suppose those voyagers, the

Argonauts, had actually been searching for gold washed down from the mountains instead of the legendary golden fleece? Still, they had ventured into the mythical mountains at the end of the farthest sea, those mounts of Caucasus where the Titan Prometheus had been bound, his giant shape rearing within reach of the predatory birds of the upper air. Present-day voyagers to the Greek colonies in the Euxine reported seeing the loom of vast mountains rising into the cloud level where their summits were covered by everlasting snow. Through this mountain barrier of the Caucasus the mariners said a gate gave access to the unknown farther east. Yonder, some Asiatics believed, lay the inland sea called the Caspian, frequented by giant bird life, by Amazons, and by unknown celestial powers.

This Caspian, if it truly existed, might flow northward to the outer Ocean.

By ancient reckoning, or surmise, Greece, and therefore Macedon, lay almost in the center of the Oikoumene. From Athens, for example, it seemed to be about as far to the water gate of Heracles in the west as to the land gate through the Caucasus in the east. But Alexander wanted rather to believe the venturesome thinkers who placed the center of the habitable world much farther to the east.

In this unknown area of the east Alexander believed that the true gods might still exist.

Patiently he gathered together all the threads of evidence he could find, reading through legends and stories of eastern voyagers in the study hours of the night while Aristotle buried himself in the laboratory experiments. He no longer pored over Homer before blowing out the lamps. Still he did not confide much either in his companions or in the scientists.

By following the track of his idea, as if tracing a way through a Cretan labyrinth, he made certain of some points.

In the histories of Herodotus facts began to give way to fables about as far east as the Caucasus. The farthest great city to be fully described by this Herodotus was Babylon, whose lofty terraced gardens and sky-scraping towers were a wonder of the habitable world. Yet one Phoenician related that the name Babylon meant actually *Bab-il*, the Gate of God. Alexander knew nothing about the Phoenician language, but he caught at the mention of a gateway. For Babylon lay, it seemed, at about the same longitude as the Caucasus mountain barrier which also had a gateway opening to the east. What lay beyond?

Then, following out Aristotle's method of tracing land shapes by the course and size of rivers, Alexander satisfied himself that two such rivers flowed by Babylon, the twin Tigris and Euphrates. In what area, then, did they have their source? In the heights of the Caucasus or in unknown heights farther east? These twin rivers emptied, without doubt, to the south, into the stream of outer Ocean. But where did they take their rise?

What if the greatest mass of mountains lay beyond the known limits, rising far above the earth's atmosphere into the heavenly ether? What if the twin Tigris and Euphrates flowed out of this immense height beyond which the sun rose out of Ocean itself? What if *this* elevation far above earth's surface were the abode of the Powers, whether men called it Parnassus or Olympus, or Paradise, as the Asiatics did?

Most legends, he discovered, originated in the far-distant east. There, men said, the very Waters of Life flowed out of the ground—the waters that preserved life forever in those who drank of them, There, too, was situated, by all accounts, the Tree of Life, the fruit of which imparted celestial knowledge to humans.

Surely the traces of the gods all led toward this unknown side of the earth. The older shrines stood toward the point of the sun's rising. In every case this was true. Delphia, down in Greece, was younger than Eleusis on Asia's shore; Apollo's temple in Athens had been built long after the sanctuary of Apollo Ammon in Egypt, and that in turn had not existed—so Alexander conceived—when the Chaldeans and Magians of Babylon first worshiped their sun god.

Very soon Alexander discovered that Mieza possessed a drawing of the image of the world by Hecataeus that actually set in place the lands and rivers and seas as if the Oikoumene were visible in its entirety, seen from a vast height.

This he copied painstakingly, adding to it his notes upon the shrines, the routes of the legendary voyagers, and the gates opening into the goal of his imagination, the unknown east.

Unfortunately he could not resist tracing along the eastern border a vast height that dwarfed all other mountain ranges. Upon this he wrote a name *Parapanisades*—the Greatest Wall—as being the only proper name for the homeland of the gods.

Inevitably other eyes saw his world picture, and whispers about the Parapanisades began to be heard in the halls of Mieza. Harpalus, who followed the prevailing fashions, posed on the roof looking through the tubular height finder zealously, explaining that he had dreamed that the summit of the Mightiest Wall that pent in gods and demons had appeared to his sight above the clouds.

Some of the assistants argued with Alexander about the folly of sketching distances on a chart until the distances were paced off by surveyors on foot, in stadia, or steps. Only the seacoasts, they said, could be sketched in, since these were fairly well determined by the transits of ships which, driven by the winds, sailed at a uniform speed.

The Parapanisades talk must have reached Aristotle's ears. Instead of arguing directly with his rebellious pupil he contented himself with pointing out one evening in the garden that the frontier of knowledge was being pushed back steadily, so that more of the habitable world was known with the passing of each century. And in his dry lisping voice he added that, in the time before Homer, Mount Olympus, which they could all see from southern Macedon, had been thought to be the home of the gods. Until, after sufficient explorers had climbed it, this mount was seen to be quite ordinary bare rocks. Then the mythical Mount Olympus was placed, in men's imagination, east of Troy, where some high summits pierced the cloud level. This in turn became known. Now it seemed that men imagined Olympus to lie within the far-off Caucasus. And exploration there, in turn, might reveal only another natural even if lofty mountain chain. He did not mention the word "Parapanisades."

He simply pointed at the garden in which they sat. "Here also are the gods. The impulse of life is here, as it is elsewhere."

But when they were alone he did say something more. The unknown, he explained always seemed mysterious, and on that account both fearful and wonderful. Then he added thoughtfully: "And when men are most alone they hold most closely to myth."

As soon as he could get back to his cell, Alexander took a knife and cut his drawing of the world image into ribbons, ripping them apart in a paroxysm of anger at himself. His labored reasoning, his reaching out toward the unknown, had been no more than a child's citadel of sand built in front of the incoming seas. Aristotle had dismissed his Parapanisades as myth, and the others in Mieza were laughing at his stupidity, as so often happened. The fury of his self-accusation left him silent and shaken.

After that no one spoke again of the ill-fated Parapanisades. And the assistants explained that Aristotle wished his eccentric pupil to concentrate upon politics rather than on cosmography. Alexander did that without protest.

There was no meeting ground between the mind of the middle-aged scientist, intent on his tabulation of natural causes, and the young daydreamer, stubbornly determined to track down Mysteries. Yet pupil and master had mutual respect for the other's capacity to work. Neither one cared to waste time in argument.

Four centuries later matter-of-fact Roman historians mentioned the violence of Alexander's passion for learning. Yet even under Aristotle's guidance he showed no ability to master a single science. He merely gave to his books the same devotion he had given to the shrine at Pella. Left to himself, he might have become a hermit of the academy, following out a labyrinth of thought. If so, he would have lived longer.

Or he might have become a physician, as Philip had intended. It is clear that Philip tried at first to safeguard his visionary son through Aristotle's guidance and the protection of the great commanders of the army. But Philip by then had heard the gossip of Pella, and Philip also had a temper not to be trifled with.

Perhaps because of his loneliness and introspection, perhaps because of his stubbornness at that time, Alexander never forgot and never gave up what affected him closely. Trifles that others passed over struck in his memory. He kept the annotated copy of Homer close by him; he fed and groomed the black horse Bucephalus, now full grown; he practiced the medicine he had learned. And along with the poems he had memorized, he kept the riddle of the mountains that fed the river Nile, and his mythical Parapanisades.

He was sixteen years old when he plunged into the examinations of politics, or city rule—his last work under Aristotle's tutoring.

The philosophers from Anaxagoras to Plato had concentrated upon the problem of designing a perfect state in theory. And that in turn meant to them an ideal city government. Plato had gone so far in his *Republic* as to develop a perfect model, wherein aristocratic thinkers could exist with slave laborers to their mutual benefit.

At Mieza the experimenters pointed out that Plato's city plan was the finest of the Greek attempts to meet the problems of reality by an ideal solution.

Aristotle on the contrary refused to speculate upon what might be the best form of government. He limited his effort to an attempt to determine what *had* worked out best, and when and how and why. So his assistants were at work examining the constitutions and histories of all governments of record—and they had singled out more than one hundred and fifty. These included the various Greek cities, from the Athenian democracy, or rule by the people, to the Spartan military communistic state, or rule by a select warrior group. Among the examples also appeared the tyranny of Crete, or rule by one head, and such oddities as the priesthood rule of the celebrated Delphic oracle which supported itself by payments from visitors.

Going far afield from the Greek cities, Aristotle was also examining the tribal communities across the great river Danube. He compared such rule by the leading family in the tribes to the reign of the Pharaohs in Egypt. The first, he believed, was a primitive form of the second. The barbarian tribes maintained themselves by an economy of war, raid, and some trade. So they were still devoted to the leadership of individual warriors, while the Egyptians sustained themselves by long-established agriculture and handwork, reaching a much higher intellectual level.

Midway between these Danubian tribesmen, with their herds and huts, and the great metropolitan centers of Egypt, Aristotle placed his own people, the Macedonians.

The Macedonians were still young, still barbaric. Only yesterday, in historic time, had they migrated down with their herds out of the northern forest and river lands to these hills at the edge of the sea. They still retained the rude independence of a hunting people. By constant struggle against the invading Scythian tribes and the highly equipped armies of the Greek cities, they had kept freedom, in the sense that they had not been made slaves. Yet they were still subservient mentally to the educated Greeks, and actually inferior to the more sophisticated Cretans, Egyptians, and Phoenicians.

The Macedonians still retained traces of tribal life;

the Kinsmen were no more than blood kin of the royal Amyntas family; the Companions or individual nobles consisted of the great landowning and cattle-breeding families. Any important question had to be decided by the meeting of the commanders of the army, just as generations ago the leading warriors had assembled in council to decide what was best to do for the tribe.

And Aristotle's examination had raised some startling questions. It seemed as if different peoples had been shaped not so much by their governments as by their physical surroundings. Going back to the history of natural things, the assistants at Mizea pointed out, as a shore was eaten away or built up, fertilized or made barren by the action of water upon it, so aminals evolved according to the sources of food or conditions of safety or peril around them. Certainly forest animals differed from those of the grass plains; while they in turn developed differently from the beasts of desert regions.

So in the case of men. Herdsmen on half-barren hills did not develop as the dwellers within a fertile river valley. Apparently a human group domiciled upon a natural stronghold evolved different ways of protecting, feeding, and sheltering themselves from those of a similar group settled upon on an open shore. Had not the different Greeks all sprung from a common stock, in tribal times? Had they not, thereupon, built many small cities separately, because the peninsula of Hellas offered them only small and isolated valleys?

For protection's sake these Greeks had each built their separate stronghold or *polis*—city. They had done so out of necessity, and not because in that pioneering stage they had believed the single city-state to be the ideal state. Moreover, developing in different ways, the cities facing upon the coast tended to rely on sea-borne trade and to hold most firmly to democracy because the building and handling of ships required the co-operation of the community—on shipboard were not all men equal, like the ancient Argonauts, except that they chose someone for leader?—while the land-bound cities tended toward aristocracy or leadership by the elite few who commanded or planned for the armies.

These questions seemed small and irritating beside the grandeur of Plato's ideal city. Moreover, they hinted that the fortunes of a people did not depend upon fate alone.

As to the Macedonians, it was apparent that they had developed no such elaborate city-state, since Aegae and Pella were no more than poorly sited towns without trade, dignity, or the great academies of the more advanced Greek centers. The Macedonians had been confined to peasant life and animal breeding because they had been cut off from the trade routes and even from the coast itself. There seemed, according to Aristotle's reasoning, no possibility of making Pella into such a city as Athens.

In fact he laid down no rules by which a people could progress or a city be well governed. While he pointed out that the environing country influenced a city's growth, and the energy of its inhabitants its welfare, he left unanswered the question, toward what should it progress. Nor would he admit that its future was predetermined by fate or the will of the gods.

Yet Alexander sensed the answer toward which the Stagyrite was working with infinite patience. If human beings could be shaped by their environment they could change themselves in equal measure by their own efforts. If so, they would not be dependent on fate.

Aristotle was working with reality, divided down to its smallest atom. And he—Alexander—had evoked a dream world, real only to his imagination, and then only because it lay out of human sight.

Among the hundred and fifty cases Aristotle made a notation upon Thebes: that the city had been raised above others in the last generation by the supreme ability of one man—Epaminondas—who had created a victorious army and had known how to gather in the fruits of victory—*For the organization of a peace after war is more difficult than the winning of a war*.

And in discussing city rule (politics) he made a further note: *If there exists in a state a person so far above others in virtue that neither the virtue nor the political ability of any other citizen is comparable with his . . . he will be wronged if treated as their equal. Such a man should be held to be as a god among men.*

In reading this, it seemed to Alexander that the Stagyrite believed the spark of divinty lay still within human beings.

He was deep in a study of the influence of sea power upon the overseas expansion of the Athenian state when a rider from the Companions appeared at Mieza and entered his cell. The horseman said that Alexander would join the main army on its march along the Nearer Sea. Engrossed as he was in making notes, Alexander replied that he would be ready to leave at the end of the month.

"You are leaving with me today," the rider informed him. "This is an order."

Instead of making preparations to depart Alexander, exasperated, threw away his notes, caught up his sleeping robe, his copy of Homer, and his knife, and started out to get the black horse, saying in that case he was ready now.

He never returned to Mieza as a student.

If Philip had brought his son from Pella to remove Alexander from Olympias's influence, he did not say so. The one-eyed leader of the Macedonians never spoke about his wife nor did he mention Cleopatra to his son. This gulf of silence between them Philip might have bridged, but Alexander could not.

Nor did Philip himself try to instruct the student from Mieza how to behave when he joined the Macedonian field army. The Macedonians marched. They marched in drifting dust along the coastal King's Way and over goat paths; twenty miles and sometimes twenty-three they covered between the dawn trumpet and the sunset meal. With full equipment and five days' rations they marched faster than any Greek phalanx, outdistancing the news of their coming. And no distance covered seemed to satisfy the impatient Philip. When his Macedonians were on the march Philip circulated through the columns, as he had limped around his building projects in Pella, having apparently neither tent nor headquarters of his own. At night he could be found guzzling by a teamsters' fire or gossiping with the advanced cavalry patrol.

If Alexander had fancied that he would be given a white mantle and the gold-adorned chest armor of an Achilles to wear, riding Bucephalus with the elite Companion cavalry, he was rudely enlightened. He marched with the transport wagons, clear of their dust, carrying his pack and shouldering the responsibility of men and animals and loads. Sweating and swearing, he fought against time to gain distance, struggling with the strange circumstance that a company could not or would not move as fast as one man, and that a line of carts could be held up by one broken wheel. He discovered that horses did not haul their weight unless fed and cared for in legs, hoofs, and guts. Luckily he was a hardened walker, and stubborn.

These Macedonians marched, but not in any apparent direction, or for any discernible purpose; at times they loitered on the open coast, swimming and doctoring the horses; at other times they kept on without stopping for a day and a night. They encircled a seaport and made all preparations for a siege, only to march away when a fleet appeared at the anchorage. By night they moved into a city, only to give it up and start off elsewhere. Seldom did the teamsters of the transport get up close enough to see what the head of the column might be doing.

On the day that Cleopatra visited the column they halted and held races, horse and foot, and wrestling bouts with wine served after. The teamsters swore that Cleopatra was a fortunate girl. Alexander saw her at the games, wearing a half veil over the loose knot of her curled brown hair, close-wrapped in a single *peplos* without a cloak, swaying as she walked—a girl of fourteen at the heels of her uncle Attalus, who pushed arrogantly ahead of other men. Still, Cleopatra kept her eyes half closed, demurely. In passing Alexander she glanced up, as if measuring his strength, then gave a skip, hurrying after Attalus. Small and weak she might be, yet Cleopatra, the niece of Attalus, had the look of Olympias about her.

That night she poured wine for Philip, and the soldiers wagered whether she would go into bed with him. They offered tetradrachmas against drachmas she would not, estimating that she was an ambitious virgin, holding herself for a great price. Then they offered Alexander fruit, which he took, and wine, which he disliked, because they were vaguely aware that Philip's son should have been invited to the feast instead of being left to mess with them.

These soldiers, as Alexander discovered, knew much about the whims, habits and abilities of the commanders, discussing them without mercy, calling Philip the one-eyed Fox and the lame Goat. At all times, whether foraging or fighting or bathing, they grumbled. Mostly they complained of short rations, scant pay, prohibition against looting the coast towns, and the state of the roads which they had to repair as they advanced eastward toward the Dardanelles. Of Philip they complained that he kept them in the field during harvest and planting time, and expected them to carry the loads of mules.

Yet they seemed to find sense in the twisting and turning of the marching. Philip, they argued, was trying to get hold of the coast ports for Macedon, which had been cut off from the sea by these Greek trading settlements. When the Spartan fleet put in, and the army marched away, they had an explanation. The Fox didn't want to waste men in a hot siege now that the city was reinforced. No, he would take another city someplace else and trade it with the Spartans for that one. The Fox always had a new trick to play, and he would waste gold bullion rather than loss of life—which the army thought a most important matter—and he would use up his new machines before he would

57

send men into battle. They explained this, taking care that Alexander understood, since he might command a regiment before long.

They were resting on the path above the gray water of the Dardanelles, trying to make out the round hills of Troy in Asia across the way, when an officer of the Agema—the favored companies that served as guard for the king-commander—laid odds against Alexander's chances of commanding the army itself. The gambler, Hephaestion by name, was young and reckless with the fine manner of an Athenian—he said trade had been the ruin of his family, so he had sold his sword into service. He had a way of mocking at sacred things. Even money he offered that Alexander would never be king, not realizing that he spoke of a man who stood beside him. "For it all depends on Philip's whim, and the Fox is not pleased with his girlish, bookish offspring and may get him another one. What do you say?"

The men said nothing, waiting to hear how Alexander might break out at Hephaestion. They knew that the carefree captain of the Agema was blood kin to the king's son.

"Moreover," Hephaestion pointed out, our Kinsmen, except that tutor-milk-sucker Leonidas, have a feeling against the son of the woman they think to be a witch, and counting Philip out, this army isn't minded to obey anyone except the generals. Those are my points. Who of you teamsters has hard money to lay against me?"

Alexander was looking through the haze over the gray water, seeing red creep into the haze as blood pounded through his veins, when a runner came down the column and stopped before him, saying that the king-commander had been hurt. Philip had sent for his son. Hephaestion looked once carefully at Alexander, hesitated, and drew his short sword, balancing it on the palm of his hand. "It was one chance in ten thousand I should pick you to wager with. But—I lose, and here it is." He smiled, his dark eyes mocking. "Don't make

58

me wait while you make formal complaint of my insubordination. I don't want a hearing—eh, Alexander?"

He could not have thought out a better way to save his life. Alexander sensed the recklessness of the captain and felt that Hephasetion had appealed to him. He touched the sword hilt awkwardly. "I don't want a burial here," he said, "because of a few words."

Philip's hip had been broken in a skirmish up the road and he lay on a stretcher where water flowed from a shrine's font, with his leg stretched out, tied to a javelin; nor would he let Alexander feel around the broken bones.

"More delay," he grumbled, wiping the sweat from his eyes. "We won't see Pella before snow comes. I'm not going back like this." His glance leveled on his son's face. "What's this new rumor that you're wishful to rule in Pella while I manage the army? Would that, be to your liking?"

Parmenio, chief of the staff, and the silent Antipater were listening. If Philip had called them in, it meant that he was having his son judged upon some doubtful point.

Head tilted, his blue eyes troubled, Alexander explained that he would like best to go back to the studies from which he had been taken. As to the talk in Pella, he knew nothing of it.

"It's all through the camp—down to the ranks. Doing as much harm as a plague." As always, Philip's staccato speech followed the swift current of his thoughts. "The *pezetairi*—the phalanxmen—like you, and they are hard as devils to please. Did you know that?"

"No, sir."

A side glance toward the two silent commanders assured Philip that Parmenio did not believe Alexander, while the matter-of-fact Antipater did. "I've been away too long from Pella," he muttered, easing his leg. "Can't be helped. But it *can* be helped. That gossip has sense in it, after all. Yes, you can go back instead of me." Abruptly the wounded Macedonian chuckled. "I'm serious, boy. Don't bury yourself in a doctor's den"—he still thought of his son as a medical student—"but go back and do the honors for me at Pella. In my name, of course."

As if pleased with his new thought, Philip explained to the commanders that from this moment the seventeen-year-old Alexander was appointed regent, during his absence from the city.

Alexander started to object and thought better of it. "Just what authority are you giving me? And what do you expect me to do?"

Impatiently, because the broken bones in his hip tormented him, Philip handed his son the small royal seal with the lion's image on it. "Full authority. Make payments, sign letters. But be careful about making promises. Don't ask me what to do—find out for yourself what you *can* do. Didn't I lay out a cartload of gold so that Aristotle might teach you? Consult with him about politics. Take along a military adviser too—take Antipater here. You'll need an escort, now, so pick a company of the foot Agema. Neither Aristotle nor Antipater will sell you out, boy, and the army will see you don't get in a scrape over a girl." And he added thoughtfully, "You'll have to strike some more coins from the mine bullion, for cash."

With his orders given, Philip hesitated, not knowing how to show personal feeling to his son. At that moment Alexander would have chosen to stay with the wounded man and the troops.

"Kiss me, and farewell," Philip muttered. His dry lips touched his son's cheek, and Antipater motioned the boy to leave.

Tucking the seal absently into his girdle, Alexander wondered if he had been dismissed because he had failed at soldiering or whether Philip actually wanted him at Pella. He felt a surge of gratitude, realizing his father had defied gossip by honoring him openly. But he had no illusions about his ability to manage affairs at Pella. (Later Olympias declared that Philip, who was infatuated with the girl Cleopatra, had wanted to be rid of his son, especially when he found that Alexander was becoming a favorite with the troops.)

When he started the journey home with Antipater the following sunrise he remembered Hephaestion and named that reckless individual to be his guard officer.

Hephaestion towered above Alexander, who was tall enough. This young aristocrat had the strength of a Heracles and the easy laughter of a Dionysos, whether drunk or sober. In most respects he was the very opposite of the single-minded student—relishing fights more than sports, and the wine cup best of all. Where Alexander worried himself into black depression over difficulties Hephaestion took no thought of them, preferring to play the flute instead. Philosophy he dismissed with a grin, quoting Euripides: "*We are slaves of the gods, whate'er they be.*" In proof he cited his own elevation from culprit to commander of the prince's guard within half an hour. "If that isn't a miracle, show me a better one."

His easy good nature delighted Alexander, who kept Hephaestion close to him, having found at last a friend. Ptolemy said spitefully of the pair that Hephaestion was the man of the two.

As Antipater looked after the policing of Macedon, and Olympias immediately assumed the direction of the palace, Alexander was free to spend most of his time in the olive groves of Mieza's gardens, where the Stagyrite worked at his problems.

Still the philosopher would lay down no axioms to his pupil. Greek philosophy, he thought, had stagnated because it had become too abstract in its search after values. Socrates had turned it aside form its quest after pure reason, by his rough questioning. Until Socrates, too many Greeks had limited their efforts to the past—to the *how* of creation, and the nature of the divine powers. Almost for the first time this stubborn Athenian questioner had refused to wonder how human life had come to be, and had asked instead what it

61

might make of itself. His objective had been to find the purpose for which the world existed, not the source from which it came. And in his lone quest of this objective he had been forced to commit suicide.

Aristotle, with his hard peasant's head and his work-stained fingers, was following out this quest. In his reasoning the mystery of the world soul might be impenetrable; but human evolution could be measured and directed, like that of animals—of which he was compiling his history. Men, whole peoples, had developed from something and were changing continually into something else. That process of change could be measured and directed. It seemed as if this process were for the sake of the thing evolved—for the end result, not for the automatic process itself. And if this were true men might be freed forever from the fear of a predetermined fate. Men might be free to shape their own evolution. If they could understand the process . . .

So the Stagyrite discussed with his pupil the first of the Mysteries that he had kept secret until then in his mind. And Alexander, understanding little as yet, was fired by the purpose that lay behind the endless experimentation.

It was Olympias who insisted that he should lead an expedition against the tribes beyond the frontier, who had become troublesome in the absence of the field army. "The people like to see you as a leader, not to hear that you are reading books."

Antipater made the preparations, and Alexander went without enthusiasm. But his mother made the departure a parade, closing the shops for that day and riding at his side in her light chariot—having sent Antipater ahead with the foot soldiers. Bareheaded, on the great horse Bucephalus, Alexander drew enthusiastic shouts from the watchers.

When they were alone, beyond the streets, Olympias drew him close beside her, whispering as she kissed him that she knew he was not as other men. It had been her secret, she confided, but now he had the right to share it.

She had always been devoted to the shrine at Samothrace, where the gods appeared to mortals. And on the night before her marriage she had dreamed that the night wind of the island rushed by her room; the light of the stars had been dimmed and sudden thunder had shaken the house—until light flashed down upon her and spread, kindling flames along the room, until she waked. Upon that night she had been impregnated, and not in Philip's bed.

"Certain it is, Aristander the diviner tells me, that you are a child of the gods."

So Olympias left him, crying to him to bear himself as became his birth. Sighting Hephaestion behind them, she paused fleetingly at the Companion's side, whispering, "That boy! Protect him, but tell him he must stop slandering me to Zeus's wife!" And off she went, waving back, fair to behold as Nausicaa in her chariot.

And so Alexander rode on his first expedition, silent and afraid. He dreaded ridicule, and he felt coldness settle on him like a garment when they began to climb the hills. But he found that he had to do nothing more than ride in the center of his small force, for Hephaestion, who looked on this as no greater matter than a chase after deer, was ready with a word or a jest to help him out of any hesitation, and the veteran Macedonian commander gave all orders.

The highlanders—the Maeti tribe—withdrew to the heights, only annoying the Macedonians with arrows, while they tried to save their heads. On Antipater's advice Alexander did not destroy the deserted town of the Maeti but brought in settlers from the nearest farmlands and built defense towers for them. Hephaestion suggested naming the place Alexandria—Alexander's City—as Philip had recently christened a captured city Philippi. It was a quiet spot in the mountains, where wood smoke drifted through the trees. Alexander reflected that by the Stagyrite's reasoning he and his Macedonians had been like these cattle-breeding Maeti, a few centuries before.

As soon as he returned to Pella he searched for the diviner Aristander and questioned him about Olympias's dream. The man from Telemess did not seem surprised, pointing out that other omens confirmed his mother's belief and that even Philip had a portent in a dream—that he had sealed up Olympias's body when he slept with her, and the seal had borne the impress of a lion's head on it. This portent Aristander had interpreted to Philip as meaning not that he must look closely after his erotic wife but that he must know his son would have more than mortal courage. "These are portents," declared the soothsayer, "that, taken together, may not be questioned. Philip is not your father."

In some fashion word of the diviner's announcement spread through the market place and hostels of Pella. People questioned the priest of the Delphic oracle who was also waiting in Pella at that time. This agent of the Greek oracle would neither confirm nor deny the statement of Olympias and Aristander. Now when Alexander made the dawn sacrifice at the altar facing the east he had to push through a crowd of servitors and slaves who waited in reverent silence for a sight of the golden-haired prince as he made sacrifice to his father, Zeus.

Before one moon had waxed and waned Antipater brought Alexander a message, delivering it himself because it came from Philip.

"Philip, King-Commander of the Macedonians," he said without emotion, "divorces Olympias, Princess of Epirus, daughter of Neoptolemus. He has taken to wife Cleopatra, niece of Attalus."

III. DEMOSTHENES AND THE GRAVES OF CHAERONEA

Philip very soon called his son back to the army, allowing him to serve time with Hephaestion in the elite cavalry.

During that year, the year 438 from the first Olympiad [or 338 B.C.] the conflict between the Macedonian army and the Greek city-states came to a head. It was really the conflict between Philip's ambition and Demosthenes's determination—the issue being the rule of the Greek cities.

Because Greece as a whole did not exist. The Hellenes, separated among their dozen cities, had been united only by the shock of the world war, when the armies of the Asiatics invaded the waters and homeland (from the first meeting at Marathon to the sea and land victories of Salamis and Plataea). When the threat of conquest ended, the Hellenic cities fell apart like the spokes of a broken wheel and involved themselves in the long civil war which became a merciless struggle for mastery between, in one aspect, the land and sea powers, the north against the south, and in its final phase the test of mastery between Athenians and Spartans. Strangely, throughout the raids and sieges, the plague and the final mobilization of manpower at the height of this conflict, Athens had been touched by the splendor of the age of Pericles.

Then had followed the political prostration of the postwar generation, with its weight of taxation, its expanding trade, and its weak efforts to form peace leagues. After a century and a half of wars the famous city-states, dependent now on slave labor, had tried to protect themselves by professional soldiery, which could be maintained by money. Leadership had descended to individual tyrants or dictators or to a religious council. Toward the end of this decline Philip of Macedon displayed his astute leadership—lacking since the death of Pericles—while the Athenian orator Demosthenes used his great persuasive power in an effort to rouse the city-states to their danger.

The conflict for control now centered in these two individuals—Philip, opportunist and realist, seizing every hold upon the disorganized cities of Hellas, posing as protector of the religious council, champion of the Delphic shrine, and benefactor of *demos*, the common man; and Demosthenes, lashing at the inertia of now wealthy Athenians, whipping up the ghosts of Marathon, calling upon a true citizen army to defend the last of the democracies. In this death duel between two personalities the actual antagonists seemed to be two irreconcilable ideas—the fading concept of the free city-state and the nascent concept of monarchy. For Demosthenes in his *Philippics* argued not so much against the human Philip as against the incarnation of power in Philip? *If Philip were to vanish tomorrow, you would find yourselves another Philip. I want an army of the Republic.*

Did the Athenians fear Philip? Demosthenes lashed their fear with scorn. Was Philip a strategist? So was a wolf, slinking out of sight, feeding on dead bodies. Was he handsome and hard-drinking? So was a woman, and a sponge. Would the immortal gods, watching from the skies, bestow favor upon such a lecher, a schemer, a bloodsucker?

Already, Demosthenes explained, the gods had vouchsafed an omen to the Greek patriots. The seeress of the Pythian shrine had given them a verse:

> *The eagles shall see, watching from the skies,*
> *The conquered weep, while a conqueror dies.*

Unmistakably this prophecy meant that the Macedonian invaders would mourn Philip, who would be killed in the coming war.

By the driving force of his emotion Demosthenes got

his army of patriots. He got it into the field by persuading the Athenians that their advantage lay in making war as far as possible from their city, and by shaming the Thebans into becoming allies of the Athenians. (And in these Thebans lay the strength of the allies. The Theban phalanx, formed sixteen ranks deep under guidance of Epaminondas, had overthrown even the celebrated Spartans—the Theban Sacred Band of hoplites, devoted to a life of war, was believed to be supreme on the battlefield.)

So, reassuring, promising, inspiriting, the great orator marched toward Macedon that year with his citizen soldiers, who seemed to him to be the resurrection of democratic power. He marched with the hoplites, his bronze shield on his arm, his only insignia of rank the gold letters on his shield, spelling: "With Fortune."

And from that moment Demosthenes ceased to exert any more influence upon the event than the hoplites trudging beside him. Philip, the trickster, the play actor and consummate commander of men, made his presence felt. The Macedonian army disappeared. At least it could not be found by the Greeks, who advanced in high spirits when they intercepted a message that Philip had departed for the Balkans. The Greek citizen soldiers were bewildered when they discovered that Philip was actually behind them with his Macedonians. The message had been a simple trick.

Anxious and tired, the Greeks hurried down out of the mountains into the long valley near Chaeronea and found the Macedonians there. Even then these Macedonians did not seem like an army ranged for battle. They moved at ease along the valley, not crowded together, and they seemed to have no servants or baggage. They stopped and sat down as if waiting for the foot-weary Greeks to hurry into formation against them.

Far out on the Macedonian flank files of horses moved through a grove, led by men sheathed in bronze down to the hips.

They did not look at all dangerous.

67

The Greeks hurried on. The Sacred Band of Thebes went into its phalanx. Past a small temple dedicated to Heracles, past the village of Chaeronea they went, toward the winding stream that divided them from the horsemen waiting at this rendezvous.

By midafternoon the sun was in the eyes of the horsemen. They had mounted, but they still waited on the rise among the scattered oaks.

These Companions, all Macedonians and noble-born, had been put—all three regiments of them—under the command of Parmenio, chief of staff. From past experience they knew that Parmenio would wait for Philip's order to advance. But no such order had come from the lame leader, who was off somewhere in the battle opposite the Theban phalanx. From the sounds on their left the Companions judged that the Macedonians there had given way and were moving back up the slope. That meant the Thebans had not been checked.

The strain of waiting told on the armored horsemen, even though they were accustomed to it. Through the trees and the drifting dust they could see only that the small regiment of Hypaspists, or Aids, was engaged on their left. At times clouds of kilted Cretan bowmen moved across the slope in front of them, screening them. The level sun, striking into the dust, made it difficult to see more than that.

Restlessly the riders adjusted the shield straps on their cramped arms, shifting their weight, not speaking because they were listening intently. Nonetheless they would have waited in ranks until a command reached them, if one rider had not broken ranks. And if this rider had not been Alexander, the son of Philip.

Alexander had waited on the black horse until his nerves jumped and tore at him. He had been assigned to the Companions with Hephaestion, with the rank of regimental commander, although Philotas, the experienced son of Parmenio, actually commanded the regiment. Beside Alexander a big warrior sat his horse patiently—one Cleitus, called the Black because most of his body was burned to the hue of charred wood by the sun. Cleitus had been told off to guard Alexander's body, so he stationed himself knee to knee with him, pushing Bucephalus over when the black horse moved restlessly. Cleitus the Black had no more nerves than an oak tree.

But Alexander strained to keep his bare knees from quivering; he wiped the drip of sweat from his right hand, tortured by anticipation of plunging into the maelstrom beyond the drifting dust, where sounds rose and fell like the pounding of surf. He breathed quickly, his throat dry. This grip of fear upon him was like a chain tightening with each moment, and with the glare of the sunlight against his eyes. Behind him he felt the other riders were watching him, noticing how he was being overmastered by fear.

Cold gripped his stomach, nauseating him until he had to swallow and cough to keep from retching. Lazily Black Cleitus picked at a scab covering a scar on one brown arm, and the noise beyond the trees changed to the screaming of gulls. But there could be no sea gulls screaming here. . . .

Alexander had to move, to hold down the rising sickness. Jerking at the rein of the black horse, he tightened his knees, and Bucephalus plunged ahead. Cleitus called out something, and a tree branch whipped across his face. He flung up his shield, bending down, as he passed a group of archers who looked over their shoulders, startled.

Other horses followed after him, but he could not see them. Metal grated against his shield, and Bucephalus swerved, so he had to grip hard with his knees. Suddenly he felt the horse rise in a jump. A knot of men rolled and crouched against the ground beneath him. He realized how fast he was going and tried to steady the frantic horse.

Through the dust a group of men took shape, standing as if pressed together, turning a line of spear points toward him. Crouching behind his shield, he felt the black horse stumble and lurch and then race on, fighting for his head. Two wounded men, sitting back to back, held out open hands to him, making a sign. . . .

When at last Alexander was able to rein in the black horse he found himself deep in brush at the edge of a stream. Listening, he heard no voices over the humming in his ears. But he felt desperately thirsty and dismounted to limp to the water, wrapping the rein around his wrist. Lying down, he drank, and then shoved his head into the water. When he wiped his eyes clear he saw Bucephalus drinking beside him. So he waited for the horse to finish. He was breathing easily now, and the sickness had left him. But he did not want to move. Somewhere beyond the encircling brush voices echoed and carts creaked.

Then he noticed that the sky had changed. The glare had gone, and the clouds over the hill were darkening. He stretched his arms and got on the horse, turning back through the break in the brush. When he reached a path he followed it, through an orchard, past a white stone temple where men lay as if flung into piles, motionless.

Alexander could make out only objects moving against the afterglow of the sunset. He tried to account for the missing hours but could not.

Over this cluttered land, he realized, the battle must have passed. It had disappeared now, except for the watch fires that winked into light ahead of him.

A man moved jerkily over the ground, bending down when he heard a voice from the wounded. Alexander noticed him because a squad of armored shield-bearers moved methodically behind the erratic searcher, and then he saw that it was Philip. His father peered at him and yelped, "Praise to the almighty gods!"

He gripped Alexander, felt him over for injuries, and hugged him. "Philotas swore you vanished into the village as if snatched up by a demon. They couldn't find your body. Now I'll give gold to thieving Delphi!" Philip was royally drunk. Suddenly he swore. "Boy, what made you start the Companion regiments off with-

70

out an order? Parmenio had no order. It wasn't time. They said they followed Philotas, and Philotas says he followed you. What devil possessed you, eh?"

"I don't know. I was frightened."

Philip turned his scarred head, to peer at his son, his breath reeking of wine. "Frightened? Don't say that. It wasn't easy, no Chaeronea ridge. Parmenio looked like a ghost—I was scared through my guts. You can't escape that before an action. Only keep your head clear, until your work's done. . . ."

Relief flooded through Alexander, who had dreaded his father's anger. It seemed that Philip felt what he had experienced in the oak grove. Suddenly Philip began to curse, peering into the darkness. Too many men had died in those hours. No such battle as this should have been fought. It was the fault of the charge of the Companions, before the turn in the battle.

Holding to Alexander, and stumbling across the bodies lying in the darkness, Philip went on cursing, tongue-lashing himself and the mistakes that had been made. He had planned to let the Theban phalanx come through—he had placed only a screen opposite that phalanx. When the Athenian hoplites followed, he had meant to wait until they lost formation, believing themselves victorious. *Then* he would have launched the Companions, with the Hypaspists and Thessalian cavalry supporting. . . .

Alexander never forgot that moment when Philip, dead-drunk but clear in his head, led him over to the slope where men searched for weapons among the dead. "The Thebans stood here. At your age I used to watch them drill. They didn't break, like the Athenians. We had to kill them—they had iron in them, the dumb bastards."

Staggering through the darkness, Philip began to mutter. Then abruptly his words came clear, in Greek, repeating words of Demosthenes which he seemed to know by heart: *"By the springs of our land, by the rivers that water it, by the hills that have made our home . . ."*

71

They found on the field the shield of the orator with its legend, "With Fortune." Men related how Demosthenes, throwing away his weapons, ran with the others, helplessly, from the valley of Chaeronea.

Afterward, in Athens, when he was urged to speak to the people, he refused, saying, "It was Chaeronea that spoke, not I."

Stunned by the disaster at Chaeronea, hearing with dread that the Macedonians had taken over and garrisoned Thebes, the citizens of Athens would have yielded up their orator and the other instigators of the war to pacify Philip. When Demosthenes appeared in the streets he was hissed and called the Snake. Political orators reminded assemblymen that his speeches "stank of the study lamp." To one of these Demosthenes made answer, "My lamp does not give out the same smell as yours."

But Philip, surprisingly, made no demands upon the great commonwealth. For this city of the Acropolis he felt unspoken admiration. His was the awe of the highlander for the metropolis.

Among the emissaries of this good will, Alexander and Hephaestion were sent to Athens, and the eager Macedonian feasted himself with sight-seeing—thrown as he was for the first time among masses of educated people, visiting the old Tower of the Winds, sitting in the cool of nights in the front row of the marble seats with armrests in the Dionysos theater, discussing politics in the lamplit gardens of the more exquisite prostitutes, who had at their tongue's tip the gossip of the sea trade, the fashionable ideas of the Sophists, and tales of wonder from ancient Egypt where the Sphinx had been heard to utter prophecies.

The Macedonian youths walked with the pupils of Plato in the Lyceum—named after the hero Lykos, the Wolf. And Hephaestion as usual found amusement in this. "Behold," said he, "here is your evolution of man, entire. From wolf to hero to philosopher. What next?"

Nor was Hephaestion impressed when they sat with the politicians in the city council on the hill under the Parthenon. "These citizens draw a dole to feed themselves, and they sit here all day to argue about what to do with themselves!"

And Alexander must have remembered the complaint of the dour Stagyrite, that these Athenians had become too abstract in their ideas and in their search for an ideal.

They met with gray-bearded men who had joked with ugly Sophocles, and had attended the first nights of Euripides's plays which, like the *Troiades*, dramatized the story of females as well as the dominant males—an effort speedily lampooned by the uninhibited Aristophanes in *Lysistrata*. In fact the companion-ladies of the metropolis were more modern in their thought than the men, expressing themselves in deft quotations: *"When I behold how filthy rich the gods have made me, why should I question them?"*

These educated ladies made agreeable companions, superior companions, in fact. They concealed their amusement at the uncouth Macedonian mountaineers, because it was quite apparent to them that these same mountaineers were becoming the most influential men in Greece, if not yet the richest. The *hetaerae* had great interest in such a change in the political wind.

Alexander missed seeing children around their apartments. For this lack Hephaestion had a ready explanation. "They don't want children running around and begging for bread, and calling all the visitors 'Poppa.' Anyway, they don't have many because they practice that new thing called abortion. It may be good or it may be bad, but it certainly keeps the population down. It's different with our women: they have litters. Did you see that girl called Thais? Imagine her having a child. She's a child herself."

Hephaestion saw no harm in the influence of these public women. "I've sold my body for what—only hard knocks given and taken; they sell their bodies and also provide an education."

73

Athens differed from provincial Pella in other ways. Wealth flowing in from taxation, payments of tributary islands, and the growing overseas trade had ringed the city with new boulevards and vast public works.

The *chink* of silver coins was heard constantly along the shop fronts, where prices seemed fantastically high compared to Pella. Down at the harbor round merchant craft disgorged grain from the Euxine, lumber and metals, and groups of black and white slaves from the outlying islands. The sharp odor of wine hung over the hot waterfront. Alexander, taught by the insistent Aristotle to examine into causes, satisfied himself that this money prosperity came from the constantly rising prices. Goods increased in value, while labor remained cheap, owing to the great numbers of unemployed soldiers and the continued influx of slaves. More than that, Athens was drawing the materials for its new industries out of the east, from the islands and the coasts of Asia. This wealth had created a new aristocracy in Athens, three generations after the civil war.

From every crowded street he could see the gigantic statue of the goddess Pallas Athena, shining with gold and the pale splendor of ivory against the sheer blue of the sky. And he thought of the small altar of the God-Father under the window in Pella.

Many people spoke to him of the centenarian Isocrates, who had been buried that year. Isocrates, the philosopher, had devoted his life, like Demosthenes, to the ideal of democracy. But unlike Demosthenes, he had believed the Hellenic city-states to be in decline.

How could that be possible, the citizens argued, when statistics showed that the foreign trade of Athens had never been so great, nor the colonies—except for those ports taken over by the Macedonian—so flourishing? The figures for population, the silver reserve, the numbers of schools and civic works, all showed that Isocrates lied. Isocrates, they explained, merely remembered, owing to his great age, the earlier, primitive city-state, at a time when most men were farmers,

74

before the advance of modern industry in the new commonwealth. Isocrates complained that in Hellas the city-states now could not maintain peace within themselves or between themselves. All of them—Sparta, Athens, Argos, Delphi, Corinth, and Thebes—had struggled first for supremacy and then for trade, and now were divided internally between the moneyed class and the laboring class. So said the doting Isocrates, and it was rumored that he had committed suicide by starving himself to death after Chaeronea.

Certainly this aged philosopher had accused the modern city-states of surrendering to Persian power, more than a century after Salamis. For Persian statesmanship and gold, he argued, had won the victory that the Asiatic fleets and armies could not obtain at Salamis and Plataea. The all-powerful Persians had induced the Spartans to sign a mutual assistance pact; the Hellenic colonies in Asia had yielded to this empire's control, while imperial fleets dominated the seas and imperial gold decided the elections, even in the Athenian Assembly.

Under such conditions, Isocrates maintained, the Hellenic city-states could only survive if they united in an effort to free themselves from this golden yoke of the Asiatic empire. By making open war upon Persia and advancing their forces across the sea to liberate the colonies the Greeks could preserve their democracies and regain their ancient heritage.

To unite in this fashion for the Asiatic war, Isocrates admitted, it might even be necessary to accept the mastery of Philip of Macedon, who was very close to being a Greek and who alone could direct the course of such a war. This last advice the Athenians remembered, after the funeral of the aged Isocrates.

In their hysterical relief at being spared the fate of Thebes after Chaeronea, the Athenians voted Philip a citizen of their city. They managed to forget all of Isocrates's warnings except his last counsel, to accept Philip. When Alexander and his companions appeared in the city, instead of the dreaded Macedonian army, the Athenians made much of Philip's striking son. Only the friends of Demosthenes remarked that a wolf cub was not the less a wolf.

And Philip, using his son as emissary of good will, achieved a miracle of statesmanship in the year after Chaeronea. Informed by his spies, acting so swiftly that the rival cities had little time to weigh his actions, he called their representatives into a congress at Corinth.

Apparently Philip merely listened to the problems of the Greeks as they argued before him. For each problem he had a solution.

They were disunited: he formed a league of all the cities except Sparta, to be known as the Hellenic League, to have its own council, with which he would not interfere except in time of war. The constitutions, the private properties, the privileges of each city were guaranteed. Nor were the cities called upon to pay tribute. Any major dispute need not be referred to Philip; it would be decided by the supreme judgment of the religious council.

Moreover, Philip agreed to Isocrates's plan. Having united all Greece, he would lead all Greece in a war against Persian dominion, to free the seas, liberate the colonies, and restore Hellas to its true grandeur. He would lead as captain-general of Hellas, not as king of the Macedonians. Upon each city he would call for a detachment of volunteer infantry. Sparta alone was excepted, as being the ally of the Asiatics. And the Spartans refused to join the new Hellenic League, assuring Philip, "we are accustomed to lead, not to be led."

With nothing to pay to the conqueror, and nothing to lose, and with prestige and power to gain, the representatives of the Greek cities accepted Philip's plan for a greater Hellas with enthusiasm.

Alexander, sitting through the sessions in the theater at Corinth, saw his father acclaimed a liberator and the statesman of the hour. Hearing the decision of the congress at Corinth, Demosthenes went into voluntary exile, declaring that he could not endure being a spectator of the end of Greek democracy.

Philip arranged for the levies from the Greek cities to join him the next year upon the King's Way, en route to the Dardanelles. Meanwhile he sent Parmenio, his chief of staff, with task forces ahead, to secure a bridgehead across the strait, on the Asiatic side. Alexander he kept at his side, to observe these manipulations, while he arranged for his weak-minded son Arrhidaeus to be married to the daughter of a minor noble on the Asiatic shore.

Then at last Philip was satisified that he had compensated by negotiation at Corinth for the wastage of lives at Chaeronea. This greater victory over the assembled Greeks had insured the kingdom for the Macedonians.

With so much accomplished by inspired forethought, Philip allowed himself to relax, and his Macedonians to feast when he came home to Pella.

Then, at the full tide of success, he was assassinated. And men recalled the prophecy of the Pythian seeress, that at Chaeronea the conquered should weep and the conqueror die.

After receiving notification that she was no longer the king's wife, Olympias had retired with her personal servants to a separate house near the cemetery, to be out of the way of Philip and his girl bride. In this seclusion Olympias put on dark mantles, abandoning her bright silks. She took to spinning thread from wool, sitting at the wheel for hours in implacable silence. When she did go out she made use of a covered litter, so that no one in the streets of Pella saw her face—although her litter attracted attention enough in its passage. People began to say that the Princess of Epirus, who had never secluded herself as a wife, now screened herself properly as a rejected wife. Others observed how she walked abroad only at night, like a second Medea in the graveyard during the hours when the power of Hecate waxed great.

From her window Olympias watched the new influx

77

of people thronging into Pella—merchants from Tyre or Carthage with war gear to sell, ambassadors from the barbarian tribes, Greek prostitutes and agents. Within a year Philip's court had become the axis of Hellas. Often had Olympias imagined for herself such a triumph as this.

To Alexander, when he at last arrived home, she made no complaint of her misfortune, saying quietly that fate struck down those who had been raised too high by success. Her hope now lay in Alexander, and she only feared that she could not shield him from Philip's drunken violence.

"Long since," she murmured over the threaded wool, "when I carried you under my heart, I vowed to the Father-God that never would I cease to protect you in life."

Especially she warned him against the overbearing manner of Cleopatra's Kinsmen. Now that the girl was with child they acted as if their family had become the arbiter of Pella. To Alexander this mildness in his passionate mother seemed strange.

"I fear for your life," she admitted, her fingers tearing at the ball of loose wool.

Alexander noticed that Philip, who had a habit of sitting alone on the lion-crested bench at the feasts, now kept Attalus, uncle of Cleopatra, beside him, even though Attalus grew foul in talk when he drank. As for Philip, no one could be certain when he was actually drunk. When Attalus goaded Alexander with a barbed word Philip fell silent, as if observing the two of them. Cleopatra did not pour the wine now, when they sat together, being far along in pregnancy.

Attalus disliked Alexander's way of leaving his wine goblet untouched.

"You pour out enough on the sly, in sacrifice to *your* Father-Zeus," Cleopatra's uncle remarked repeatedly. And one night he stood up, lifting his wine bowl and shouting out, "May Cleopatra give Philip a son who'll be a legitimate heir!"

Suddenly Alexander's temper flared, and he saw

78

only the bearded mocking face of Attalus, challenging him. At that head he flung his own wine-filled goblet, and reached back of him for a weapon, shouting, "Do you say I am a bastard——"

Empty-handed, he stepped on the table, to leap at Attalus. Instantly Philip jerked his sword from the bearer behind him and threw himself at his son. Muddle-headed with drink, he slipped, sprawling on the stones.

Shaking with anger, Alexander stared down at his father, then leaped across him, to the door. He shouted, "That's the man who'd take you across into Asia—he can't move himself from one bench to the other."

Looking down at the staring, gaping faces, at his father getting up from the stones, Alexander turned and raced out of the hall. He ran through the guards, beyond the torchlight, into the street of Olympias's house.

He found her awake, at her wheel, and without explanation he hurried her with one maid out to the stables. Within an hour he was out on the black horse beside her chariot on the dark path to the forests of Epirus.

But he left her at her old family home and rode on alone into the northern mountains. Freed from Olympias's importuning, he could more easily forget that night at Pella. While he pictured Attalus ridiculing his flight, he pressed on deeper into the forests, afraid to face Macedonians. Until messengers from Pella tracked him down, giving him a letter from his father.

Philip wrote that the Greek counselors were asking him how he expected to keep order in the new Hellenic League when he could not hold his own house together—and he wanted his son Alexander back to resume duty with the army.

Somewhat to Alexander's surprise, his mother made no objection. Although she distrusted Philip's letter, saying that the man who was called Fox by his own soldiers was never so dangerous as when he appeared most friendly. But her son should face his enemies, knowing that he was under protection of the Powers that had shielded the hero Achilles through all dangers. Alexander should trust in these Powers, which were not perceptible to other men.

At Pella, Philip greeted the exile as if nothing had happened at the wine cups that night. Immediately he began discussing a new kind of wheeled transport for the demountable catapults that Deiades had designed for the Asiatic expedition. Olympias distrusted this warlike activity. Usually, she pointed out, Philip did the opposite of what he discussed openly. Why should he depart just now, leaving Greece half pacified? More likely he intended to remove Alexander, with this transport, sending him across the sea to join Parmenio—at least until it was known whether Cleopatra's child would be a boy or a girl.

Ptolemy also felt worried, hinting to Alexander that his idiot half brother was being married into the family of an eastern governor—while another bastard, a half sister, was betrothed to a prince, yet Philip had mentioned no forthcoming marriage for Alexander. He was being kept in the public eye, Ptolemy thought, because the rank and file of the army fancied, after Chaeronea, that he brought them good luck.

Worried by this advice on a matter he little understood and fearful of some outbreak from his mother, Alexander tried to intrigue for himself, sending a companion—an actor, of the new theater—to offer to marry the eastern girl himself, in place of Arrhidaeus. Yet he felt instinctively that Philip would neither send him away nor forgive him this attempt at amateur statesmanship. It gave relief to his jaded nerves to yield to his advisers.

It seemed as if Philip discovered his secret before his actor-envoy could return. Limping into Alexander's room with Philotas behind him, he sat down moodily, rubbing his untidy head. Philotas, the leader of a Companion regiment, stood at the door as if on duty, although by then he was intimate with Alexander.

Philip, perfectly sober, looked tired as he surveyed

the books, the night lamps, and the half-finished drawings that littered the study. "When will you cease to be a moon calf," he muttered, "filling your mind with other men's writings, and gossip? You neigh like a filly when a man stamps his foot or takes a sip of wine." His good eye blinked and his voice gentled. "By all the dog-headed tykes of hell, I wish you'd never had tutors. Can't be helped now. Listen. Arrhidaeus was a problem. I wanted to marry him off somewhere. You'll command the army, someday, with Parmenio. I wanted you to be able to grasp problems and master men. You can't do that by making sweet music like Orpheus or reasoning about mathematics. Or by waiting for a god to come out of the stage machine to help you, like in a tragedy. I wish——"

Under Alexander's silence he seemed to feel that he was lecturing a stubborn schoolboy. He seemed to try to reach across to the boy. He only said awkwardly. "No use worrying—I'm cracked here and there in the body. Have to get used to it."

Alexander remembered how he limped out after their talk, pushing his head, clumsily clear of the door curtain. In that moment he believed Philip had no thought of putting him aside.

But a few hours later Philip issued an order for Ptolemy, Harpalus, and Nearchus to leave Pella and stay in exile, depriving Alexander of his close friends.

And then, on the day of his half sister's marriage, Alexander never forgot how the Kinsmen, and the silent Antipater, and the great families of Macedon had gathered in the half-ruined hall of the elder kings at Aegae, with their retinues waiting outside and the flutes playing. He had waited alone with some officers near the hall, until the trumpets sounded. They had not seen Philip limping out of the gate of rough stones, the trumpets calling, and people pressing back to make room for the king.

And Philip had fallen to his knees, with a bare-headed, screaming man stabbing a knife into his back, killing him.

81

IV. THE MOUNTAINS
AND THEBES

The moment life left Philip's scarred body Macedon ceased to be. It was not as if a ship had lost its captain; rather as if a ship, half timbered on the shore, had lost its builder. For Philip, son of Amyntas, had been the brain, the driving force, the general, and the supreme court of the Macedonian clans. No assembly survived him, no experienced ministers existed, to carry on the semblance of a government, nor had Philip named an heir to succeed him. Even his plans for the future remained uncertain, because in his caution he had been at more pains to deceive his enemies than to enlighten his lieutenants.

The next day, from Aegae and Pella agents of the Phoenician merchant houses, the Greek city governments, couriers of visiting ambassadors, and spies of the Illyrian and Thracian barbarians slipped away along the roads, carrying the news of the end of the Macedonian regime.

At Pella the elder Kinsmen and heads of the great clans met with the general officers of the army. For the old tribal custom required that the gathering of the clan heads should decide the question of blood guilt. Over this gathering Antipater and the one-eyed Antigonus presided.

Investigation revealed the murderer to be a young Macedonian, Pausanias. He had been killed immediately by the spectators in the courtyard at Aegae. This Pausanias, it developed, had been injured by followers of Attalus and Cleopatra, who had stripped him and outraged him in public after a drinking bout. It was proved that Pausanias had gone from person to person to claim retaliation from the older Attalus; refused by Philip, he had been seen to visit both Olympias and Alexander.

And Alexander testified that he had dismissed Pausanias without discussion; this quarrel had nothing to do with him. He denied giving to Pausanias the Celtic knife with which the murder had been committed.

Yet clearly someone had instigated the half-crazed youth to attack Philip. Pausanias had belonged to Alexander's circle of companions—some of whom had just been exiled by Philip; Alexander had quarreled openly and violently with his father; he was known to have an ungovernable temper; he had been near the scene of the murder. Moreover Cleopatra had given birth to a son who might in time have displaced the erratic Alexander.

The investigators did not presume to question Olympias, who was both priestess and Princess of Epirus, widow of Philip, and mother of the man under suspicion, Alexander. Servants testified that Olympias, on being told of the murder, had murmured something like "*Upon husband, upon father, and upon bride,*" which proved to be a line written by Euripides but was hardly understandable or in any respect evidence.

At that point the investigation ended. By clan law the killing of a member of the royal family by another of the same blood was an act that could not be judged or atoned by Kinsmen or generals.

Those same Kinsmen and generals remembered only too well how blood guilt had laid upon Philip's family before now. Philip's mother Eurydice, an adulteress, had arranged the death of his elder brother, Perdiccas.

While a group of Macedonians headed by Attalus believed Alexander guilty the majority felt then and believed thereafter that Olympias had egged Pausanias on to attack Philip. The knife of Pausanias had been diverted in some way from Attalus against Philip. Of the assassination itself Alexander would say nothing.

Passing over, in this way, the question of the blood guilt, the council of the clans had to name a new ruler of the Macedonians. From that moment of Philip's death *someone* must reign in his place, if the great clans were not to revert to their isolation in the highlands. The army officers would take over Philip's task of organization, but the army—especially the men in the ranks—had to have a titular head of the blood of Philip. Most conveniently the idiotic Arrhidaeus would serve as figurehead, the older Amyntas would carry on the royal name. Or Antipater and Antigonus could serve as regents for Cleopatra's newborn son.

Against choice of Alexander there were several counts: the rumor that Philip had not fathered him; his anti-social absorption in study and inexperience in command; the open blood feud that had started with Philip's murder. For such a death among the clans would lead to others.

The veteran generals insisted that a decision had to be made instantly, and held to. And they made the decision, in spite of all argument. Afterward Antipater and Antigonus went to Alexander's study. When he looked up from his books and offered them benches they remained standing. They explained to him the verdict of the army. Philip had named no successor, but Philip had assigned his twenty-year-old son Alexander to duty with the army, and after Chaeronea Alexander had performed such duty. Now he was King of the Macedonians.

When the versatile and all-competent chief of staff, Parmenion, hurried back from the eastern frontier he approved the choice of the others at Pella. Probably the three great commanders felt that the Macedonian army believed the youthful Alexander to be favored of the gods, if not born of a god. And this army of farmers and mountaineers would follow no leader of whom it did not approve. The three generals thought that the daydreaming student would hardly interfere with their plans. Of this triumvirate the diplomatic Parmenio made an indispensable link between the arrogant and ambitious Antigonus and the loyal Antipater, whose thoughts did not rise above carrying out orders.

The three commanders knew what Alexander soon discovered, that after Philip's death Macedonian power had shrunk from an expanding Hellenic federation to a small kingdom. On three sides of this kingdom the highland tribes reverted promptly to their natural independence. Beyond lay the threat of the barbarian Celts along the Danube, pressing toward the sea, and the roving Scythian steppe clans. The Greek cities deserted the Hellenic League promptly. Athens held public celebration of the death of the man she had made a citizen only a year before. Consigned to leading Athenians, a weighty shipment of gold coin arrived mysteriously from Asia. Demosthenes was again acclaimed as the leader of Greek democracy.

On the other hand the staff knew only too well what their resources were. Philip had piled risk upon risk. His *tour de force* in wresting leadership from the Greek cities under the guise of captain-general now yielded nothing tangible. There was no longer a captain-general, and no longer a Hellas. True, the Greeks did not know the weakness of the Macedonian army. By his rapid maneuvering the astute Philip had allowed foreign spies no opportunity of observing its numbers. Yet the staff realized that the Macedonian core of the army—the *pezetaeri* [phalanxmen], the Companions, the Hypaspists—numbered no more than seventeen to eighteen thousand. Other detachments, such as the Thessalian cavalry and Agrianians, with the lighter allied contingents, had been linked to the army by Philip's leadership alone.

The condition of the treasury was more alarming than that of the armed forces. It had some seventy talents' weight of bullion and coins, while it owed thirteen hundred talents. Philip had gambled on getting new revenues from the rich Asiatic coast. Pella did not have money enough to meet expenses for more than two months.

Philip had gambled on creating a greater state and had left the original Macedon in danger.

In this crisis Aristotle agreed with the generals on the first thing to do—reassert mastery over the restless tribes. So Alexander left Pella almost at once on this mission with the field army, leaving Antipater to hold Pella.

He rode off with the generals, irresolute, uncertain how to meet the responsibilities Philip had borne so carelessly. His familiar world of study had been lost, not to be found again. Demosthenes said at this time that the student had come to his graduation.

Shy, introspective, the Macedonian had been accustomed to trust people at sight, to take the advice of friends. His world had been one of imagination, with cities that lay beyond the horizon, and mountain ranges that were Parapanisades, peopled by kindly gods. In questing toward this dream region he had followed Aristotle upon the still untrodden track of study of the evolution of human beings. As with Demosthenes, his knowledge smelled of the study lamp, yet of no ordinary lamp.

In other respects he was normal as Hephaestion or Ptolemy—both of the blood royal—being, however, more stubborn, feeling responsibility more deeply, and having greater physical beauty.

So at twenty years of age he started on his journey.

In little more than a year he had changed into a man of decision, distrustful of advice, going headlong at danger and determined to lead his army into Asia, away from his homeland.

And in the following years he developed a capacity for inspired leadership, an ability to shape events on strange lands and seas, and the determination to achieve what had not been attempted hitherto.

What influenced him and what forced his thoughts into new channels during this brief year is little known. Certainly he received very quickly the news of the deaths in Pella. His cousin Amyntas had been poisoned, and Cleopatra's infant son had been found strangled.

With those two out of the way, he had no male blood kin except half-witted Arrhidaeus.

Olympias alone would have wished for the deaths of those two. He remembered the words she had spoken, of retribution upon father and husband and bride. After that he never went back willingly to Pella. The palace and the new city must have been, in his imagination, antagonistic and terror-filled.

Pushing rapidly through the high valleys near the summit of Mount Haemus, the Macedonian army threaded through the barbarian peoples, who watched from hiding, judging its strength suspiciously, eager to close in upon the disciplined force that restrained them from looting the lowlands. Alexander had to ride with his officers through thick forests, where they might be shot down from cover. He learned that he could not expect warning. The Macedonians were among folk as merciless and unpredictable as animals, who could be controlled only by discipline and by force. Some of them, the highland Agrianians, volunteered to serve in the army.

There were conflicts as sharp as the attack of wolf packs. Nearing one pass, the scouts in advance brought back information that the tribes in strength had barricaded themselves behind a wall of wagons, which stood at the summit of the slope, in readiness to be rolled down on the advancing column. There was no other approach to the pass. If the advance regiment scattered it could not force the wagon wall; if it massed to attack with spears the wagons might be launched down the slope upon it. Since Philip's son was with them, the regimental commander waited to receive an order instead of giving one.

Alexander felt five hundred men stolidly watching him and knew that he could not hesitate. To halt and wait for a more experienced commander would be to admit his incompetence. So he caught at the first solution that occurred to him. "Go forward as you are. If the wagons come down, divide and take shelter and let

87

them go through where you can. Those men who can't move out of the way should lie down and lock their shields over their backs. Let the wagons go over the shields."

It amazed him, as always then, that the infantry should go forward at a word. Long experience in battle had accustomed them to facing risks, providing their officers had weighed the situation and decided on their action. And Alexander's quick imagination had taken count of all possibilities. So the men went up steadily, and the wagons crashed down from the summit, breaking the ranks and thudding over the prostrate men who lay under shields and spears. They got to their feet, shaken and badly hurt, and went on—those who could walk. Alexander never again ordered them to lie down under wagons. But he noticed that the horde on the hill, terrified at seeing the decimated men moving up again, fled into the forest.

By experience and by watching Parmenio and the veterans, Alexander learned how quickly decisions must be made. His commanders attacked at night, they attacked across rivers; they marched for two days to arrive without warning before a mountain city like lofty Pelion. But they kept always in motion, so that no observers knew where they might be next. They pushed on where the tribes had not looked for them, to the Danube; on this barrier river they seized the only ships within sight—some Byzantine galleys—to ferry a force across, in darkness. Going with them, Alexander made his way through fields of standing corn that hid the men, picking his way by the stars, shivering with the damp and chill and the weariness of anxiety, until they came to the wooden wall of a sleeping city at sunrise. And the inhabitants thought it a miracle that men in armor should be posted around them at the first light.

Bearded Celtic chieftains, in leather riding breeches, with hair plaited over their shoulders, came out with gold bowls and the jewelry of their wives as gifts to the soldiers, saying that they brought tribute to the king of the Macedonians, because they were afraid.

"Of what?" Alexander laughed.

"Of only one thing."

"What is that?" He felt proud that they should fear *him*, being young.

"That the sky might fall on us."

To Hephaestion he said, "They seem to be brave, yet they are great boasters."

"Most men are boasters," Hephaestion assured him, "and few enough have any courage for business like this."

Alexander remembered how his father had said the same thing in the reaction after Chaeronea. Fear itself could not be driven from the mind, and Philip had been fearful, besides, for the lives of his men. Philip had guarded his *pezetairi* jealously, scheming to get every possible advantage for them before risking them in action. Philip had shunned fortification and the uncertain sea, plotting, deceiving, breaking his promises, to win an objective without an engagement at close quarters. How he accomplished this was a mystery to every commander except Parmenio. And the chief of staff, while understanding Philip's methods, could not get the same result from them. This mystery of supreme command was as baffling in its way as the science of the evolution of life that Aristotle had solved.

In two respects, their grasp of higher knowledge and their reliance upon reality in its minutest forms, Aristotle and Philip had reasoned alike. Otherwise they differed sharply, for Philip acted upon intuition that was close to genius, while the Stagyrite would reach a conclusion only when evidence had pointed it out.

Alexander brooded over this problem of leadership with his immense persistence. By watching the veteran Parmenio he learned only expedients and tricks. This master of the staff could move his brigades from place to place with inimitable ease, to gain some specific advantage. Beyond that he trusted to the discipline and experience of the Macedonian soldiery to profit from the advantage.

The one-eyed Antigonus, caustic and conceited, had Philip's gift of deception. By terrifying an enemy, by bribing a political figure, or by coaxing his antagonists upon a stage set for peaceful negotiation, Antigonus prepared the way for a sudden massacre of any force that opposed him. "Don't march up to 'em," he growled. "Don't be fool enough to parade your strength and intentions beforehand. Get hold of a few of 'em, slice the guts out of those, and the other thousands will stampede like a herd of cattle. When you have them running you can execute all you need. That's the thing. Strike a spark of terror and the fire will do your work. The turn of a battle comes when more of the enemy are afraid of your men than yours are of them. Wait for that turn."

Yet Alexander discovered that few Macedonians really trusted Antigonus. If he made a mistake in his scheming he sometimes sacrificed a Macedonian regiment to extricate himself.

Although Alexander could not ride into a danger zone without feeling weak and cold he was able now to keep his nerves under control. So many men watched him, their own nerves taut, taking alarm or courage from his least motion, that he had to act as if he were certain of himself. So he formed the habit of leaving off his helmet. For some reason when he did this the men around him, helmeted, felt more at ease. In the same way, to cover his own anxiety, he had a way of laughing much and talking to them. For the rest, he trusted to guessing aright as the situation around him changed and new difficulties cropped up. Distrusting his own ability, he seldom thought out beforehand what he should do, although his mind was constantly preoccupied with what might happen. By degrees the ranks learned to watch the golden-headed youth on black Bucephalus for a sign of what might be doing next. Alexander now mounted Bucephalus when there was prospect of any action.

At this time he developed a tendency to push forward recklessly. He learned that it was safer to move quickly than to delay in the mountains. The Macedonian infantry, mountainbred, was at home in such marching. And it happened that in the Dalmatian heights he pushed his column forward blindly into a boxlike valley, to find that the heights around him were held by formidable Illyrian barbarians who promptly cut off the column's road of escape. The Illyrians remained out of reach, while other tribes hurried up to strengthen the mountain trap. Parmenio, outside the valley with cavalry, forced his way in to Alexander and managed to open an escape route back along the valley to a river where the infantry was out of danger.

"In spite of what men say," Hephaestion assured Alexander, "you have a mistress and she is that slut Tyche."

Tyche was the goddess of fortune, much importuned by the soldiery. The careless Hephaestion never seemed to be disturbed in action. He said that every Macedonian had a hundred-to-one chance of coming out alive, although he might be hurt, in such affairs. At such odds, why should anyone worry?

Alexander laughed in sheer relief. After fording the river on the black horse with the rear guard and watching the masses of barbarians halt at the bank behind him, he was soaked with perspiration. "I have never seen Fortune's face."

"Well, they say Tyche follows you everywhere."

"If I have been lucky I would like to know when."

For once Hephaestion fell serious. "If you don't know—well, you are *protected* in some way. Either you number the gods among your—ancestors—or the gods set the seal of Philip's good fortune upon you at his death. Fate. You can't argue about it. The phalanxmen have it all figured out. If you don't grab the best-looking girls or lap up wine from the jug, or knock a chap down who steps on your toes, it's a *sign* you're something more than a plain mortal, like Hephaestion, who does all those things. So does Perdiccas and he is a grand soldier.

They don't know why you are different, but they

91

know you *are* different. Why else don't they call you High-Born or Commander or Straw Thatch? Eh? Nothing of the kind. You are Alexander, and that's the sum of it."

So Alexander found himself compelled by circumstances to do what he least liked to do: lead men in conflict. Tormented by his own inability and reckless now of physical hurt, he dreaded the time when he would make some inexcusable mistake, and his companions, like Hephaestion and Perdiccas, would see the feet of clay in the statue they had erected themselves. Already it seemed to him that he had failed and Macedon was breaking up. These men in the ranks saw in him only the reflection of their own ideal of a fearless and invincible leader, favored of the gods. When they discovered his weakness they would jeer at the yellow-headed fool who acted the part of a soldier. They would tear the mask from him and laugh and bid him go back to the waiting murderess, Olympias.

With all his stubborn determination, he set himself to postpone that unmasking. For he knew now that, except in Aristotle's academy, he would meet with no mercy in Macedon.

Perhaps the destruction at Thebes was inevitable. But it shook Alexander, and the memory of it never left him.

It developed while they were still on the Dalmatian coast. Couriers came up from the south, to report that a new defense league was forming around Athens. Orators had taken the stand in Thebes, calling on the citizens to mobilize to defend their liberty and freedom of speech. At a rumor that Alexander had been killed in the Illyrian forests the Thebans assassinated two Macedonian officers of the garrison left by Philip in the Cadmea, or citadel, of the city. Now the Macedonian garrison was holding out in the Cadmea and the Thebans were calling on Sparta for alliance against the invaders. The Hellenic League was mobilizing against its masters.

At Pella the councilors felt the need of conciliating the Greek cities. Aristotle warned that the Hellenic cities must be won over by diplomacy.

But the garrison in the Cadmea could not be sacrificed to gain delay for negotiation. The Macedonian generals started for Thebes at headlong speed, keeping to the highland roads, out of observation, and covering nearly three hundred miles in thirteen days, taking Alexander along.

They went into camp upon scared ground at the cemetery outside Thebes, hoping to relieve the battalions inside the city and to put an end to the resistance movement there before other armies could take the field against the wearied Macedonians.

By selecting the cemetery for a camp site Parmenio made clear that he was not seeking battle. Wanting time to rest his men, he sent envoys over to the city to offer the Thebans a truce if they would surrender the fortifications and release the garrison. The envoys came back looking grim.

"The Thebans," they reported, "will give up nothing. They offer *us* a truce if we will surrender Parmenio and Philotas."

When he rode around the city to inspect its wooden wall, raised on an earth rampart, Alexander could think of no way out of the dilemma except a siege. Above the city rampart he could see the square of the stone citadel where his garrison waited to be released. "How would you get in there?" he asked Perdiccas absently. This brigade commander had served with the army all the years that Alexander had been at Mieza.

"Any way that suits best," Perdiccas answered, occupied with his own considerations. For to the combat officer it seemed necessary only to break into the wall at one point. To Alexander the great city with its monuments of the past and its tens of thousands of human beings presented a more complex problem.

For a little after that he was occupied with the skirmishing of outposts. Then he was startled to hear a report that Perdiccas had got over the wooden wall by a sudden rush close to the Attica gate, near the Cadmea, and was tearing down a stretch of the wall. Alexander sent the Cretan archers and Agrianians, the least weary of his units, to support Perdiccas's brigade. By the time he arrived opposite the point of entrance the Macedonians had thrust deep into the streets, heading for the temple square. The supports had followed.

It was soon clear that the forces inside had been locked in close fighting in the narrow streets. And Alexander waiting irresolutely with the armored infantry outside, hung back, against Parmenio's advice, unwilling to order the phalanx into the narrow entrance, uncertain about making an attempt to carry the wall elsewhere. Perdiccas was carried out badly wounded. A runner reported that the Cretan officer was dead with some eighty men and that the Macedonians were retreating.

They boiled out of the break in the wall, pressed by close-packed Theban shield infantry and severely cut up. When the Thebans continued to pour through the break Alexander ordered in the phalanx. When the mass of long spears came down and the phalanx front moved forward the experienced Cretans gave way to the flanks, and the Theban wave, following on, broke against the solid wall of the phalanx. At once Alexander and his officers, within the ranks of the spearmen, ordered an advance. The massed infantry plowed forward through the disorganized enemy. Once in motion, the phalanx pressed on like an inexorable machine harrowing the earth, treading underfoot what stood in its way,—changing front to push through the break in the wall, into the crowded streets, to be caught there in the delirium of the house-to-house fighting. Breaking up into squads and scattering through the alleys and over the flat roofs, the Macedonian infantry fought its own battle, being now out of hand and beyond recall.

At this point the Macedonian garrison broke out of the beleaguered Cadmea and joined the attack. The

Theban soldiery, entangled in a mob of women and children, retreated desperately toward their temple. The city wall being now deserted, other Macedonian contingents streamed in, with volunteers from Phocis and Plataea who had a feud of their own to settle with the Thebans. In another hour the streets had become runways for human herds that struggled, died, fled and followed, suffered and ravaged. That night Thebes burned.

Next day when the ruins could be policed and graves dug, four thousand bodies of all kinds were counted. In a garden out of the drifting smoke Alexander sat with the regimental commanders to hear reports. Most of the soldiers were still searching for coins or gems and herding in the prisoners. The city of two days before had changed into a devastated area, policed by the Macedonians and without other life of its own. Some of the officers complimented Alexander on the timeliness of his counterattack with the infantry, the judgment he had shown in waiting until the right moment. As if he had planned in cold calculation, to wait for what Antigonus called the turn of the battle.

Alexander had made no such plan, nor could he make one now.

This city could be left as it was, to heal its wounds; or it could be demolished. Antigonus and most of the commanders argued for the destruction of the stronghold that had twice stood in the way of the Macedonians. To make an example of one enemy, they pointed out, would have an effect on all other Greek cities. Alexander agreed.

Among the prisoners in the garden awaiting judgment, he noticed that the least excited was a well-dressed woman, unusually lovely, with two children holding to her. She was accused of murdering an officer. The Theban woman had admitted the murder, explaining that the officer had been a Thracian barbarian who broke into her house and used violence on her. Then, instead of leaving, the Thracian had tried to find out if she had hidden any jewelry away. She had

95

told him yes, in the garden well, and when he had taken her there to examine the well she had pushed him in and had thrown stones from the coping at him, killing him before the soldiers could come up.

"Who are you?" Alexander demanded.

"I am the sister of Theagenes, who held command against you at Chaeronea and died there for the liberty of Greece."

She waited, unmoved, to be sentenced to death.

"Release her," the Macedonian ordered. "Escort her with the children out of our lines."

As swiftly as he had dealt with the Theban woman he ordered entire destruction of the great city, its buildings demolished—except for the temple, the house of Pindar, and the homes of those who had befriended Philip or himself—and the mass of the survivors sold as slaves. He would not hear any more individual cases.

This annihilation of one of the member states of the Hellenic League, almost before the others were aware that the Macedonian army had returned, stunned the volatile Athenians. The revolt died out before it gained headway. Athens sent envoys north who were known friends of Alexander, to urge that in this crisis the Greek cities looked to him for leadership. Alexander needed only to ride to Corinth, they explained, to be greeted as captain-general by the councilors of the Hellenic League, as Philip had been acclaimed before him.

On that ride Antigonus treated him with grudging respect. After the storming of Thebes that day Alexander required that orders to the army be given by him alone. If mistakes were to be made he would make them himself.

In Athens the friends of Demosthenes reproached the peace party, saying, "Even sheep would not surrender their watchdogs to the wolves."

Yet the delegates and philosophers who gathered hastily at Corinth, above the blue waters of the gulf, made a great ceremony of Alexander's arrival, devoting their efforts to persuading him to lead the united forces of the cities in the *revanche*, the attack upon Asia. (Uncertain of the young captain-general's disposition, they felt the safest course was to urge him toward the glory of military conquest elsewhere.)

The philosophers reiterated that this had been the hope of Isocrates and of Philip himself. Once, when they were climbing the height above the theater, they passed a man lying in a worn *chlamys* on a stone in a corner out of the wind. Those around Alexander mentioned to him that this was Diogenes, who liked to be alone. Going over to the hermitlike figure, Alexander stared at the sunburned cynic who was one of the most talked-of philosophers. When Diogenes stirred restlessly he asked, "Is there anything you want?"

Diogenes looked up without emotion. "Yes," he said, "stand out of the sun."

The others laughed and Alexander went on without speaking. Yet he remembered how Diogenes, at the council of Corinth, had wanted only sunlight.

It was pleasant, resting by the waters of Corinth, sitting in the theater on the hill in the warm evenings and hearing Greek orators and statesmen urge him to play again the part of Achilles and cross the sea to Troy, to lift the torch where Philip had laid it down, to become the champion of Hellas. By now, so quickly did his moods change, he was troubled by the terror at Thebes, the blotting out of life around that temple on the hill. He felt that at Thebes he had broken into the shrine of a god. And when an exile from that city made any request of him now he granted it. At Thebes he had struck against something more than a human enemy, and he felt the need to make good the harm he had done. His eyes searched the crowds for the woman of Thebes, without finding her.

Some of the philosophers understood clearly enough that Alexander, who had established himself so unexpectedly and rapidly in Philip's post of leadership of the new Hellenic League, had accomplished it only by brutal action, where Philip had relied on masterly persuasion. Among these was Aristotle.

V. THE ROAD TO TROY

There were many who in after years pointed to signs and portents that appeared throughout the Greek lands during the months from the sinking of the Pleiades to the rising of the star Arcturus that spring, when it was not certain whether Alexander of Macedon would lead his army to Asia.

In the market place of Pella fishermen related how the seeress of Delphi had refused to prophesy whether the Asiatic venture would succeed or not. When Alexander had insisted that she speak she had only said cryptically, "Eheu, Alexander, you will always have your way!"

The fishermen wondered if this were a true prophecy or not, and whether Alexander were truly their king, the son of Philip, or the son of the God-Father, born out of the witch woman Olympias. Had he not in three days reduced mighty Thebes to fly-infested blood and charcoal and broken marble—a fate more catastrophic than the hero Achilles had administered, aided by the gods, to Troy itself?

In their highlands the hardheaded Macedonian farmers likewise began to wonder about the soft-spoken man with the beauty and strength of a Heracles, who held his head on one side and listened to them, his blue eyes eager and friendly when he told them how to doctor the ills of their horses and how to brew fruit juice and balsam for their own fevers. With the build of an athlete, able to break a sarissa's wooden shaft between his hands, he avoided the physical struggle of pugilists or wrestlers; shrinking back from a battle's engagement, he had plunged three times into the heat of a battle, at Chaeronea, at Pelion and Thebes, like a drunkard rushing to a feast. These peasants and horse-breeding nobles of Macedon had understood Philip; they did not understand his studious, absent-minded son who wrestled with dilemmas in his tent by lamplight, poring over manuscripts as if performing the ritual of a strange shrine before plunging into monstrous action.

While the common people wondered, the generals of the army told Alexander he must lead the Macedonians into Asia, and they told him why.

His father had decided on the venture, the staff had worked out the logistics of the campaign that would take one half the manpower of Macedon—about twenty-five thousand men—across the Dardanelles. Parmenio himself had gone ahead to prepare the bridgehead to be thrown across that strait at Troy. (Antipater would remain at Pella to safeguard the homeland with overage soldiers, while he trained recruits and kept Olympias quiet.) To sap the resistance strength of unstable Greece they would take along with them contingents of the more venturesome Athenian hoplites and cavalry from Thessaly. It had all been worked out; it would succeed; it could not be abandoned now.

"Why not?" Alexander asked. "General Xenophon could not stay on in Asia with his ten thousand. His book is not called the *Journey In*—it's the *Anabasis, the Journey Out.*"

Parmenio knew that Alexander had read the book. But Parmenio was getting on in years, and his three sons were rising to high command in the army. He wanted to retire after this last victorious campaign and leave the direction of the armed forces to his sons. If the army were disbanded, what would happen to them?"

"The risks have been calculated," he explained patiently. "We can assume that our field army will defeat any force sent against it."

"Even if that is so we have no hold on the sea. The Persian fleets are in all the waters."

But, Parmenio pointed out, their route would be along the land, except at the narrow Dardanelles, and he had provided against failure there. By running a slight risk they could win immense gains, they could liberate the rich Ionian coast opposite Greece, with its historic seaports of Miletus and Ephesus where Seven Sleepers slept, Halicarnassus where Mausolus lay in his tomb, Sardis, where affluent Croesus had reigned . . . they could control the grain route into the Euxine.

"Philip said all that in two words," Olympias remarked. "Gold and glory."

Olympias distrusted the generals, because she could not influence them. She warned her son against them, saying that he must profit by them and not allow them to become as powerful as kings. And the final event was to justify her suspicion.

The elder Kinsmen came to sit with Alexander, to drink his wine and to urge him to take action with the army. Had not Philip educated him and trained him to do just that? The Macedonian nation was young and must fight for its existence against the antagonistic forces surrounding it. Among those forces, the old men said, the most dangerous was the professional soldiery. They had seen that danger grow.

Before the world war the professional soldier had not existed in Greece. The hoplite of that remote day had been in truth a citizen soldier, keeping his weapons in his home and going forth at need for a month or more to serve in the armed force of his native city without pay—then to return to his farm or shop. This exercise of arms had been to him little more than the training for the arduous Olympic games. (The first Marathon race followed the course of the runner who had sped from the battlefield of Marathon to carry the news to Athens.)

During the exhausting civil wars that followed, however, the hoplite had been kept longer in the field; his family, thus deprived of his all-important services, had been given at first a dole of food or supplies to enable it to survive, then a regular dole in money during the absence of the hoplite. By degrees the citizen soldiery had begun to draw pay.

Moreover, as campaigns lengthened and armies were expanded, more recruits were drawn into the ranks of the phalanx, until finally even in Sparta the helots, or slave laborers, were enlisted in the ranks and—eventually—paid. This change-over to total mobilization also took place with the crews, the rowers and fighters, of the warships. This change could not be undone. At the end of the Greek internecine conflicts the citizen volunteer, who was also a homeowner, had become no better than the physically powerful helot, or freed slave, in the ranks. Or the barbarian from forest or sea who enlisted for pay.

Moreover the citizen who did return after demobilization often found his farm destroyed or his shop burned; he usually found a foreigner or slave doing his work as harvester, shoemaker, or druggiest, for a smaller wage than the citizen could live upon. He found prices of clothing and luxuries much higher than before.

More often than not unemployed soldiers demanded subsidies from the state or hired out in other armies. These professional forces tended to form within all cities, where conflict broke out—as where the proprietor class of a city defended itself against the newly landless. The hoplite volunteer of Marathon, who owned his spear, shield, sword, and bronze helmet, had become as legendary as the warrior Achilles by the year 400 B.C. The wealthier cities now hired military forces, paying the highest rates to the best-trained troops. The newly rich citizens, the merchants and landed proprietors, no longer served in the phalanx; they hired professionals instead to take their places.

As with the men in the ranks, so with the officers. The elected leaders of the early citizen levies had been replaced by professional officers who made a career of warfare as doctors devoted themselves to medicine.

About 400 B.C., Xenophon's ten thousand, with their officers, had ventured as far as Babylon, in the service of the Asiatic king. And a king of Sparta, Aegesilaus, had hired out with a thousand veterans to the Egyptian Pharaoh.

This diaspora extended to all skilled classes of the turbulent Greek cities; technicians streamed away from the mother cities toward the colonies and vast capitals of Asia—teachers, prostitutes, architects, and philosophers emigrated toward the market for their skill. The artists of the Parthenon, men like Phidias who had ennobled the temples of their home, gave way to statue makers, carvers of jasper and agate gems, designers of bathtubs and fountainheads and pottery figurines of the gods. These artisians of the new postwar world were no longer devoted artists; they gave their loyalty to a profession. They followed the sea lanes and caravan routes to foreign employers, as the notorious Thais voyaged to Egypt, after the Spartan soldiers.

These mercenaries of the Nile served an officer instead of a city; the officer served the man who paid him. Moreover, being professionals in the business of war, these hired hoplites had skill and rigid discipline.

As with the men, so with the machines. During the long civil war period expert engineers from Tyre and Syracuse had perfected machines to cast javelins, burning oil, massive balls of stone—*apparata* to tear down walls, and other machines to defend walls. Projectiles such as these, discharged from a distance, began to be more devastating than the shock of an advancing human battle line. These new engines of destruction could be built by money power.

Philip had understood this danger from money power and the professional soldiery, the wise old men reminded Alexander. To train the Macedonians he had hired professionals like that Theban veteran; he had bought Deiades's brain to devise more efficient mobile machines. In consequence his Macedonian highlanders had a fine spirit, a very fine national spirit; yet they were still at heart farmers, thinking of their homes. All

102

around them extended the danger of the professional regiments, fleets, and machines. At any time the money power of the great Persian king of Asia might assemble these scattered forces and crush little Macedon. At any time, now that Philip was dead. Did not Alexander understand the danger?

And then the managers of the royal silver and gold mines at Mount Pangaeus came up to talk with Alexander. They talked to him about money, telling him that a new force had come into the world with coined money that had not been written down in the textbooks of the academies like Mieza.

Coined money had become in a peculiar way not merely the symbol of power but power itself. In the shadowy elder world of Troy, when the Macedonian herders had been emerging from the northern steppes, coins had not existed. Human beings had been accustomed to exchange one kind of thing for another, or food for service, and had very gradually begun to use such well-known valuables as sheaves of precious iron rods as a standard of value, to exchange again for something else. Then certain weights of rare metal like copper or electrum had been used as standards, stamped with the mark of the owner or maker. Only two centuries before, much smaller weights of gold and silver had been stamped as true coins of fixed value and used for exchange in cities like Sardis, Rhodes, or Argos. These coins bore on them the images of gods or the totem of a city, like the Athenian owl.

Now traders were spreading coined money through the Mediterranean world—chiefly the fine Athenian "owls"—yet the supply of new silver was limited to the yield of a few mines. Values began to be reckoned in terms of the silver Greek drachmas. But a strong feeling persisted among ordinary folk that it was unnatural to make a profit out of money itself. Such unnatural profit contraverted fate and would bring retribution upon the offender. Had not Midas, lord of a small city, come to a bad end through his craving to hoard gold?

Even Sparta, which had long maintained itself without use of money—by communal sharing and a common kitchen—was now on a money basis. And Sparta, sustained artificially by Persian gold, had become the servant of the will of the Asiatic king. Demosthenes, the orator of democracy, had confiscated the silver coins of a shrine to outfit an Athenian army, and Chaeronea had been the result.

Had not the wars deprived the common folk of food, fuel, and clothing, and loosed epidemics among them? Now the cities like Athens built large public works, to employ discharged soldiers—paying them in coin. All this had driven up the price of necessities like wheat, sheep, and cloth. A barrel of wheat now cost five drachmas instead of two, and a sheep sold for five times as much as before the wars.

This foreboding about coined money on the part of common folk was not shared by the intelligentsia, who realized the immense leverage to be gained from possession of even a few of the bright minted coins. (All coins, to be accepted at this time, had to be full *weight,* of pure silver or gold; counterfeit, token, or fiat money still lay in the distant commercialized future,[1]

---

[1]It needs an effort of the imagination to realize that in this age before the financial machinery of the Roman Empire the Mediterranean world was still on a primitive money basis. Banking as such did not exist, and only in a few markets could *coins* be exchanged for *things.* Taxation was something new under the sun. City-states had small budgets, which were met by contributions from the citizens, more or less forced. If an army was to be equipped or a fleet outfitted or a play staged in the theater, the citizens were called on to raise a fund to pay for it. While landowning classes had existed for some time, property owners still remained rare, and money owners were only just beginning to appear.

Such valuable *things* as horses, weapons, grain, or cloth—or slaves—remained the commonest property; while precious metals, by weight, served as the commonest means of exchange, Iron, the most useful, was still rare enough to be worked into setting for jewelry; solid gold, silver or copper bracelets, chains, cups, and caskets had great value because of the weight of metal in them.

along with paper currency, price fixing, manipulation of the currency. Usurers and moneylenders had not yet taken their places, with their scales, in the doorways of the temples.)

A handful of Athenian owl coins could *buy* for the possessor a stone house or a half-dozen labor slaves from the Euxine or Thrace. A single talent could build a trireme (a "destroyer" or bronze-beaked narrow warship, powered by great oars with three rowers seated on three tiers to drive it into action). Such a talent of coined money could acquire the grain crop of an island, or a ship's load of girl and boy slaves who could be trained to cultivate land, weave cloth, and who would in time increase their number by bearing children.

A store of coins accumulated by a tyrant or the keepers of a shrine in a *treasury* or locked chest could be seized entire, to be spent by the new possessor for an infinity of valuable things.

While Greece itself, except for the always wealthy Delphic shrine, had little enough of such treasuries, Asia seemed to possess an unlimited store of gold as

---

While the Greek drachma equaled an English shilling of later times in nominal value, its actual value before Alexander started the expedition into Asia was more than thirty times the English prewar shilling. Thus it is estimated that an Athenian family of four needed some two hundred and fifty drachmas for its minimum yearly subsistence. A talent, nominally about eleven hundred dollars, had a purchasing power of closer to forty thousand dollars. But almost no price standards existed in the west.

The flood of Asiatic gold *darics* had already driven down the silver exchange ratio from about 13 to 1 to 10 to 1, in the west. In entering Asia, Alexander encountered the problem of the infinitely greater wealth structure of the east.

One specific problem he solved in lightning fashion. Since the gold in the east was beating down the value of the silver in the west, the two currencies conflicted. In Greece one gold stater was worth twenty-four silver drachmas, in Asia one gold daric equaled twenty silver *sigloi*. Alexander struck an equilibrium between the currencies by simply demonetizing gold, making silver standard, at the rate of one gold daric to twenty Greek drachmas.

well as silver, drawn from the mines in the Taurus Mountains, in farther Arabia, and in that most distant unknown east that voyagers named Ind.

The Macedonians, poor in coined money, were also weak in trade.

Out of Asia, with the ever-increasing flow of coins, precious metals, ivory, alabaster, onyx, and rarer stones, came traders and slave dealers, in fleets of ships westward bound. Out of the Greek peninsula passed a constant stream of emigrants, goldsmiths, vase painters, settlers, vagabonds, doctors, and musicians, eastward bound toward the wealth in Asia. Trade had mounted with each postwar generation, and the peninsula of Asia Minor now became the junction of the new trade routes from Tyre and Sardis, to Syracuse and Carthage in the west. Industrialized and commercialized, the Greek cities now imported their grain and timber and metal, serving as great clearinghouses of trade, dealing increasingly with money.

But the great trade routes did not enter the Macedonian mountains. The Macedonian treasury had no store of bullion. Although Philip had gained for his people a strip of the coast, with seaports, they had no fleet, nor could Philip make these agriculturists into traders. The growing prosperity of the Mediterranean world had not touched the Macedonian highlands. It would be necessary for the Macedonians to go and possess themselves of the wealth of the Asiatic coast.

So urged Harpalus, the sickly peasant's son, who had become fascinated by the possibilities of coined money. And Alexander understood those possibilities. He could solve problems of economy more quickly than most men could think about them.

Many fears held him back from the venture. Distrusting his own ability profoundly, he shrank from putting himself at the head of thirty thousand men. When he paced the groves of Pella, out to the shrine that had served once to measure a run for him, he watched the hard line of the distant sea, hostile and unknowable;

106

when his glance touched the wording on the shrine, *I am an immortal god, mortal no more,* his imagination conjured up the distant, antagonistic gods of Asia. He had no one to advise him—rather he had too many advising him. And always behind him in the halls of Pella's residence he felt the ghosts of Cleopatra's murdered child and his cousin Amyntas.

Until the morning when Parmenio and Philotas walked with him out to the shrine, urging again that he must give his consent before the expedition could start. Alexander listened, saying nothing, holding his head aslant.

"With the rising of the star Arcturus," he said at last, "we will march to Asia. You have the plans. Carry them out."

When they left him to hurry back to the palace with the news he stayed to look long at the line of the sea. Hostile it might indeed be, but beyond it far to the east he might find the Parapanisades.

Aristotle opposed this. And during the last of that winter Alexander sat much with the Stagyrite, who was then at work upon his *Politics*.

The philosopher who was to become the criterion of human thought for many centuries advised the young captain-general of Hellas to limit his activity to Macedon. Here Alexander could control events. Here Alexander's privileged class of noblemen could exist in security, maintained by the peasant class, while it educated itself—and Aristotle had reason to know the ignorance of the mass of the Macedonians. Even Plato, in *The Republic*, had assumed that only a protected few could reach the heights in human endeavor. The ideal state must be like a garden, sheltered to allow the growth of the finest plants.

This was the qualitative argument, and Aristotle pressed it because his own standards were so high. If only a few could be enlightened by exact knowledge of their purpose in life, still that few could govern the mass of the ignorant.

107

Perhaps there existed no World Soul toward which Plato's speculation had tended; yet surely there existed within space the Immovable Mover—the directing source of energy. Toward that forever stable source human thought should be turned.

Sitting on the bench under the stone nymphs, Aristotle prodded the damp earth with his staff. "We must find the good for which life exists on this earth of ours," he lisped, blinking his eyes, overstrained with work. He relaxed, a smile moving the wrinkles of his set face. "We can grow good fruit trees in this soil, within this garden. Even if the Tree of Life does not grow here."

Worried, his mind encompassed by the ever-growing multitude of notes that he kept upon a half-dozen sciences, his words confused when he tried to explain the greater mysteries toward which he labored—his notes on metaphysics being poorly written compared to his treatise on physics—the Stagyrite gave voice to his fears. This garden in which they sat, the mountains of Macedon, the narrow seas around this land, could be no more than one small corner of the greater Oikoumene. The limits of habitable land might stretch for vastly greater distances than philosophers had supposed around the globe of the earth. Those distances might be peopled with barbarian hordes unseen as yet by Greek eyes. If Alexander led half the manpower of Macedon eastward the voyagers might be swallowed up in these multitudes or lost in the vast distances still unmapped.

Perhaps in speaking against the departure overseas Aristotle may have been influenced by his knowledge of Alexander's heredity. For Olympias showed evidence of incipient mania, being never at ease unless she dominated those around her. And Philip, a drunkard, had sired one idiot. Alexander, at twenty years of age, still showed restlessness in meeting ordinary people and a tendency to escape into a dream world of his own.

Stubbornly the captain-general of Hellas refused to change his decision about the expedition. Aristotle

108

himself had admitted that men, like animals, could alter with their physical surroundings. Why, then, could not Macedonians develop in this way, in a kindlier land? The Greeks had extended to the east by sending out colonies. Why could not new cities be built on more fertile hillsides than the bleak slopes of Pella?

"By Macedonians?"

"Yes."

Aristotle shook his head curtly. "There *is* no Macedonian people as yet. Your father has created the idea of Macedon. Around that idea, out of tribes, he has formed an army. Without the army, there is no Macedon. He made conquests, yes; but he failed to administer them properly. The nation he imagined has not yet evolved."

The laws of such evolution, Aristotle held, were inexorable and not man-made. Men could not hunt happiness as if it were a winged bird.

"Yet mariners seeking land, and men crossing a desert, guide themselves by the flight of birds," Alexander laughed.

With the first warmth of the sun at the rising of Arcturus he felt an overmastering desire to start this journey that had been made by Argonauts and Achaeans before him, toward the rising sun, seeking something better than their old homes, whether gold or glory, or a new land. Of nights he read himself to sleep with the *Troy Tale* and the shining loveliness of Helen. *Small blame to the Trojans that for such a woman they long time suffered hardships, for she was marvelous like to an immortal goddess to look upon.*

"Perhaps," said Ptolemy, who was skeptical about the expedition, "but men go questing for immortal beauty in women, and they are snared by bright-eyed girls in a garden——" He checked himself, remembering a Scythian girl in a garden. "At least Euripides knew that much. What did he say of Helen? Something about joy . . . *died beside the streams of Troy—for the phantom of a face—and the shadow of a name?*"

He could not change Alexander's mind, and it

109

worried him. Because it seemed as if Alexander was thinking of the beauty that had set Helen apart from other women, and not of finding a second Helen. It was a dangerous thing to have preying on your mind. You could not resurrect a ghost. "At least," Ptolemy comforted himself, "we're not launching a thousand ships. We haven't got them."

Having agreed to go, Alexander surprised the staff officers by examining and testing all equipment. His imagination, it seemed, probed into everything that might happen to the army; he studied the journal of Herodotus and the world plan of Hecataeus, questioned insatiably the spies who had been over the roads in Asia, trying to picture the actual lands that lay ahead. He pondered details endlessly.

Looking over Deiades's new machines, he tried the weight of the long ladders that the engineer had mounted on two sets of wheels and all the heavy ropes and light cords, neatly coiled for packing. Such ladders, Alexander thought, could not be moved over streams easily; Deiades would have to do without them and make new ones when necessary.

The temperamental engineer dashed the sweat from his chin and roared. "So, I am to conjure up a forest of such fine seasoned wood, when you call, 'Deiades, bring ladders!' I am to sow acorns and grow oaks, all in a breath, when the trumpet——"

"You can knot the ropes together," Alexander, who had been studying the cordage, said mildly. "Yes, Deiades can make ladders of cords. And they can be carried easily."

The engineer hated to lose his ladders. "And I suppose," he breathed ominously, "you can make ropes climb a wall, like a snake."

"No," Alexander chuckled, "but you can."

Nevertheless he instructed Aristander, the seer, to be ready to go with the expedition. Ptolemy was to command a brigade. And Alexander added strange figures to the army—two surveyors, who were to plot each

110

day's march, a mineralogist, a weather expert, and scientists who were to keep a record of all animal and plant life. Alexander planned to keep his own journal of the trip and asked Ptolemy if he would not like to do the same. "As if," the son of Arsinoë complained, "he were taking the academy along. Not one woman to go, mind you, but a plenty of bigwigs, musicians, and bug hunters, not to mention the doctors."

It seemed to veteran Macedonians as if this was to be more an exploring venture than an invasion. Who had ever heard of a general keeping a daily journal?

Moreover, their captain-general insisted on preparing for a year's absence or more. He checked over the personal means of the higher officers and Companions and offered crown lands—he had no money—to those who needed help. Among them was Perdiccas, now recovered from his wound.

"But what are you keeping for yourself?" asked that experienced trooper.

"My chances."

Perdiccas thought that over and said he would take his chances with Alexander. He had noticed, with the others, that the erratic and inexperienced Alexander, having announced that he would give all orders, had also assumed responsibility for all details.

At the same time he freed himself from one dominating influence. When Olympias, who was to be left in Pella under the unimaginative care of Antipater, stormed at him for his recklessness in giving away the family lands to powerful officers—"You are making them the equal of kings!"—he would not listen to her. When she wept, then, working herself into a spasm of self-pity, he spoke suddenly, harshly.

"I think I have paid rent enough for the time in your womb."

Astonished, Olympias fell silent, drying her tears. "My letters will follow you," she assured him, "wherever you go."

At the rising of the star Arcturus in that year 442 of the Olympiad, the Macedonian army set out on the

King's Way toward the Dardanelles. Alexander walked in the column in the dust, with the black horse Bucephalus led behind him.

He never came back.

TWO

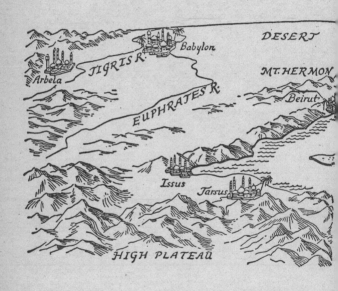

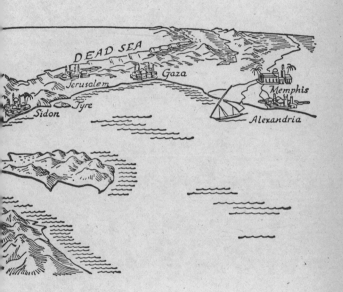

VI. BRIDGEHEAD

The crossing had been a jolly one. The weather had been perfect, with the breath of the north wind caressing the troubled waters of the strait, and a clear sun warming the reddish earth of the Asia side, and the hill of Ilium [Troy] visible against the higher ridges of the land's backbone. Only friendly gulls skimmed the water, without a sign of enemy ships. Even the most superstitious of the Greek allies conceded that the omens were good. The gods most certainly favored the expedition in its crossing, and that was an indication of success to come. A whole flotilla of fishing smacks and merchant craft ferried back and forth across the gut of the Dardanelles, and men shouted, "Hail!" as they waded ashore and turned to glance back at the familiar northern shore.

Someone had thrown a garland of ivy over Alexander as he jumped ashore in his armor, with the white plumes on his shining helmet. And already they had set up marble blocks as altars to Zeus, the God-Father, protector of wayfarers, and also to Athena, to honor the Athenians with the expedition. At these altars they had poured libations out of gold cups, and they had hurried in a festive mood to the fallen towers of Ilium, to look for the historic Skaian gates and hunt for souvenirs, amazed to discover how small was the hilltop upon which heroes had performed immortal deeds.

Here the merchants and fisherfolk who still inhabited the hill showed them relics. They stared at the dark shield and broken harp which the temple attendants swore had been Achilles's, and they took it to be a favorable omen when Alexander, after inspecting the

117

shield, kept it to be carried with the army and left his own in its place. The festival, in fact, became general that evening when the leaders drank wine at the tombs of Achilles and Patroclus the two mighty friends—until, feeling joyful, they twisted garlands in their hair and stripped off their clothes to dance in honor of these illustrious dead. Alexander when he tired of the dancing and flutes sat in the torchlight arguing with Hephaestion about whether Achilles had really been supreme among warriors or whether he had been shaped by Homer's verses into a legend. Suppose that Homer had never written the *Iliad*—what then would they know of Achilles?

Nothing, Hephaestion said. If a man did not have a mighty poet to make a song of his deeds he would be forgotten after the last grandfather of the last grandson died. They weren't dancing and drinking here to the memory of Greeks and Trojans, but to the memory of what Homer had sung.

Ptolemy objected hotly that rhetoric could not make fame. Take a gorgeous woman like Helen—why, he could feel the ghost of the long-haired Helen moving through the grove, passing with the night wind. Hephaestion snorted and said in that case he had better put on some clothes.

The Macedonian *pezetairi* said little over their wine. They felt the damp, dark earth with their fingers and looked at the numerous lambs in the great flocks of sheep and agreed that this was good, fertile soil, better than their own stony hillsides.

Although the Macedonians were disappointed by the small size and poverty of the ruins, they felt happy to be camped among the graves of the old heroes, especially Alexander, who ordered the inhabitants to repair the walls and promised them freedom in perpetuity from tribute payment. When he marched from Troy it was to battle.

Parmenio's spies had brought word that strong forces of Asiatics were moving in from the east. This did not disturb the chief of staff, who had tricked the enemy by making a surprise crossing. Leisurely now he moved on with the Macedonians, keeping to the lowland near the shining sea, with the white summits of Mount Ida and Olympus-in-Asia standing like beacons ahead of him. When scouts reported the enemy in sight the Macedonians deployed into twin columns and arrived in their own good time at a rain-swollen river called the Granicus. And there they had their first sight of the horsemen of Asia.

While the columns advanced on the river Parmenio and his young commander studied the forces on the far bank curiously—the fine, rangy horses massed in regiments, the riders strange in loose trousers and colored capes, with small shields and sheaves of javelins slung at their hips. For these horsemen were down at the river's edge, laughing at the silent Macedonians and shouting insults.

"*Yunnani! Yunnani!* Who pays you to come here? Are you women to wear kilts?"

Undisturbed by the clamor, Parmenio observed more cavalry with bows farther back, along the crest of a ridge. He saw also a phalanx of close-packed spearmen—Greek mercenaries. The whole strength he estimated to be less than his own, and the order of battle to be childish—with the best-armed horsemen, Persian chivalry, down in the valley at the edge of the turbulent stream shouting challenges.

Coldly he summed up the situation to the restive Alexander, who was tense with anxiety. "Don't listen to them," Parmenio warned, "and don't try to move out across that water—it's treacherous and deep in places, and they could maneuver against us where they like. We would lose alignment and have to climb out of the water—what did you say?"

Alexander was muttering: "You didn't turn a hair at the Hellespont, and now you're afraid of this bastard of a stream."

"All you have to do," Parmenio went on, making no sense out of the mutter, "is to do nothing. Hold the formations here—go into camp. They've only one good

119

brigade of infantry, and they won't dare stay near us after dark. They're cavalry. They'll be gone in the morning and you can cross as you will without hurting a man."

"And what then? They'll be laughing at us still."

This burst of temper seemed to the chief of staff as childish as the behavior of the Asiatics—challenging veteran Macedonians to a cavalry skirmish in a river, as if it were a new game. But Alexander would not let the challenge pass. He ordered the skirmish line ahead of the columns, down into the Granicus, and rode off to the Companions on the right. He was not riding the black horse that day.

Tense with excitement, he pushed through to Philotas and started the armored horsemen down into the river.

"Come on," he called, leading his regiment down.

Everything disastrous that Parmenio had predicted happened in the next hour. Alexander, plunging into flood water up to his knees, turned instinctively downcurrent, toward the center of the massed Persian horse. Losing all formation among the rocks, the Companions stumbled and plowed downstream, hard hit by flights of javelins, half blinded by spray. Slipping in the mud, caught against rocks, they wheeled up the far bank and were met by the rush of horses handled with swift skill. Their long light spears with cornel-wood shafts snapped like grass in this press of shields, rocks, and brush. Horses fell and men crashed down. The surviving Companions pressing close to Alexander's white plumes and cloak yanked out their short swords. The Persian leaders headed for the Macedonian chief. A javelin caught in a joint of Alexander's bronze chest plate, and his plumes were hacked off. He reached back to his weapon carrier for a fresh spear, and the man waved the shaft he held, to show it was broken.

A sword bit deep into Alexander's helmet, stunning him and driving the sight from his eyes. Crouching, he bent his head and never saw Black Cleitus, his bodyguard, covering him. A Persian chief, in gleaming

120

gold-washed armor, struck at his bent head, but Cleitus hacked the descending arm off at the joint and held his shield over Alexander.

The Macedonian army kept their leader from going down in this mad press of bleeding horsemen. Cretan archers put up a covering discharge of arrows over the disordered Companions, and Parmenio started the infantry phalanx across the stream in the confusion. These spearmen worked their way up to firm footing, out of the mud.

In a little the Persian horse pulled away, and the action ceased at the river as abruptly as it had begun. Black Cleitus wiped the sweat from his palms on his kilt and looked Alexander over. "Well, you are still here," he said.

Alexander could see clearly again, and move all his limbs. He said nothing, watching under his helmet brim while the Companions gathered. Then he led them headlong up the slope at the solid square of the Greek mercenaries, who had not tried to retreat in the face of cavalry. The sunburned mercenaries stood their ground like figures of stone behind the hedge of spear points. And Alexander's horse went down, killed by a spear point, and he was thrown heavily, bruised, rolling helplessly on the ground. By the time he could mount again and hold a weapon the surviving Greeks—two thousand of them—had laid down their weapons and given themselves up.

By then the swift Persian cavalry had passed out of sight into the hills and the Macedonians had started searching the ground for weapons and valuables. The turbulent Granicus brawled through the valley where men moved busily, making camp, carrying in the wounded and stacking the weapons. Alexander had to recall with an effort that his horse had died and he was riding a strange mount. Black Cleitus had gone, and Philotas, unmarked, was speaking in cold, clipped words. "Nearly a hundred of the Companions will have their graves here."

Going down to the stream, Alexander threw off his

helmet and dipped his head in the icy water. He felt shaken and suddenly hungry. With some officers Parmenio came up as he was drying himself. The chief of staff, impassive, chose his words carefully. "You took too great a risk, but you did well to angle into the river. It helped the men behind you." And then, curiously: "Didn't you know the Greek mercenaries had asked for terms when they were left alone?"

Alexander shook his head, muttering. "They were Greeks, hired—against Greece."

"If you are surprised that Greeks will meet Greeks, then you will have much amazement in store for you."

Many of the mercenaries, Parmenio explained, were Athenians. Only those who had hidden among the bodies of the dead had managed to escape. Their commander had been killed, with most of the noble-born Persians, for the searchers of the field had identified a son-in-law of the Great King, with an uncle and other relatives, a viceroy and governor of provinces, and many general officers. The commander of the Persian cavalry had committed suicide when the retreat began.

It seemed strange to Alexander that all this had happened and that so many hours had passed in what he had thought to be no more than the rush of a few moments. Already dusk was hiding the river and the sunset glow fading along the peaks.

That day had been a bloody business, Parmenio pointed out, holding in his anger. Too many Companion horsemen had died in this river. Alexander himself had escaped twice—once by Cleitus's quickness and again by sheer luck. He had endangered the Companion cavalry and risked defeat, which would have been a stunning blow to morale at the start of the expedition.

But the men of the phalanx spoke otherwise, among themselves. They had suffered less than the cavalry, and it seemed to them here at Chaeronea that Alexander had led them in person to triumph, as if indeed he had in him the spirit of Enyalios, the god of battles. After that, where Alexander went no man would refuse to go.

With nightfall reaction gripped Alexander. He went from fire to fire, watching the physicians at work over the wounded men, asking the men how they had been hurt and letting them brag of what they had done that day. He gave order that the Companions should be buried fully armed and that their families at home should be freed from harvest tithes and future service. In this emotional strain he ordered the sculptor Lysippus to make memorial statues of some of the illustrious dead, to be cast in bronze and placed about the altar pillar erected on the battlefield. The semblance of these men and the memory must survive.

Afterward, recovering from the black moodiness, he arranged for a shipment of spoil to be sent Olympias and Antipater. And three hundred suits of Asiatic armor to be presented to the Parthenon at Athens with the inscription: *Alexander, son of Philip, and the Greeks—all except the Spartans—present this offering taken from the foreigners of Asia.*

So at the same time he sent money home and paid tribute to Greek patriotism. And he never repeated the mistake of that headlong rush into the river Granicus. For Alexander learned the lessons of command quickly.

Much later a hardheaded Roman historian, Arrian, pointed this out. *He was quick to recognize what had to be done, while others were still held back by uncertainty. From observation of facts, he was most successful in conjecturing what was likely to happen. In danger, he relieved the fear of his men by his own freedom from fear. Thereafter he did quickly and boldly what had to be done, even when he was uncertain of the result.*

What had to be done after the action at the Granicus was to move quickly. Leaving a military commander at the bridgehead of the strait, the Macedonian army started south down the coast of Asia, covering twenty miles a day.

Its chief of staff was troubled by more than Alexander's recklessness. His intelligence had informed him that Memnon of Rhodes, a veteran commander of mercenaries, had escaped from the field at the Granicus. This same Memnon, alone at the council before the engagement, had argued that the Persian command should withdraw slowly before the Macedonians, avoiding battle and trampling down the crops, burning stocks of grain and emptying the villages of inhabitants, so the invaders would find no fodder, food, or assistance, on their way. They might then be led into the interior, to be met there by a greater mobilization of Persian power and cut off from their base at the strait. And this was the line of action Parmenio most feared.

Far inland and out of reach lay the main strength of the Asiatics. On the other hand, hostile fleets patrolled the coast and might either cut the Macedonian communications at the Dardanelles or make a raid upon Greece, with or without Spartan assistance. And Parmenio heard that Memnon of Rhodes had gone out to these fleets.

The Macedonians, barred from the sea and the interior, were marching down the winding coast against time.

VII. THE FIRST SUMMER, AND THE WINTER

Rapidly as the Macedonians marched, down the good roads of a smiling coast, just as quickly realization grew upon Alexander that they were failing to accomplish their first and simplest objective. As captain-general of the new Hellenic League, he was invading Asia to liberate the Greek colonies from the yoke of the Asiatic king. Well, it seemed that the Greek colonies did not want to be liberated.

There were ghosts along that fertile Ionic coast, besprinkled with orchards and pasture lands, with forests, mines, and warehouses. Concerning these ghosts his own excellent intelligence service had not advised him. And he found them both intangible and difficult to exorcise.

At Mieza they had known a little about the ghosts. How, in the twilight age after the golden age of the Titans who implanted within ancient men a spark of the divine, the Hellenic tribes had migrated down from the northern forests and steppes of the mainland, into the coasts and peninsulas of the Mediterranean. Finding little fertile soil on the western shores, many tribes had adapted themselves to the sea and had voyaged out to the islands, becoming Peoples of the Sea, like the Sardana who finally settled in the island of Sardinia.

However, these peoples who had tended east had found better soil and everlasting forests on this eastern coast, as far down as the cedars of Liban, watered by winter snow. The Dardana had stayed put at the mouth of the strait [the Dardanelles]. Other peoples than the

125

Hellenes [1] had migrated thereafter to this nearer Asia—the warlike Cimmerians coming from as far away as the steppes north of the Crimea [the Cimmeria].

So these eastern migrants had found a better land than the westerners.

Pent up in their narrow valleys, cutting down the scanty forests, so the slopes soon became bare of trees, and soon exhausting the rocky soil of the Greek peninsula, the inhabitants of the Greek *polis* had begun to migrate over the seas, to found colonies around the perimeter of the Mediterranean and especially upon this sunny Ionic coast. Here, as the Macedonians soon discovered, a great variety of crops could be grown—more than the meager olives and wine grapes of Greece proper. Here was fine clay, ready for the potters' hands, and hardwood timber growing beside the shipyards. These colonists lived better than the populace of the mother cities. They no longer cared to be citizens of Corinth, Thebes, Sparta, or Athens. They held themselves to be citizens of the new Ionian cities in Asia Minor.

Alexander had brought with him pilots' sketches of the intervening sea, the Aegean. But here on the eastern shore he was surprised to discover how close he was in time to the mother cities. A fast-sailing galley could pass with a good wind from an Asiatic promontory to Athens in thirty hours, whereas the fastest-marching Macedonian regiment could not reach Athens by the land roads in a month. Again the sea

---

[1] Traditional dates of this Hellenic expansion are: Arrival along the coasts and extension to the islands (with the Peoples of the Sea) about 1400–1100, with the siege of Troy (western Achaeans vs. eastern Hellenes) toward the end of that period. Homeric poems 800 (?). Historical extension of western Greeks by colonization, 750–580. World Wars I and II ("Persian Wars") 499–79. Civil Wars ("Peloponnesian") 460–04. Philip's campaigns to control Balkans, free the Macedonian coast, and gain supremacy among Greek cities 357–36. Alexander's crossing into Asia, 334 B.C.

here was so besprinkled with island chains that at one point sailing craft could hop-skip to Athens, keeping always within sight of land—there being no more than twenty-five miles in the widest gap between the islands of the Cyclades chain. Some of these islands of the Aegean like Rhodes and Lesbos had developed mighty cities that were now wonders of the world.

All in all, these colonies had grown up and become fecund, hostile to the barren mother cities. Having possessed themselves of all the good harbors along the coast—finer ports than the narrow anchorages of Greece proper—they had become terminals for the trade originating within the vast hinterland behind them. Caravans from Armenia and Mesopotamia disgorged their precious goods at these seaports. The shipping here, roped in masses with prows against the quays, *belonged* to the seafaring Asiatic Greeks. Goldsmiths who had emigrated from Corinth found a greater supply of the rare metal here. The actors at a port like Miletus played to bigger audiences than at Corinth's theater.

The ghosts of those half-forgotten migrations haunted this Ionian coast.

Here, too, was a fulfillment of one of Aristotle's requirements for an ideal city: a prosperous aristocracy, with leisure time to study. Slaves from the interior did all the rougher work; mercenaries supplied the garrisons. The Ionians had developed a leisure class, highly educated, dwelling in marble villas in cedarlined gardens set into the cool hillsides. Women of this class, like the legendary Semiramis, often ruled the cities. They entertained the Macedonian officers at luxuriant feasts, served by deft slaves to the music of harp and flute. They liked to quote Aristophanes's satirical verses, they kept their inner thoughts hidden, they had traditions of great wealth-producing kings—Midas, Croesus, Gordius—they could gamble a dozen talents upon the throw of dice. Their women shone with garlands of matched pearls and jasper chains—Lesbian and Chian women, sweet with the dry scent of nard

127

and myrrh. They were drifting upon a tide of wealth, proud of their family ties, secretive, conscious of vast opportunities unknown to the barbaric Macedonians.

While the aristocrats of the seaports still spoke classic Greek, some of the inland folk had forgotten it, and along the water fronts a new trade-talk vernacular, the *koiné*, had developed. These easterners had only faint, hostile memories of the glories of Marathon and Salamis. They agreed courteously that a united Greece, a revived and powerful Hellas, was desirable, to join together all the Aegean world. Free democracies were a splendid thing, no doubt. Yet they were vitally concerned with their trade, and this came from the hinterland ruled by the Great King, who imposed no greater hardship upon them than the presence of his tyrants—Greek officials who served him—the payment of a light tithe, and possibly the service of their warships at intervals.

Very soon the sensitive Alexander realized that these Ionians were aliens, willing to sacrifice nothing for the liberty and glory of Greece, only agreeing to his plans because he had for the moment the greater military power on the scene, and because they were not sure exactly what the next turn of fate would bring.

"They are worse liars than the Corinthians," the blunt Nearchus summed up, "but they have grand ships."

Faced by this open acquiescence and secret opposition, Alexander moved very cautiously, deeply disappointed, becoming aware that here was a moral, not a physical, state of war.

At first his progress had been something like a triumph, and it had seemed certain the Macedonians were winning their race with time. Sardis, the terminus of the eastern post road and headquarters of the Persian administration, had sent out its councilors to welcome the Macedonian with flowers and songs—the garrison having fled with the Persian tyrant. He had been escorted within its triple walls, to the summit of the citadel. Wishing to set up something of his own here, he had arranged for the building of a new memorial temple, and he had left Sardis the richer for the contents of the Persian treasury. At Ephesus the hostile garrison had taken ship, the Greeks improvised a democracy happily on the spur of the moment, and Alexander surprised them by turning over the revenues to the new Temple of Artemis—for which he had a friendly feeling, the old one having burned upon his birthnight. Aristander the seer, who was now approaching his old home, assured Alexander that the omens were excellent. Cities were setting up triumphal pillars, inscribed with their new accord with the captain-general of Hellas. He was careful to levy no impost on these cities. They were free, he said, and meant it.

But as he pushed south he began to meet with delay. It seemed as if these Ionians were more concerned about bargaining for privileges than in planning for their new liberty. Certainly no volunteers of any account joined the Macedonian army. Miletus, the oldest colony, closed its gates to bargain the better—and to observe the movements of a strong fleet that appeared along the coast.

"Memnon of Rhodes," Parmenio told his king, "is in command of that fleet."

The Macedonians had a few craft converted into warships, and these were used to close the narrow entrance of the harbor while negotiations went on with the city. The Milesians would only offer the Macedonians the same rights as the Persian forces enjoyed.

The men, in high spirits, wanted to storm the wall. Deiades set up new machines. Even the ever-careful Parmenio urged Alexander to man the ships in the harbor with a few regiments and go out to engage Memnon's battle fleet. He argued that the Macedonians could win against odds of two to one, afloat as on shore, that a victory over the main Persian fleet would impress all the coast, while a defeat could cost only limited casualties. He offered to command the extemporized fleet himself.

Probably Parmenio was right in his argument. But Alexander, distrusting the situation, had become the soul of caution. He refused consent.

Parmenio insisted, pointing out that he had an omen in his favor. The men had seen an eagle come down from the sky and alight among them on a rock under the very stern of a war galley. So the eagle had presaged victory, indicating a ship.

"If the eagle stayed on shore," Alexander told him, "we will stay put on good firm land."

The consequences were not happy. Weeks went by in skirmishing, while the Macedonians took over all the nearby sources of drinking water along the coast and Memnon's fleet, weary of trying to keep up a blockade without water, drew off to occupy the great island of Lesbos. This, his first encounter with a battle fleet, gave Alexander much to think about.

After Miletus resistance increased on the part of the Ionians. Memnon, moving over the open thoroughfare of the waters, appeared in the monumental city of Halicarnassus with a garrison of Persians and mercenaries. Alexander was forced to yield to his officers and set up siegeworks on the heights around that city, where the Macedonians beheld the towered tomb of Mausolus, the Mausoleum. Yet he made his Macedonians put on an act rather than a siege by making a great show of setting up their elevation towers, breaking down sections of the wall with stone engines, and generally impressing the inhabitants with the certainty that they were about to launch a terrific assault.

One incident almost led to a second Thebes. Two warriors of the phalanx, messmates of Perdiccas's brigade, bored with demonstrations, engaged in a drinking bout in which each tried to outboast the other. When really drunk, this highland twain conceived the idea of proving which was the best man. Putting on full equipment, they paraded out toward the city wall, followed by an interested gallery. Under the wall the two heroes bellowed a challenge to all Halicarnassians, and they got results. Soldiers streamed out to annihilate the profane messmates. The two took up a strong position among some rocks, launched a protective flight of javelins, and held off the attackers. The gallery plunged in to aid the duellists, and other *pezetairi* charged up to extricate the gallery. Before the soldiers could be pulled away, bringing with them what was left of the two champions, a miniature battle had been fought outside the gates of Halicarnassus.

In the end Alexander had to break in, when Memnon started to burn the city's engines and stores, and to evacuate the walls. Memnon escaped out to the omnipresent fleet, while the garrison fortified itself anew in two rocky promontories that could not be surrounded by the Macedonians. Alexander's officers were ordered to put out the fires and not to enter the houses of the city.

He had managed to preserve Halicarnassus, but only at cost of time and lives. And he had to leave some regiments to block off the strongholds of the garrison. The city itself, with its monuments intact, he turned over to a woman to rule for him—to a sister of Mausolus, Ada by name. He paraded the Macedonians through the avenues in her honor, and when the grateful Ada insisted on adopting him as her son he agreed cheerfully.

After Halicarnassus offers of tribute and even a symbolic gold crown were brought in by envoys from neighboring towns. The Lady Ada sent a woman's gift, of preserved fruits and rare seasoned dishes, along with cooks to prepare and serve such palatial food. This Alexander shared among his officers, informing his adopted mother that years before his tutor Leonidas had not allowed him such food from his real mother.

By courier he sent word up the coast that now the Ionian cities were free to manage their own affairs.

But in his own mind he discarded forever his designation as captain-general of the Hellenic League. He had lost all hopes of uniting the Greek cities against the Great King. Perhaps he realized that if these highly separatist cities were welded into a nation they would forfeit the vestiges of their individual democracy. To these vestiges they still held stubbornly, content often to be administered by tyrants, so long as the tyrants were of their own *polis*. He was neither the first nor the last organizer to be baffled by the complexity of the Greek spirit.

Unwilling to plunder the wealthy Ionian cities, yet needing funds if he was to go on—assuming responsibility for their protection, and needing the services of their seaports—he had convinced himself that he would get no aid from them. Stubbornly he held to the splendid coast, determined to work out some solution for it. Meanwhile he had to work his way down this potentially hostile shore.

His first move was to dismantle his miniature fleet that had been hugging the harbors and to land the crews—explaining that he had no money to pay them. He would not risk his Macedonians on the sea, even after learning of the death of the enemy commander, Memnon of Rhodes, at Mytilene.

Yet the sea itself came inland to menace the army in so strange a fashion that the Macedonians took it to be an omen for certain. The coast road down which they were marching wound around an arm of the sea. At the end of the arm the road disappeared.

Here the land rose sheer from the shore, and the way led across a slimy rock shelf. Surf, beating in through jagged rocks, swept over the narrow passage, except for brief intervals. The natives called this gantlet the Ladders of the Sea. They said that here the deep waters climbed up the rock upon the land, to destroy men—unless Fate protected them. To risk the column of the army upon the Ladders of the Sea seemed to be a most dangerous thing to do, but Alexander did it.

Taking advantage of an offshore wind, he rushed the column, wagons and all, across the arm of the sea. The deep waters licked at the legs of the men but did not destroy them. "Alexander's luck," said some, and others pointed out that now the sea appeared to be friendly and no longer antagonistic.

Nearchus knew that as long as the favorable north wind blew they had been reasonably safe. "If the wind had changed," Ptolemy observed, "you would be singing a different tune. The dice fell for us, that's all."

Beyond the Ladders of the Sea they became aware of the activity of human enemies.

Persian gold appeared along the water fronts, and mercenaries slipped past from the sea toward some destination inland. No visible enemies emerged from that vast hinterland, where a destructive power was making its presence felt. One of the Companions was caught with gold darics on him, and proof that he was sending information to the enemy. This officer was placed under arrest—Alexander would inflict no greater punishment because the Companion had been the first to come to him, with arms, after Philip's death. There had been no case of treachery before; now Parmenio warned Alexander that enemy gold had been paid for his assassination.

When the Pleiades sank in the southern sky and autumn cold set in the Macedonians prepared to hold their gains along the coast of Asia Minor. The newly married men were given leave to march home—a highly popular measure—under command of a certain Coenus, himself separated from a bride. They had orders to gather what recruits they could in Macedon and Greece and bring back the new levies with them in the spring.

Alexander started inland with the toughest of the infantry for a winter's march over the snowy plateau.

This was not so reckless an exploit as it seemed to the Ionians. The tribal folk of the plateau's ranges, Phrygians and Pisidians, descendants of stocky Hittites and Cimmerians, were startled at the appearance of disciplined army columns climbing the heights in winter. The Macedonians, being highlanders themselves, could find their way over mountains, and Alexander had discovered that mountain people were more accessible in winter when snow prevented them from re-

133

treating to the summits. As on the coast, he blarneyed and paraded his way among the barbaric folk and the gigantic monasteries of strange cults, avoiding serious conflict.

Moreover his highlanders felt at home among pine forests and sheep, and got on with the Phrygians, who were kindred of the Macdeonians. The people of one city evacuated it, upward to a cliff stronghold that looked hard to take. The experienced Macedonians encircled it and sent word to its defenders not to be fools but to come down and make a treaty. They answered that they were not fools because they expected to be reinforced within two days. Alexander then inquired: if they were not relieved within the two days would they come down? They said yes. And when the two days were up down they came and talked over the situation. From such folk as this Alexander got more volunteers than from the aristocratic Ionians. They were even more superstitious than his Macedonians, and he heard how a wagon was preserved in the palace of Gordium, the largest of the mountain cities, because its founder was supposed to have arrived on the spot driving a wagon. Age had sanctified that wagon, until the priests of the palace at Gordium maintained that it would rest there until a man should come who could untie the knot that bound the yoke to the wagon shaft, and if any man could do that he would become a Great King of Asia.

The mountain folk were curious to see if this impetuous Macedonian would dare attempt to loose the knot, because that country had bred many fine seers and omen-takers like Aristander.

There was a deal of talk about this wagon among the neighbors, Arrian the Roman relates. *When Alexander arrived at Gordium he was very keen to go up into the citadel and see its wagon, and the cord and yoke of the wagon. Because the saying had gone around that whosoever loosed the cord from the yoke would rule Asia. This cord of cornel bark was so tied that its ends were tucked inside and could not be seen.*

134

Alexander could find no way to loosen the cord, and he was afraid now if he failed it would have a bad effect on the watchers. Some say that he drew his sword then, and cut it through. But one who was there with him says that he pulled out the pin of the wagon-pole. As this was a wooden peg driven through the yoke and pole. As this was a wooden peg driven through the yoke and pole, when he drew it out the yoke was free and the cord came loose. However that may be, he and his men went out, as if he had fulfilled the oracle. And that night the folk heard thunder in the sky.

During those winter months the rumor spread over the snowbound plateaus of this Asia Minor that the golden-haired Macedonian youth had in him divine power and that he was destined to become the monarch of these lands. So thought the peasant folk, and the Macedonian *pezetairi* agreed. This popular rumor had one unexpected result. Thereafter Alexander's appearance in person upon a scene had something of a shock effect.

Meanwhile bad news was coming in to the Macedonians resting at Gordium. The enemy fleets, unhampered by the mild winter winds, had been systematically taking over most of the island chain in the Aegean and had finally established a base at Tenedos, near the entrance of the Dardanelles.

When Coenus came back, at the melting of the snows, with the new levies—some three thousand infantry and three hundred Macedonian horse, with several companies of Thessalians—Alexander learned that these enemy fleets had also appeared close to his homeland. Antipater had outfitted a few galleys to patrol the Macedonian coast but was fearful that the Persian fleet would join with the Spartans to take over Greece. The Macedonians at home also worried because Alexander's army seemed now to be cut off.

Whoever made the decision, Alexander announced it. The Macedonian army would not retreat; it would advance and try to eliminate the dangerous fleet by capturing its remaining seaports along this coast of

Asia. Such ships as these could not well keep the sea for more than three days at a time, because they had to put to shore for water or to cook a meal and let the men sleep.

Alexander understood that he could not match the Persian fleet upon the sea, Arrian relates. *He believed that he could break up the Persian fleet by capturing the maritime cities, because that would deprive it of ports in which to recruit crews or supply its shipping.*

That meant, however, running the risk of meeting the main Asiatic army, which he knew to be mobilizing somewhere on the plains south of them. If the Macedonians lost a battle on this far coast it would be hard to find an escape route back to the Dardanelles.

All this was explained to the general council of the army, the officers and Companions. They voted to go ahead.

VIII. ISSUS

Their first night of the southland was a bit ominous. Through the knife slit of a gorge barely wide enough for a wagon to pass they looked down upon an immense plain where the earth was the color of blood, sinking down and away to far mists and a green scum of tropical growth. They stood at gaze in the semi-darkness between gray granite cliffs, whipped by an icy wind even in midsummer, and contemplated this nether region of unfamiliar aspect.

The gorge itself they knew to be named the Cilician Gates. Alexander had occupied it by one of the lucky turns that were to be so common later. Holding back the main column with the supply train, he had tried to surprise the force occupying the gut of the gorge by leading up a few companies of Agrianian highlanders late at night. The trick had not worked. The Macedonians were sighted. But when Alexander was discovered advancing, his white cape showing through the darkness, the defense force had evacuated at once.

Now it seemed to the Macedonians as if this red plain might be an approach to Hades, a descent toward the inner earth. Down there, the seers of Gordium had told them, strange gods held power: Dagon and Baal, before whom children were burned as an offering. Of nights, at the edge of the sea, seraphim passed, borne upon three pairs of wings, and the great god Kronos had two pairs of eyes, so that he slept while he watched, and watched while he slept. Out on the breast of the sea a city, Tyre, had been built upon columns of rock by a Semitic people, the Phoenicians, who burned their dead and worshiped metallic stones that had fallen in flames from the sky and now lay like blackened iron upon the face of the earth.

One of the meteorites lay within the city called Jerusalem, covering an opening that led down into the middle of the earth. The walls of Jerusalem had been built by a man named Nehemiah, above a salt inland sea where plants were poisonous and the earth was salted, and the very stones were tortured and blackened.

Moreover, as the Macedonians descended from the gate into the red plain, the heat of the sun increased markedly, bathing them in sweat. They sighted a yellow rock upon which an inscription had been carved in wedge-shaped marks instead of writing. The officers were not willing to pass until the strange writing had been read to them by a scholar of the countryside, who said it was Assyrian.

Sardanapalus . . . built Tarsus city in a day. But do thou, stranger, eat, drink and lie with women, for that is best in human life. So said the inscription. On top of it stood the figure of a man in strange, kingly robes, with his hands pressed together as if praying.

The Macedonians, who relished both a jest and a philosophy, laughed and debated whether it was best to do as Sardanapalus had said or as he had done.

When the army passed through the Cilician Gates and entered the zone of unseen enemies, a change of mood took place. Alexander seemed to be anxious, while Parmenio suffered from nerves. They moved warily, weighing all the information that came in. During the last winter they had arranged a very useful intelligence service. The records here mention spies as well as scouts. How this secret intelligence was formed is not clear. Perhaps traders, pilgrims, and seamen went in advance, leaving information at the villages along the roads for the army to pick up after them.

Then again the Macedonians kept up continuous observation as they advanced: observations of the familiar constellations of the stars at night, surveys of the distances marched, investigations by the physicians of new diseases. Both Alexander and Ptolemy tried to keep up day-by-day journals of such findings. Regularly they sent home collections for Aristotle's laboratories—new plants, shellfish, animal skins, insect life, and birds. By interrogating the inhabitants as they advanced they gained some idea of what lay ahead—of the roads, food stocks, and peoples. By sending a flying column ahead the Macedonians reached Tarsus, on the river Cydnus, before the enemy could either defend or demolish it.

There Alexander was laid up for weeks by fever brought on by his own carelessness. They had raced through the hot, malarial valley and Alexander had stripped and plunged, sweating into the river fed by the melting snows of the mountains. He was seized with cramps and racked by a stubborn fever, and the officers feared he had been poisoned.

Then he indulged in one of the dramatic byplays that set all the camps talking. When the physicians with him failed to check his fever he called in a certain Philip of Arcarnia, who prescribed a strong purge. At the same time a courier brought in a secret dispatch from Parmenio warning Alexander not to trust this same Philip, who was supposed to be an assassin in the pay of the Great King. Alexander—so the story is told—read the dispatch and said nothing. When Philip brought in the medicine prepared in a goblet Alexander took Parmenio's message from under his pillow, handing it to the physician as he took the goblet.

While Philip read the warning the Macedonian drank the medicine. Those in the tent reported that neither man seemed disturbed as they looked at each other.

"If you follow my directions," the physician said, handing back the letter, "you will get well. Otherwise I can't answer for the result."

The purge prostrated the weakened Alexander, but he kept Philip in attendance. At that time he placed full trust in those around him. Harpalus, for instance—being too sickly for field service—had been put in charge of the small bullion reserve at Sardis.

The illness of the twenty-one-year-old king-commander seemed to have changed the luck of the army. Carrying Alexander in a litter, it could move only slowly across the fever-ridden plain stretching from Tarsus around the Gulf of Issus. The sick list grew. The Syrian inhabitants of the coast began to jeer at the columns feeling their way through the heat haze of marshes. Secret agents of the invisible enemy stirred up rioting in the towns.

All the signs pointed to misfortune to come, and the spirit of the camp sank accordingly.

The anxious Parmenio took the strongest units up into the hills bordering the sea, without finding a trace of the field army of the Asiatics, which he knew to be within two days' march of him. Alexander tried to shake the army out of its moodiness. Seizing on the excuse of favorable news from the north—Ptolemy had come in to report the surrender of the enemy garrisons at Halicarnassus—he declared a field day, paraded all forces to music, allowing them to hold games followed by a torch relay race and a feast at night. After that the sick were left in quarters at the town of Issus, and the army pushed on along the coast road with the sea washing its right hand, the hills pressing close on the left.

And, as if in evidence of the power of hostile gods, rain deluged the marching men for a day and night.

When the skies cleared, incredible news came in. The evasive army of Asia had materialized at last, *behind* the Macedonians. It had circled them and reached the coast, cut their road back, and massacred their sick at Issus. The Macedonian officers could not believe the news.

They sent back some Companions in a fast thirty-oared galley to observe what might actually be in the valley of Issus. And the galley came back with white foam flying and definite report that the enemy was massing around Issus, filling the coast between hills and sea. They were cut off.

Certain of that, Alexander held a quick conference

140

of commanders, and went out to the regimental officers to announce the news. His own nerves on edge, he talked volubly, he talked too much. But he convinced them—if he did not convince himself—that this near disaster was their great opportunity.

"You have never been beaten. You will not be beaten now."

He argued, laughed, and praised. The strength of his purpose went out from him into them with almost physical force.

"Instead of a cavalry division and the Asiatic governors who were at the Granicus, you will meet here the full array of the Persians and the Medes, and the Great King. You will have luck, because they cannot make use of their numbers on this narrow front, while you can make full use of your striking force. You don't have to worry about the flanks—the sea and the mountains will take care of them."

He reminded the barbaric Thracians and Agrianians of their individual exploits, pointed out that the Macedonian Greeks were free men, going against the mercenaries—Greeks also—of an emperor. And in his anxiety he made a promise. "Go through with this conflict, and you will find your long labor at an end. After this your only task will be to occupy the lands of Asia."

Then he had supper served to the men. As soon as it was dark he about-faced the column and started back, without trying to re-form on that narrow roadway. About midnight they reached the narrow pass that opened out into the great bay of Issus. And here he halted the column and let the men sleep a few hours. With the first light they advanced again, opening out as the hills began to fall away from the shore. They were going into their fixed battle formation against—as they soon discovered— three or four times their own strength.

To understand what happened then, so unexpectedly, at Issus, it is necessary to understand that these Macedonians were following out a fixed plan of action. The Macedonian army could do that because it had been seasoned by a generation of campaigning. Moreover each unit had been recruited from one segment of the people. The Agrianian highlanders made up the best skirmishing regiment, and so forth. So each unit knew its place, its task to perform, and had gone through with it several times before. The whole made up something strangely modern, an experienced fighting team.

Ancient battles before then had consisted usually of two masses of fighting men which pushed at each other until something gave way—or, as Antigonus had said, until one side became more afraid than the other and ran away. Such a disciplined mass had been shaped into the hedgehog-like phalanx to give it power; in it the Spartans had prevailed over others because they excelled as individual fighters and because they could not be stopped unless they were killed.

But a phalanx became useless when it was broken into. And Epaminondas the Theban had devised a way to break up the enemy formation by making the extreme right of his own line heavier and more powerful than his adversary's. For a time this Theban thrust-by-the-right had prevailed on fields of battle.

Philip of Macedon had studied the Thebans and improved upon them. The best infantry phalanx could only attack at a walk and push with its massed spears. Philip had devised a way to use horsemen for the break-through. He had horsemen and he armed them heavily. And either he or his commanders worked out a way to conceal this flying wedge of horsemen until it broke loose *behind* the enemy lines and broke up all resistance.

This was the secret maneuver of the Macedonian army which had given it victory until now. Alexander had gone no more than lead this spearhead of attack through an opening prepared for him. And Parmenio was justified in saying that the Macedonians need fear no other army in an orthodox battle.

The maneuver was worked in this way.

As seen by an enemy's eye, only weak units were visible on the extreme left of the Macedonians—only some archers and skirmishers. These served as a screen for the brilliant and fast Thessalian horse. (Under Philip's tactics this Macedonian left wing might put on any kind of an act but was only supposed to hold its ground, to protect that side of the phalanx.)

The phalanx was the core and center of the Macedonian formation, with the Greek hoplites nearest the Thessalian cavalry, their countrymen. Though Macedonian peasantry formed the bulk of the *pezetairi,* the spearmen. When it closed up, this phalanx usually stood eight men deep, with the rearmost carrying the longest sarissa, or pike, of some sixteen feet. The front rank had the shortest weapon—so that all eight weapon points projected beyond the front line. (Internally the phalanx was formed in *taxis,* or regiments, of 1536 men, also made up of units down to the *stichos,* or squad, of eight men—a double file, in the close order).

In numbers the phalanx was about fourteen thou-

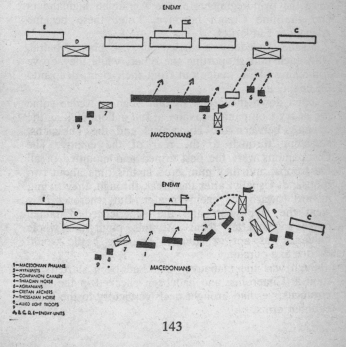

143

sand strong at this time, and it was nearly invulnerable to attack. Beside chest plate and metal helmet and narrow shield, each man was equipped with a short but heavy sword for close fighting, if any occurred. (Each man carried his own kit on the march.)

This particular phalanx, however, did something unusual and barely noticed by the enemy. It edged forward on the right—advancing, as soldiers say, by echelon on the right.

As it did so a most unusual unit appeared on that side of it—the Hypaspists, or Aiders. They were on foot and heavily armed, but could fling themselves forward, some three thousand strong, almost as rapidly as horsemen.

When these Hypaspists advanced Thracian horsemen farther out also moved ahead. Beyond the Thracians, screening them and supporting their movement, were the twin regiments of the Agrianian highlanders and the fine Cretan bowmen. Later these became Alexander's favorites.

So the Macedonians carried out their plan of battle, with each unit supporting the other, while they drove something like a wedge out from their right, deep into the enemy lines.

Then down the center of that opening wedge came the heavy Companion cavalry at full gallop, picking the opening between the Hypaspists and the Thracians, smashing through to the rear of the enemy. The Companions were the best armed and mounted of all the troops, and they numbered at this time about two thousand. Usually, after the break-through, they swung inward toward the enemy center. But wherever they went the Hypaspists and the experienced Thracian horse raced after them. At this point the whole phalanx was apt to advance and the battle would change to a pursuit.

Such was the maneuver that had been started too soon at Chaeronea and had been checked in the river Granicus, yet had brought decisive victory to the Macedonian arms.

Of all the contigents, only the Cretan bowmen served for hire—although the Greek allied units had not come along too willingly. There were auxiliary units: the talented engineers, who also operated Deiades's siege train, the physicians, and scientists. On the arch some barbarian horsemen like the Thracians served as teamsters, while the light-armed skirmishers doubled as body servants of the elite Companions. This compact army of about 27,500, had almost no supernumeraries. Alexander's Agema, or personal guard, was made up of selected companies of Companions, Hypaspists, or phalanxmen, in rotation. The staff then consisted of seven brigade commanders like Perdiccas, who stayed close to Alexander until an engagement began, when they went to their commands.

This morning, as usual, Alexander went with the attack forces toward the hills on the right, while Parmenio took the left flank, which he was to anchor against the sea.

Alexander, who had probably not slept at all in the night, showed evidence of being very nervous, as he had reason to be. His first sight of the half-moon bay showed him such masses of enemies awaiting him as he had visualized only in dreams before. This was an army of nations—Greek mercenaries, Kurdish infantry ranged on the far side of a large stream, with other forces spreading over the slope of the hills on his right, and a cloud of cavalry poised there, as if waiting for the Macedonians to advance. Behind this battle line other masses of the Asiatics stretched back to the distant town of Issus.

The shore of the bay was itself like an amphitheater, and not too large a one, with a narrow entrance gate through which he had come, and a corresponding gate—another narrow pass—at the far end of the bay behind Issus. He must have seen how he was outnumbered in horsemen. His infantry could not retreat now.

Within this natural arena there could be fought no delaying or holding action. Inevitably one army would be driven back against a narrow exit, much too small for its passage. Apparently the Asiatics had been following him down the coast road, and his rapid march back under cover of darkness had caught them on the shelving bay shore. Only along the shore itself, on his *left*, was the ground level enough for a massed cavalry charge.

For an hour or so in the morning he and Parmenio watched what was happening at the far end of the half-moon, keeping the Macedonians back, out of good observation by the Persians. They observed the withdrawal of the cloud of cavalry from the hillside back over the stream—changing its ground to the lower shore. At the same time the Persian center began to fortify the steep bank of the stream with wooden barriers.

To counter the move of the Persian cavalry down to the shore Alexander added the Thracian horse from his own to Parmenio's command, cautioning them to keep out of sight as they moved. Then he added the Cretan bowmen, because at all cost Parmenio had to hold the anchor of the Macedonian line there, on the level beaches. If the Thracians and Thessalians fought up to their belts in salt water they had to hold the left flank!

Then he advanced his battle line, to attack. As much as possible, in the rolling ground, the horsemen were kept out of observation, behind the infantry. When his men approached the stream, coming into full view of the masses on the other side, Alexander rode among them, at high tension, on Bucephalus, reining in for a quick word with company commanders. The men cheered. They wanted to go on.

But Alexander kept the four thousand Greek hoplites back of the phalanx as a reserve. On this narrow front he did not want his Greeks to meet other Greeks. And always he watched the mountain flank. They were moving past the Asiatics posted under the crests, and Alexander must have studied the slopes, the rocky gullies, and the hollow of the stream ahead of him. For he sent the Agrianian mountaineers, with bowmen in support, to clear the slopes above him.

146

They did it by driving the light forces of the Persians up into the crests.

With these slopes cleared temporarily, Alexander had completed his observation of them. It was after midday, and he halted his advance to let the men eat the rations they were carrying.

While the dense Persian ranks were kept under arms, foodless, he waited. But during this interval he was withdrawing the Agrianians from the upper slopes, adding them to the Hypaspists at the right of the phalanx. He thought that two or three troops of horse would hold the Persians up on the crests, and by now he was satisfied that cavalry could move over the shoulders of the hills above him.

Then he started the phalanx forward, in echelon to the right.

These first regiments had to cross the stream at the foot of the hills where the banks were steep. They got across and forged up the other bank. When they checked, the companies of Hypaspists ran in, drifting to the right. Behind them at a foot pace Alexander started the Companions moving in. His spearhead of attack was now crossing the stream, tending uphill.

The center regiments of the phalanx had been stopped at the barriers behind which the Greek mercenaries massed. But always, as ordered, they edged to the right, away from the shieldside.

What Alexander had feared then happened. Down on the shore the strong Persian cavalry attacked, crossing the stream and driving into the much weaker Thessalian and Thracian horse. Still the Companions were held back, while the infantry gained ground, yard by yard, in front of them. The horsemen began to come under a heavy discharge of arrows and darts that set the horses surging.

It was too dangerous to hold back longer, and the Companions were sent forward along the lane that had been cleared on the hillside. They broke through resistance there and swung sharply left, racing downhill. At full charge they struck the rear of the Persian

147

phalanx, with the Hypaspists following after them. The close-packed Greeks and Persians, trying to re-form, were driven back.

At this point one man gave up the battle before it was lost. Darius, the Great King, in his chariot behind the center of the Persian line, saw the Companions breaking through. He ordered his chariot back and when it was checked by confusion along the road he abandoned it and fled on a horse with his personal guards past Issus.

It was luck that Darius should be a coward. But the deadly attack that frightened him had been anything but luck. What might have happened if he had kept his place, in front of his strong reserves, will never be known. What did happen, as he raced away, was that those reserves, backed up as far as the town, were thrown into a tangle of cross movements. Other units started back. The center phalanx, half enveloped now, began to give toward the shore.

There the Asiatic cavalry had been having things all its own way. But it became aware of the panic behind it and swung around.

It swept past the center, now in full retreat, and plunged through the infantry drawn up along the road.

Alexander had checked the Companions' advance and waited until he was satisfied that Parmenio's forces were safe, even if battered. Then the Companions took up the pursuit along the foothills, while all the Macedonian units pressed along the road.

The fleeing Asiatics piled up in the narrow pass at the end of the bay. Ptolemy wrote in his journal afterward that in the terrible congestion there horsemen suffered as much as men fleeing on foot, and when the Macedonian cavalry reached the pass they had to ride over the piled-up bodies of the dead.

The pursuit continued until it was too dark to see what was underfoot. And the soldiers brought Alexander the shield, mantle, and bow of the Great King, which they had found in the abandoned chariot.

At Issus Alexander had extracted the Macedonian army from an almost desperate situation. This had been accomplished by no inspired gamble but by painstaking, relentless efforts. It had taken him until early afternoon to work the column of Companion cavalry up to the vantage ground of the hillside—where, incidentally, the Persian cavalry had held free tenancy early in the morning. It was an extraordinary feat to launch a charge of mounted men down this mountain slope, like a landslide. But this was the only path possible for the maneuver of the heavy horse upon which the Macedonians relied, and Alexander cleared it in time, but only just in time.[1]

---

[1]Most military historians have followed a pattern of comment, in pointing out that Darius made a fatal mistake by penning up his much more numerous forces on a narrow front, in rough terrain where cavalry could not easily operate, and where his superiority in missile fire was largely nullified.

This is all true, but Darius could hardly have anticipated that a full-scale battle would take place precisely there, on the shore at Issus. We have some record of the factors influencing his generals. Some three days before Issus a decision was made not to assume the defensive by waiting on the open Syrian plain but to go in to attack. The Persian commanders accomplished the difficult feat of maneuvering a much larger army across the communications of the Macedonians. They were closing rapidly on the Macedonians when Alexander turned back sharply to meet them. He caught them still extended in march column and turned what had been up to then a strategic defeat into a decisive tactical victory.

As to the argument that the Persian commanders forfeited their best advantage by leaving the open plain, the Macedonians showed later on at Gaugamela what would happen on ground not only open but artificially leveled for cavalry action.

While the Macedonians had superiority in discipline, they had overwhelming superiority in command, not only in Alexander's leadership but in the quality of the brigade commanders. Alexander could not have made the difficult move over the shoulders of the hills if Parmenio had not held the left flank together against great pressure; Parmenio could hardly have managed this if the Thessalian horse had not accomplished a minor miracle by fighting a successful defensive action along the open beach.

He had shown here none of the nervous excitement of the Granicus. Midway through the engagement he had been able to check the advance of his striking arm, the Companions, backed in this instance by the Hypaspists and Agrianians, until he had made certain that the other flank had not been driven from the edge of the sea.

But it was the relentless and rapid pursuit by the Macedonian forces that had broken up the Asiatic army of Issus. Nothing so terrifying had been encountered by armies of the east before, since they had met with nothing more speedy or destructive than small masses of Greek hoplites such as Xenophon's ten thousand.

This army of Issus lost all its equipment and was scattered so widely that it never reassembled. Darius—who had lost his side arms, tents, family, and servants—gathered together no more than four thousand disciplined men in his rapid retreat east the next day. That retreat continued without a pause until he had put the Euphrates River between him and the dreaded Macedonians.

After Issus the young Macedonian leader gave no evidence of the hysterical reaction that followed the fighting at the Granicus. He seemed both tired and thoughtful, and was bothered besides by a painful sword wound in the hip, so that he had to be helped around and did not mount Bucephalus for a few days.

The next day at the burial of the dead and the selection of new officers he paraded the forces to music. He included the townspeople of Issus in this solemn thanksgiving by remitting the tribute due from them and not yet paid. A large part of the Persian treasure found in the abandoned camp—some three thousand talents—he ordered distributed among officers who had distinguished themselves. Discovering that the main Persian baggage train, corps of servants, and treasure had been left at the base at Damascus beyond the coast range, he asked Parmenio to go after it at once, taking the Thessalian horse who had managed to hold the beach that day—thus giving the warriors of Thessaly first chance at greater loot.

When Parmenio unearthed at Damascus a group of envoys from Greece who had been negotiating with the Great King, Alexander made a point of including them in his gesture of liberation, dismissing the charge of treason laid against them by Parmenio. He found odd reasons for such amnesty. The two agents from Thebes, he said, were guiltless because Thebes itself had been destroyed by Macedonians (so that in seeking aid from the Great King they were acting as patriots). Other agents he dismissed because they had won honor in the Olympic games. Finding Iphicrates, the son of the great general of mercenaries, among the Athenians, he kept the soldier with him as adviser; even the Spartan agent he kept only under observation.

He wanted no more enemies along this coast of Asia, and his policy of sheer generosity—utterly unexpected, after the near disaster at Issus—impressed these suspicious people strongly. Shipbuilders sailed in from Cyprus to investigate the new state of affairs and to offer their services. Keepers of the ancient shrines on the islet of Aradus petitioned him to make sacrifice at their altars, and emissaries of the merchant-trading houses of Beirut brought gifts and an invitation to visit their garden city built against the breast of the mighty Lebanon—founded, so they said, by the sea nymph Beroë or perhaps by the goddess Astarte who had appeared out of the forest riding a lion. (Actually Beirut is a Semitic name, its meaning, The Wells.)

It seemed to these easterners that Alexander possessed a power which could derive only from the gods. Besides, they estimated that he would influence the course of trade for at least two years.

151

IX. THE WOMAN
OF DAMASCUS

If the young leader showed only healthy gratitude when darkness came down on Issus and they learned that the defeat of the Asiatics had been a complete rout, the officers became nearly hysterical in their excitement. While Alexander had been returning along the escape road, many of them had been investigating the immense Persian field camp, captured intact with its tents standing and food ready to serve.

Promptly they led Alexander within a barricade—now without guards—to a group of pavilions where lamp flames flickered through colored glass. They walked in on carpets, showed Alexander an onyx bath filled with scented water. He started to take off his arms.

"Let's wash off the dirt," he said, "in Darius' bath."

"Not in Darius'," someone corrected him, "in Alexander's."

Stripped, he examined curiously the silver water jars, wrought-gold ointment vessels, and glass scent throwers. They put him in the portable tub, sluiced him with fresh water, rubbed him down with nard, and saturated the air with rose water.

"So this is royalty," Alexander said. The towels were immense and soft as duck down. The colored lights shed illusion over the hard sunburned faces of his friends.

Draped in one huge towel, Alexander laughed, shouting for cooks and supper.

"Well, look," yelled the Companions.

They led him through a curtain. There low tables of hardwood inlaid with ivory figures had been loaded with fruits, spiced meats, and rice, in gold dishes. Embroidered quilts lay around the tables. Surveying these, Alexander ordered most of the rich food carried outside to other officers' mess. Even in Corinth he had never seen so much food in one room. He lay down on a quilt, peering at the embroidered pattern of heraldic beasts fighting each other, his injured hip swollen into a knot of torture.

Pouring libations, gulping wine, snapping dirty jests, the Companions reveled, wiping at their own hurts. Coldly scheming, ambitious, they were gifted builders, and deceivers. They felt that night something like awe for the big tired man with the unchanging, questioning blue eyes who had grown up with them. Between goblets they called him Achilles, and Heracles. They had seen sacks weighted with *gold* coins, they were eating sweetened food from *gold* plates, and that man in the towel had driven the Great King, the King of the Lands of the Earth—driven him headlong, on a racing horse into the night. Why, Darius I had merely stopped trying after Marathon and had turned back with his armada; the royal Xerxes had gone off after Salamis in state with the Phoenician fleet. But here, this night, on Asia's soil . . .

They called him Enyalios and got up to pat his shoulder and kiss his cheek. They had found Asiatic women in the camp, slender Syrian girls, small, trim Cypriotes, half-negroid girls from Memphis and other kinds they did not identify. Besides, they had Alexander's promise that the last great battle was behind them, and usually they could prevail on him to keep a promise.

Sipping his wine, Alexander listened to them, not caring to drink but feeling warm and comfortable in their exultation. Then he heard the shrill wailing of women.

What was that? Only, they told him, the women of the Great King in the tents next this dining pavilion. The women who had seen or heard of Darius's shield

153

and bow brought back from that road. . . . So they thought he was dead, and they wailed.

Who were they?

The mother of Darius, the wife of Darius—whose name sounded like Statira, who had a better figure than Thais, a real beauty—and a couple of daughters, along with an infant son.

Calling over Hephaestion (or, as some say, Leonnatus) Alexander gave instructions about the royal women. "Tell them all I have of Darius' *are* the shield and bow. Darius is alive. Tell them. And"—he made decisions swiftly—"give them my assurance that they shall be now as they were before. Have they servants? Yes, well, they are to keep those servants——"

"Eunuchs too?" someone asked.

"All of them. What money was paid them before they shall have in the future. And they shall not be approached without ceremony."

Even the drunkest of the company fell silent at this. It meant that Alexander would keep the royal Asiatic women hostages, apparently for a long time. It meant that all Macedonian officers would have to avoid the sanctuary of these women, because highborn Asiatics secluded their females even more closely than the Greeks. It meant, lastly, that Alexander did not intend to enjoy physically the heaven-sent opportunity of having the daughters and the wife of his enemy.

"But," objected one, "the beauty of these Persian women!"

"Their beauty," said Alexander, "is a torment to my eyes."

The Companions found no comfort in these words. The physical attraction of the oriental women was no torment to them. Most of them had been separated from their homes for a year and a half, except for some of the newly wedded, and most of them had had only longing for companionship.

They did not understand Alexander.

Few of them seemed to believe what was often said, that Hephaestion and the king were inseparable, and lovers. Such homosexuality among the Greeks was common enough—had been more common than not in the Sacred Band of Thebes who had died for the most part at Chaeronea. Besides, there was often a mystical soul fellowship shared by two men. That would not have troubled the army officers.

Alexander, however, appeared to be an ascetic. His thoughts were bound up too much in sacrifice and fasting and nightly study. Yet they felt that he had too much vitality in him to be a true ascetic. And the army had no desire to practice such asceticism.

A few days later Alexander laid down another premise. He sent a written order to Parmenio to try, and to execute if found guilty, two of his officers who had violated the wife of an allied officer. The women of allies, whether barbarian, Asiatic, or Greek, should be respected as their own. "Such men as those two are to be treated as wild beasts," the letter ended.

Just about this time one of his own staff wrote to say that a certain Theodorus of Tarento had two lovely boys for sale. Alexander, reading, was heard to mutter, "What filth have all of you observed in me, to offer me such boys?" And he dictated a short answer to his lieutenant: *"Alexander to Philolexus, greeting. This Theodorus and his merchandise can go to hell with my good wishes."*

When he received another offer of a Corinthian boy, he lost his temper. And Parmenio, getting wind of the army's talk, rode in for a discussion with his young commander on the subject of women.

Probably the chief of staff pointed out that Alexander had no wife, mistress, or child, or even a Greek prostitute. He, Parmenio, had sons of his sons Philotas and Nicanor, serving with the army. Even Harpalus had a son who was an officer.[1] Without a son to

---

[1] Boys in that Hellenic age often married at fifteen or sixteen. And they might serve as cadets in the army even younger. Often men of twenty-five were veterans of ten years' service. The Macedonian commanders were young, on the average, but had seen almost continued service.

succeed him when he died, Alexander would become more alone. Such a condition was abnormal, and bad for his health. Besides, there was the question of succession to the throne, et cetera. . . .

"You call these barbarian women soulless dolls," Parmenio reminded him. "Since you would not marry in Macedon, it is better to take a common barbarian girl into your bed than a woman of royal Asiatic birth."

Alexander had seemed to avoid women. Undoubtedly, after freeing himself from his mother's morbid domination, he saw something of his mother in other women. The death of Cleopatra's baby and his father's obsession with mistresses might have influenced him, sensitive as he was. It seems also that he did not like to have prostitutes following the tents of the higher officers. To this he could not well object if he had such women of his own.

Whether Parmenio's advice decided him, or whether he was attracted to her, soon after that he did take a woman into his tent, on the coast. He singled out Barsine, the widow of Memnon of Rhodes, who happened to be among the captives taken at Damascus.

Of Barsine it is known that she was quiet and gentle, daughter of a noble Persian house but educated in a Greek school. She must have been a few years older than he.

Certainly Barsine did not try to influence Alexander. Placidly she kept to her own quarters, working with her few servants, listening to such talk of the men as she happened to hear, and making no demands for herself.

Calm in her seclusion, the widow Barsine accepted Alexander as neither an honor to her nor a punishment. To other men she appeared as a shadow in the curtained space that was her portion of the pavilion. Yet Alexander seemed to find rest in her tranquillity.

The quick-witted Ptolemy noticed this. And he quoted a verse describing the loneliness of the King Menelaus beyond the seas: *"So much he grieves, this queen beyond the seas—this phantom queen will walk within his halls and guide him on the winged path of sleep."*

Yet the army as a whole was pleased that he had taken Barsine into his tent. Alexander did not find it so easy a matter to dispose of the question of women in the army camps.

Probably Alexander never understood Barsine. Before him, she had known a brave and shrewd man, Memnon of Rhodes, a state builder who had nonetheless given his loyalty to the Great King. The Macedonians had respected Memnon; now they had no such respect for Darius, who left his army, his women, and his weapons behind him when he had become afraid. Greatly as Alexander had been afraid, in the chill anxiety of stress he knew now that he would never turn and run, to escape. The force driving him on toward danger was inflexible; it was greater than his own dread or foreboding.

Not that Barsine shared such thoughts. There was little in Alexander for her to share. Before sunup he made sacrifice alone, at the rocks outside the pavilions, overlooking the sea. When he flung himself down in the tent entrance to eat grapes and barley cake, officers would be sitting around to talk to him. When he took his stand outside the Agema post, bareheaded, in the sun's warmth, there would be groups of soldiers or country people with charges and pleas and petitions. For Alexander, when he first entered a country, made a point of hearing civilian cases as well as the military matters of routine. By discovering the problems of individuals he thought he could begin to understand the needs of the country.

No lawmen appeared to argue at such times, nor did spokesmen present the views of a class; because rights belong to the individual, who must accordingly explain his own point of view. Most men here could speak Greek or the universal *koiné*; those who spoke only Aramaic or the Semitic dialects brought interpreters.

Even when no officers or petitioners stood before the

157

tents Barsine did not find the Macedonian idle; he dictated letters to a young Greek—as swiftly as he had heard the judgment cases. Once he had made a decision it passed from his mind. But he kept a multitude of details in his memory. After receiving the list of treasure stored at Damascus, he sent eight hundred talents back to Aristotle for the expenses of the philosopher's new Lyceum, and he picked out a hundredweight of precious myrrh to send to Leonidas, his first tutor. He dictated a letter:

"So that you, Leonidas, will not need to skimp the offering to the gods."

It seemed that ten years ago Leonidas had censored Alexander for throwing too much incense on the embers. Another tutor, Lysimachus, now gray in the beard, had come along with the scientists, although his only skill lay in reading Greek. Alexander let the old man potter among the manuscripts that filled a chest in their sleeping room. Sometimes at night he had Lysimachus read from Aeschylus, while he lay outstretched, his muscles relaxed. Usually he did not sleep until after the middle of the night. There were mornings, after a rest period in camp, when Alexander lay with his head buried in his arms, oblivious, until the heat of noon, being drunk with fatigue, not with wine. Barsine noticed that these spells of oblivion came after a quiet day, not upon the march or when the Macedonians were debating important problems. At such times she would not wake him.

When marching, he would not use a shaded litter. Usually he walked, passing from one unit to another, talking with the men. Or he took bows and rode off to the side, to hunt game. When he was in a chariot he liked to practice jumping on and off at a full gallop— yet he did not like to watch violence in games.

Barsine noticed that when a budget of letters came from distant Macedon he opened first those from Antipater, smiling as he read, laying them aside carelessly. The missives from Olympias his mother he would let no one else see, except occasionally his silent shadow

Hephaestion, and then he touched Hephaestion's lips afterward with his seal ring, so that the other would speak no word of what he had read. Barsine understood from the talk of the men that Antipater, the military regent in Macedon, complained as bitterly of Olympias as the queen mother complained of Antipater.

"Doesn't the fool know," Alexander burst out once, "that all his argument avails nothing against one tear of a mother?"

This sudden impatience with people frightened Barsine a little. Because Alexander did not seem to be irritated by accidents or failure. He was very patient when *things* went wrong. But people could anger him quickly and seriously when they failed to do what he had expected. He had a way of looking at them, his open blue eyes questioning, not amused or puzzled, as if stripping away the mask of their flesh and thinking nothing of their words, but searching for what was hidden in them. As if he searched for something more than human flesh, and, finding it, became angered or pleased. He could be deceived easily by a clever lie, but he could not be deceived so easily as to the inner nature of men whom he had met face to face.

The quick-witted, caustic, and unscrupulous Ptolemy, son of Lagus, tricked Alexander often into doing things, and Alexander must have known it; yet he trusted Ptolemy with more and more responsibility. While the most brilliant of the Companion officers, Philotas, son of Parmenio, who went about with an escort of aids and experts, like a small monarch, and carried out orders faultlessly—when this Philotas left him, Barsine observed how he struggled with uncertainty and voiceless anger. Outwardly he treated both officers alike; inwardly he seemed to feel that Ptolemy could do no wrong—not even when he paraded a new mistress, shining with gems and silks, in his chariot—while Philotas could do nothing right.

Barsine thought that Ptolemy, who might have been fathered by Philip, was a dangerous rival—more dangerous as Alexander's power increased. Whereas Philotas was the son of Parmenio, whose loyalty only an insane man would have questioned.

She wondered if Alexander was actually as sane as other men. Once when she had put on a trinket given her by a slave on a feast day, a twisted snake of green copper, Alexander had torn it off her arm the instant he saw it. He had hurt her hand. And he had thrown it off the rocks of the shrine, down into the surf. Nor did he make any excuse to her for doing it.

After that she was afraid that Alexander would discover her own secret.

The only evidence of that secret lay concealed in a miniature ivory gem case, not locked with a key but cleverly held shut by a hidden catch. This case she kept with her more intimate possessions and never opened it unless alone in the tent, when moonlight allowed her to look into the case without the risk that other eyes might see what it held.

After throwing away the snake Alexander brought her another bracelet of gold set with moonstones, without any snakes. This Barsine wore daily, to please him, although she used no other jewelry—even the fillet binding her brown hair was no more than a band of gilded leaves. Alexander noticed that.

Then they brought him the casket. Some soldiers offered it as a gift, because it had tiny figures of winged royal heads on it, and they thought it fitting for him. Jesting with them, he asked what precious thing they had in mind that he should keep in this fine casket. And then they laughed, suggesting this and that, he took up an old manuscript book of the *Iliad* that he kept near his bed and declared he had nothing more precious than that, and it fitted into the new casket nicely. But Barsine felt frightened because, like herself, Alexander kept no private store of valuables about him. Usually he gave away the carved gems and gold images that came into his hands. Nor did he make use of Darius's ornamented pavilions or the gold plate service—only using the onyx bath because he liked it and said it reminded him of Issus.

So when Alexander placed the silver casket near his couch Barsine tried to keep the small gem case out of his sight. What it held was most precious to her.

Whether he observed that she concealed the case she could not tell. But one evening when the lamps were lighted she found him poised over her corner of the sleeping tent where her clothes chest stood and her combs, bronze mirror, and slippers were ranged. Except for ointment boxes and fibulae and a little terra-cotta model of a ship, Barsine possessed nothing more. She did not want to have about her now what she had had before, because those things of the past grieved her. But she had not been able to part with the things hidden within the case.

Alexander lifted the veil covering the ivory box. Holding it lightly in his fingers, he gazed at it, his body still. His fingers moved, searching for a lock.

"It holds no poison," Barsine smiled at him, "for you or for me."

At once his eyes probed her, looking through her face which he knew so well, seeking for what lay hidden within her. She felt as if he had pulled a veil away from her and was looking inside her body, angered. She thought of words she might say, and then she reached forward and pressed the corner of the case.

Inside gleamed the precious things, set in order, the armbands, the miniature tiara and earrings, and all the personal jewelry of a woman, each piece inscribed with minute letters, *The love of Memnon of Rhodes*. Alexander examined a bracelet of thin silver, put it back, closed the lid, and gave her the case.

"You need not wear the bracelet of Alexander of Macedon," he said, and went away, seemingly forgetting her secret from that moment. But when, months later, he began his journey to the east, he did not take Barsine, the widow of Memnon.

Still, he had been influenced by this women who had

161

first shared his life physically. She had been a woman of the east, not a Macedonian.

Alexander had spent months on the Syrian coast during the second winter watching the sea. Unable to go out on it, he studied it—the fishing craft using nets inshore, the war and merchant fleets passing far out, against the sunset, avoiding the shore now that he occupied it. For this Syrian coast was his.

It stood back against the far-off snow of mountains; it murmured pleasantly where streams flowed down to the towns almost touching each other, to the small harbors, man-made. Along the coast road threaded camel, mule, and cart caravans, the drivers often singing in the warm winter sun.

The Macedonian coast had been mist-bound, almost deserted. This shore was both a garden and a gateway to a whole world. There had been no more than forests and barbarian folk behind the Macedonian shore. Behind him, here, millions of human beings wandered over trade routes, climbed to aged shrine summits, and led their children through streets immemorially old. The rocks where he sacrificed were marked with figures that had never been made by Greek hands. This coast had changed masters but it had not changed its nature, like the shores of Greece.

In the limestone cliffs he saw where quarries could take out the stone; in the river beds, where clay could be taken for pottery. In the groves of the Lebanon the trees stood tall and straight, ready shaped by natural growth for long ships and great houses. Already his workmen were taking out the stone and timber, on sledges, down to Tyre.

These things Alexander saw because his fathers had been tribal chieftains, ordering the planting of crops and breeding of animals, ministering to sickness and compensating for death by violence among the folk who served them. Alexander, studying the strange coast with patient eyes, thought of what could be built and what could be grown here, where his ancestors had never ventured. He thought of the needs of human beings and the use of things, not of plans or laws. A barbarian himself, he had been taught in Aristotle's school to rely upon natural forces as he could shape them, and not upon abstract ideas. *In the natural world nothing exists without a purpose.*

If that purpose could be known . . .

The months after Issus had freed him from his worst anxieties. The gold reserve and valuables found at Damascus allowed him to send more treasure home and to support his expedition here for a year or so. Volunteers had come in, numerous enough to make good his losses. And he no longer had to play the part of a captain-general of Hellas.

Moreover ambassadors had arrived from the Great King, bringing a weak, bargaining letter and adding their pleas to it. They had asked the Macedonian to cease in injuring the countries of Asia, to agree to a peace with the Great King, and to return to him his family.

I am here as commander in chief of all the Greeks, Alexander had written in answer, *because your agents instigated the murder of my father and corrupted my friends. You sent money to the Spartans, to create enmity against me and dissolve the league of which I am head. You say the battle was decided by will of the gods. Them am I here in possession of your lands by the will of the gods. I am protecting the men of yours who came to me of their own will. As my father was killed, so was Arses, the ruler of this land, killed by you, a usurper, in violation of the law of the Persians and Medes.*

Come to me then and ask for your mother, your wife, and your children. Ask for what you will and it shall be granted, and you shall be safe. Only come and ask as of the King of Asia, who is no longer your equal but lord of your lands. If you dispute this, you can fight another battle; but do not run away. For wherever you are, I intend to march against you.

He instructed his envoys to deliver the letter but not

to talk about it. He did not think it would add to Darius's peace of mind.

The staff devoted some thought to Darius's state of mind. War they knew to be merciless; but war embraced more than any clash of armed forces. War could be controlled by human minds, so its success or failure depended upon human minds—that is, upon such qualities of mind as the will to resist, or to attack, or to endure. Had not these very Persians sapped the will of the Greeks by feeding them luxuries? Did not this Great King still control the seas because he had made it more profitable to the Phoenicians, Cypriotes, and Rhodians to collaborate with him than to preserve their own independence in trade? Had not the brilliant Greek generals learned the value of treachery and tricks? What else had been the famous wooden horse that the Trojans themselves hauled into the gate of Troy?

It was both easier and more saving of life to attack an enemy's state of mind than to advance against an enemy's horsemen. Antigonus had developed a whole technique of intimidation and deception, and Ptolemy was proving an apt pupil. Only Alexander seemed backward in grasping this new method of warfare.

Alexander went along, daydreaming about building, intent on exploring, until he was caught in difficulties. Then he fought his way out brilliantly. It was almost as if he believed in fate. . . .

In this war against the mind of Darius the staff—and the philosophers—had been at great pains to earn the friendship of the Syrian coast; here no traitors had been executed, no prisoners confined to labor. No payments had been levied on the rich cities, which instead were now free to choose their own form of government. Volunteers were honorably received—even the captive family of Darius was treated with exactly the same honor as had been theirs by right.

Only Darius was held up to scorn, in the open letter sent him. After receiving that letter—and not being allowed to discuss it with the envoys—Darius could have only two possible alternatives open to him: to come back to the coast to give battle with a new army, or to separate himself entirely from the coast, never venturing hither again. Alexander had agreed perfectly with the wording of this letter; in fact he had phrased it himself.

Parmenio, Antigonus, and Ptolemy guessed which alternative Darius would take. They based their guess on the facts that the so-called Great King of Asia had fled helplessly from the Macedonians in battle and that the captivity of his family must be tormenting him. So they expected him to surrender all the Mediterranean coast—to get his family back and to secure Macedonian recognition that he was indeed the Great King, of the vastly greater eastern portion of his dominion. The event proved them right.

But shrewder minds than theirs had reasoned otherwise in Tyre. And now Tyre resisted them.

X. GATES OF THE SEA

The men of Tyre were the most experienced politicians of the eastern Mediterranean world.

For a millennium they had balanced risks and seized advantage, and prospered and gained power. People called their city the mistress of the seas—not the master of the seas.

They were called Phoenicians, their city the Gate of the Sea. About them the Macedonians heard vague traditions. In the dawn of time they had controlled the caravan trade within the Red Land, the great Arabian desert now, facing the Red Sea. With the caravans they had appeared in time upon the coasts and had adapted themselves easily to shipbuilding and coastal trading by ship. They had built larger ships. They had sailed to Cyprus and North Africa. In order to lay up their great trading vessels during the winter storms they had built winter bases in the west, with warehouses to store the goods and forts to guard them. These bases had grown into colonies, and in time the colonies outgrew the mother cities, except for Tyre—which had been the offspring of Sidon, the first Gate of the Sea, where the caravan route from Damascus, passing Mount Hermon, had terminated at the coast. Now the aged mother Sidon struggled for life against the mature child, in deadly rivalry—as Tyre struggled with its own child, Carthage.

For the inhabitants of Tyre were Phoenicians, Canaanites, raising themselves to a high standard of wealth, dispossessing rivals, striving to gain monopoly of the Mediterranean trade in purple dye, in glass, perfumes, gems, and slaves. Their god had been the El of

166

the deserts, the one creator of life upon the earth. (The Macedonians thought of the Immovable Mover of Aristotle.) But now their concept of El had changed to the hot worship of god-masters, Baal and Dagon. Before the giant images of Baal and Dagon they burned sacrifices.

The Sidonian Phoenicians accepted the presence of the Macedonians gratefully, and Alexander ordered a sport stadium built on the hill behind Sidon. Their rivals of Tyre reasoned that the Macedonians were a small army, bound to move elsewhere in time, victorious, of course in the spectacular affair of Issus, but strategically in a weak position, holding to a narrow coast, between the land power of the Great King and the sea power of Tyre—or rather of the fleet of Tyre, allied to the fleets of Cyprus and Egypt.

Also their city of Tyre was situated on an island off this coast, where an army on land could not besiege it. At least it had successfully resisted other sieges.

Quite plainly the Tyrians could expect no advantage at all from opening their city to the Macedonians. On the other hand, they could foresee a great and real advantage in maintaining their strongpoint here between the sea and the land, balancing themselves between the temporarily successful Macedonian force and the ultimately victorious forces of inner Asia. By preserving the Mediterranean fleet for the Great King they could claim renewed privileges, monopolies, and rewards, at the expense of Sidon, which had gone over to the Macedonians.

So they bargained, as the Milesians had bargained, and that made Alexander furious, because he had no patience with bargaining—he wanted either friendship or enmity. There was a preamble of deception on both sides, the Macedonian commanders requesting only permission to allow the army to visit the shrine of Heracles *within* Tyre, while the Tyrians suggested visiting instead the much older shrine on the mainland *opposite* Tyre, and hinting that they would agree to bar out Persian agents as well as Macedonian soldiers.

Thereupon the Macedonian army council reached the decision to besiege Tyre for reasons given by Arrian:

To advance the expedition into Egypt would not be safe, as long as the Persians hold mastery of the sea. Nor will it be safe to advance inland. The situation in Greece is too doubtful, with the Spartans ready to move against us and the Athenians restrained only by fear of us.

But if we capture Tyre the remaining fleets of the Phoenicians must come over to us, having no ports to go to. Cyprus will then need to grant us the use of her fleet. When that happens we shall hold the mastery of the sea and its islands. Then we can make the advance into Egypt without effort. With Egypt secured, and the sea controlled, we need have no further anxiety about Greece. Our own land will be safe. And we could then, if we so decide, undertake the expedition inland to Babylon with greater security because we will hold all maritime cities and the territory as far as the Euphrates. And we will have more prestige than now.

This plan of action—if it was indeed exactly their plan, as Arrian and others relate—was amazing for two reasons. First, they ignored the probability that they might not take Tyre or that Darius would attack during the siege. Second, this plan was actually carried out in all its successive steps (although the final step was taken against the bitter opposition of Parmenio and some of the staff).

It called for taking successive risks amounting to a gamble. Yet the gamble would be for high stakes. This daring became characteristic of Alexander's actions during the next years. He began to take extreme risks for the greatest possible gain. He avoided wasting time, effort, or men for small gains, no matter how sure.

The men in the ranks felt dubious about Tyre. They remembered that Philip had never allowed them to be drawn into a major siege operation, while the oracles had foretold that the sea would be baneful to Alexander.

Perhaps for this reason, or perhaps because he actually had such a dream on this shore opposite Tyre, Alexander related how the hero-god Heracles had appeared to him in his sleep and had taken him by the hand to guide his steps down to the shore. Called upon to explain this portent, Aristander the Telemessan pondered it and declared it meant that the Macedonians would succeed at Tyre, but only with extreme labor—because Heracles had achieved miracles by great toil.

The Canaanites told Deiades, chief of the Macedonian engineers, that once the Babylonian Nebuchadnezzar had besieged Tyre from the land, and had gone away after a long time, leaving it as it was. After how long a time? "After fifteen years," said the Canaanites.

There were only three ways by which men could capture a walled city. By introducing a few men to open a gate or hold a spot on the wall so that others could get in after them—as had been done in historic Troy by a small band disguised as horse herders (not by the fabulous wooden horse)—or this might be accomplished by treachery. The Macedonians much preferred this first method, because it was much easier to open a gate than to break it down. The second method was to batter down enough of the wall to admit the head of a storming column. This had the disadvantage that the defenders usually built a second wall inside the breach, and after that a barrier within the streets. The third method was to wait outside until the defenders ran out of food or otherwise broke down.

None of these methods seemed to fit the case of Tyre.

A prolonged survey revealed to the Macedonian engineers the following situation. The island of Tyre consisted of a rock foundation, with stone walls rising sheer from the rock.

This island fortress lay about a half mile out from the shore. For the greater part of the way out the water was shallow, the bottom being rock pools and

169

reefs. Near the city the water deepened to an eighteen-foot channel.

Tyre had two harbors, also fortified. The one on the southern side, called the Egyptian harbor, was a small indentation with a narrow entrance closed by a boom. The one on the northern side, called the Sidonian, was somewhat larger but also in the nature of an interior basin, and its entrance could be closed by the prows of three war galleys moored thwart to thwart. Secured by these basins, Tyre kept a small but most serviceable fleet of warships—galleys armed with sharp brazen beaks and stone-casting engines. In addition, Tyre's merchant fleet carried on business as usual, bringing in supplies as needed—even some siege experts, later on, from the colony at Carthage.

On their part the Macedonians had no fleet. So the first and third alternatives by which a walled city could be entered were impossible. (Of course by the first—and best—alternative a few men might be landed against the walls at night, or even a gate opened by the hand of treachery. But that would serve no purpose as long as the attacking army could not follow, over the water.)

Now there is no record that the Macedonians ever attempted the impossible. Such as, for instance, expecting untrained or weak, allied troops to stand against a stronger enemy; or expecting a small garrison to hold out in a strongpoint against superior force. The Macedonian army crossed snow ranges in winter, crossed great deserts in summer, joined rivers together by canals, built fleets—eventually—where no ships had floated before, flung bridges over great rivers in flood, found food out of strange plants and insect life where no food was known to exist. It did things that were incredible but always *possible*.

And the only *possible* alternative at Tyre was to get the army inside by breaking down a section of the wall. And that meant extending the land out to a section of the wall. Constructing a mole out to the wall.

For the seemingly impregnable Tyre had the one weakness that it could not move away.

This battle of the land against the sea at Tyre became a conflict of engineering skill, of machine against machine, of the projection of massive rocks, the tenacity of cement, the height of wooden towers, the heat of flaming naphtha and bitumen, the force and the resistance of materials. During this conflict Alexander often absented himself to explore the hinterland around the snow peak of Hermon and the lake called Galilee—the Macedonians called this hinterland Arabia.

In doing so the young commander vanished one night. They had been threading through the hills above the headwaters of a sluggish river, the Jordan, when they were overtaken by darkness. Alexander kept on with his small force of Agrianians because he did not care to camp in the hills of the Samaritans, an inhospitable people who sold him supplies but attacked and robbed stragglers.

They were going single file along the heights when Alexander missed Lysimachus. The Greek tutor had begged to come along sight-seeing: Without saying anything to the men around him, Alexander dropped back to look for Lysimachus and found him a long way back—among a nest of Samaritan night fires. It did not seem as if Lysimachus could overtake the Macedonian column, nor could the two of them escape observation.

In this dilemma Alexander took the most audacious way out. With the tired tutor scrambling after, he raced down to the nearest fire, shouting, "Here are some of them!" Beholding a Macedonian soldier coming out of the shadows in full armor, the hillmen fled, and Alexander occupied their fire, sitting at ease and discussing Homer with Lysimachus. No one bothered them, until the frightened soldiers, having missed their commander, appeared in search of them.

The construction of the mole at Tyre went easily. Deiades and the engineers ripped down the old city of

Tyre on the coast for materials. Stakes were driven to form cribs to hold sand, crushed limestone, and the foundation covered with planks. About two hundred feet in width, this mole extended itself, creating a neck of land, to the deeper channel within a hundred yards of the towering wall of Tyre. There it stopped.

Missile fire from the height of the wall put an end to the construction work, in spite of protection rigged for the workers. Also the eighteen-foot depth of pulsing sea was not easily filled in.

The Macedonian engineers erected defense towers on the molehead, as high as the wall, to stop this harassing fire.

Then Tyrian warships approached the sides of the mole and with arrow, javelin, and engine discharges made communication between the towers and shore hazardous. As a defense the engineers set up heavy wooden barricades on the sides of the mole.

The Tyrians shifted to launching fire missiles from the wall engines; a sheathing of fresh animal hides was put on the towers to insulate against this annoying fire.

Tyrian science destroyed the twin towers by a most ingenious fire ship. This large vessel appeared out of a harbor, looking like anything but a ship. Weights abaft lifted high its prow. Extra masts had been stepped in this prow, with huge caldrons slung to the yards. Pitch, brimstone, and oil filled the caldrons. Beneath these masts wood and plaited straw had been stacked, impregnated with pitch. The crew of this floating combustible guided it against the towers, using a favorable wind. They flung torches into the bow, ran the elevated prow aground on the molehead between the towers, and escaped by swimming as the flames roared up against the Macedonian towers. When the fire broke through the deck the forecastle masts fell against the towers, the caldrons overturned, poured their chemicals into the conflagration, and the towers went up in smoke, while the army watched from the shore.

The Macedonian answer to the fire ship was to broaden the mole so that towers could be spaced farther apart and more engines set up. But this new construction was raided at night by small craft from the harbors, covered by the ubiquitous galleys.

To the desolation of Deiades and his engineers, the attempt to extend the molehead had to be abandoned. It couldn't be done. But a pretense of activity was kept up.

Alexander and the staff had decided long before that they would have to use floating platforms. Ships. They had declared a full amnesty up the coast, to all mariners and owners of anything that floated. This amnesty had effect because it had become clear to the Sidonian Phoenicians and the naval powers of the islands that Alexander *meant* to destroy Tyre. Shipping experts from Rhodes and Byblus joined up, the war fleet of Cyprus—a hundred and twenty sail—appeared unexpectedly off Sidon. Barges were towed down the coast, engines rigged on flat hulks, towers erected on the capital ships. One of fifty oars was brought over from the Macedonian coast.

Nearchus of Crete and the officers with sea experience drilled the Macedonian shield-bearers and the engineers at Sidon in the use of weapons and engines aboard ship.

By early summer—the summer of 332—the Macedonians had, not a sea-going battle fleet, but a floating armada of siege craft, transports, and engine carriers. It was a weird-looking navy, but it almost filled the shores, the sides of the mole, and the channel, and its appearance stunned the Tyrians.

They made, of course, thrusts with their fine fighting ships, and damaged or sank a large part of the armada. Being outnumbered, the Tyrian ships had to strike and run back to the basins. They tried to screen their preparations to go out by rigging a curtain of sailcloth across the Sidonian harbor by rigging a curtain of sailcloth across the Sidonian harbor entrance. Alexander, who enjoyed this matching of speed and wits, countered by moving out from the opposite side of the mole with the best of his fighting craft and going *around* the island to cut off the Tyrian craft by racing for the harbor entrance out of which they had come.

The Macedonian floating batteries could now approach the sea wall of the island. (The section opposite the molehead had been made so strong that the Macedonians did not trouble to approach it again.)

To use the engines they had to anchor the craft. Divers swam out from the city and cut the rope cables of the anchors. The Macedonian engineers replaced the rope cables with chain.

Tyrian engines countered by dropping immense boulders where the siege craft tied to anchor. In the offshore swell the ships broke their bottoms on these rock points.

Cranes were rigged on small barges, to clear out the boulders. Assault craft were fitted with flying bridges at their mastheads, to attempt landing men on the wall. The Tyrians countered by erecting towers that overtopped the mastheads.

But the engines had shattered and broken down the wall at two points near the harbor entrances.

The conflict no longer lay between machines; men were beginning to exert their force against men, and Tyre was doomed.

The Macedonians, impatient now, and raised to a fever pitch of hatred by the savage defense—Tyrians had been exhibiting prisoners on the wall summits, and cutting them open by degrees, then dropping them into the sea—ended the operation by a combined assault. On a day when the sea was calm, all the shipping closed in upon the walls. The fleets made feints at the harbor mouths, while small craft manned by archers and engineers were run aground at the wall breaks. Actually some of the phalanx soldiers were first over the wall, from the drawbridges.

Eight thousand Tyrians died, and thirty thousand were sold for slaves.

The Macedonians then linked up the mole to the island. They dragged the biggest war engine into the temple as a dedication. They hauled the biggest warship into the temple square as a monument. They offered thanksgiving sacrifice in the temple of Heracles within the city, and celebrated by a parade and games. Around the broken walls they paraded their new fleet.

"I took Tyre," Deiades said afterward, "with Alexander's assistance."

The siege of Tyre had lasted for seven months. The siege of Gaza took two months.

That citadel on the commercial road from the Philistine coast to the land of the Pharaohs should not have closed its gates to the Macedonians. Not after Tyre. Not as we look back upon the event now. The fact that Gaza resisted then was an indication that its inhabitants felt the power of the Great King to be nearer at hand than the Macedonians believed possible.

This resistance, however, gave Deiades and his engineering staff the opportunity to create their masterpiece: a causeway, running up from the red sands of the plain to the summit of the wall, two hundred and fifty feet above the level of the plain. The master trick, however, lay not in the construction of this gigantic ramp but in the circumstance that within tunnels beneath it the Macedonians excavated beneath the wall, so that when the causeway came within touch of the summit of the wall the wall came down. The Arabians who defended Gaza were killed, fighting, to a man. The women and children were sold as slaves. Gaza, however, had exacted a toll from Alexander. A bolt from a machine had smashed through his shield, breaking the bones of his left shoulder.

Then the causeway was taken down. But the mole now connecting Tyre's island with the mainland was left in place. It stretches out today to the rock foundations of ancient Tyre.

The Macedonians, it seems, wanted to leave citadels with small garrisons along the connecting land routes. But they wanted to leave behind them no more citadels of the sea like Tyre.

During the operation at Tyre Alexander had familiarized himself with ships. He had built them, altered them, experimented with different types, until he knew the qualities of each, and how sails were set and timbers calked. From that time on he knew what ships could accomplish. He had worked with Nearchus and other expert mariners from the islands. Although, except for his half-mile dashes around Tyre in the hit-and-run skirmishing on the water, he had never sailed out on blue water.

He had never set foot on the famous islands of the Aegean.

Those islands of the Aegean and the Cyclades chain—the steppingstones from southern Greece to the Asiatic mainland—now acknowledged Macedonian supremacy. Tenedos and Chios opened their harbors. Some vestiges of the Great King's sea power still survived where individual officers and Greeks who were shifting for themselves controlled nuclei of ships. But they were now pirates, barred from all major ports.

The Macedonian army had obtained this control of the eastern Mediterranean by marching on its own legs for more than fifteen hundred miles around the perimeter of the sea, from Mount Athos to Egypt. Thereafter no citadel of the sea or land in all the Mediterranean world resisted a Macedonian officer.

The Macedonians kept no battle fleet on blue water; they merely occupied the shores. But when Alexander moved on into Egypt he kept a fleet of galleys and transports in company. These ships drew up on the beaches at night—the crews camped with the army columns. And Alexander created a new unit of experts, shipbuilders from Rhodes, Cyprus, Phoenicia, and Egypt, with a few master mariners. With this unit, after its experience at Tyre, the army was capable of building its own fleet on strange and still unexplored waters.

Down the river he sailed until he reached the sea. Around the Lake Maeotis he sailed, and disembarked. This spot seemed to him good for the building of a city. So says Arrian.

The river was the Nile, more precisely the western mouth of the Nile. And the city he built was Alexandria—the first of thirteen or more Alexandrias.

It seemed an odd thing to do, for a twenty-three-year-old Macedonian to pick out a site between a salt lake full of rushes and waterfowl and the shore of the sea, and to order work begun on the foundations and quays of a city.

But instead of being odd it was in reality inevitable. These Macedonians were pioneers, still thrusting forth to explore and create. Alexander himself had grown up in the new capital of Pella when Philip was a-building. He had never wanted to add a cowshed to Pella itself, nor did he do so. Then he had watched how the Greeks extended across the sea by settlement cities, moving on in this fashion, cell by cell. (He had just passed by their small and noisy trading port called Naucratis.) Moreover for months he had been marching almost in the white froth of the surf, studying the way of ships upon the sea, listening to navigators like Nearchus.

Now he had come to the end of that march, with power to direct that sea-borne traffic. Moreover he had reached, at the end of his Mediterranean campaign, a quiet land, drawing life from a ceaselessly flowing river, the water of which might have been destined to flow through the desert in this fashion by the unseen gods. At Heliopolis and Memphis he had beheld cities of permanent stone—of dark porphyry and gleaming limestone, cut into massive shapes wherein stone figures of monsters and beneficient deities were so illumined by sunlight that they seemed to live and breathe. Some of these temples had stood for a millennium before stones were laid in place on the small Acropolis at Athens.

So had the people existed here, unchanging, carving their records in picturegraphs and script upon these walls of stone. They had endured, and what they had built would be destroyed by no tumult in the market place, or advent of an invader. Alexander observed

177

much and remembered much. His width of imagination came from no uncontrolled impulses of the mind but from the immense field over which his mind had passed. There was even a passage in Homer about this spot, where—*an island lies within sounding surf—an island Pharos on the Egyptian shore.*

After his exploration of the Ionian coast he had appreciation of the tracks followed by commerce. Here the Nile river traffic might meet the coastal route; at all events this mouth of the Nile lay closest to Crete and the ports of Greece. Ships could anchor in the great salt-water basin, protected from the outer surf.

Evidently Alexander meant it to be more than a port. It was to be the first construction of a new type of metropolis—although resembling Corinth in many respects—a combination of seaport, international settlement, and center of worship and study. For in place of the small pillar serving as lighthouse at the end of Pharos he planned an immense lighthouse and observatory, matching the height of the royal pyramids up the Nile, having the square, sky-scraping tower of the Mausoleum at Halicarnassus. He asked for an academy vaster than the squat stone buildings of Mieza—and apparently without the nymphs of the garden. He called for a temple to be laid down, like the one at Sardis, a gymnasium and a sports arena such as he had had built during the long halt on the coast back of Sidon. Lastly he requested a library—a whole building to house books—such as he had seen at Memphis.

If Deiades had besieged Tyre with Alexander's assistance, Alexander planned this first metropolis with Deiades's assistance. He liked to employ the engineer corps upon something more useful than destruction. It was not so strange that he should build Alexandria as that he should build it here on the shore of Egypt.

A story persists that Alexander wanted to mark out on the ground the lines of the city's wall before he left. No one seemed to have any serviceable markers on the spot, so they took the ground barley from the jars of the soldiers' kits and made heavy white lines where

Alexander paced off the ground. By the time they had finished, the birds from the marsh were flocking in like a cloud and eating up the barley.

Alexander and the builders were arrested by this unexpected omen. They called in Aristander and other soothsayers to explain it. Even Aristander seemed to be at a loss for a while. Then he said that the city would prosper, but only from the harvests of the earth. Others said that Alexandria, when built, would feed multitudes. In any event it prospered.

It prospered and it grew. Today, after more than 2277 years, it is still a great naval base and something of an international settlement; but it is no longer a world center of worship and learning.

XI. THE TURNING
TO THE EAST

The Macedonians had encountered the Semitic gods without displaying any particular interest in them. At least they had selected Heracles as the ruling deity in Semitic Tyre. But in Egypt they observed a gigantic and impressive pantheon, extending the length of the Nile.

In particular Ammon-Re, the God-Father of the Nile, possessed a series of lofty monoliths called obelisks, visible for a day's march across that level valley. Ammon-Re was also depicted in the wall carvings sailing in a ship across the sky.

This could not have escaped the Macedonians, who began to argue about Ammon-Re. If Ammon-Re were indeed the God-Father, creator of the divine in human beings, was he not in fact the Zeus of the Hellenes? True, the tall beardless figure in the sky ship did not look like the Zeus of the Athenian sculptors—Lysippus was clear on that point—but if different sculptors turned out quite different likenesses of Zeus even in Greece, might not the Egyptian artist be *trying* to represent Zeus in their own style?

It is known that Alexander argued the point with an Egyptian savant, Psammon. Psammon maintained that the power of creation was a divine power, emanating from the God-Father. Alexander had been taught that from Zeus descended, through the Titans, the spark of divinity common to the best of men but not to the masses. So, was not Zeus in fact Ammon-Re, just as Apollo might be Osiris, who was slain only to return to life again—the visible evidence of the divine power among mortals?

It was important for Alexander to be certain of this. When he heard that the oldest sanctuary of Ammon-Re lay not along the Nile but a long way out in the western desert, and that this sanctuary at the oasis of Siwah was also the most authentic oracle of Egypt, he insisted upon going there. When they warned him that the journey to Siwah was dangerous he determined to go.

The guides led him west more than a hundred and eighty miles from the foundations of Alexandria (so they would have passed the modern El Alamein and turned inland about at Matruh) before striking south into the barrens. As it was winter then, they did not lack for water, finding pools lying in the rocks. But sandstorms bewildered them, and at least once they lost their bearings—guiding themselves at that point by the flight of ravens to the south.

They gained the shelter of the olive and palm trees of the oasis, where they found cold springs and amazingly clear rock salt.

What happened in the semidarkness of the small stone sanctuary when Alexander appealed to the oracle of Ammon-Re as to Zeus is variously told. Alexander himself wrote to Olympias about it afterward but allowed no one to see the letter.

The robed priests of the sanctuary, confronting the young Macedonian, welcomed him to the presence of the God-Father. One story has it that Alexander then asked for an oracular response—had he punished the murderers of his father as they should have been punished?

"Take care," said the priests, "whom you name as your father."

"His name is Philip."

The priests accepted this name and said gravely that the murderers of Philip of Macedon had met full punishment.

Alexander then asked whether he would be successful in what he undertook next, and the oracle responded that he would succeed. Alexander made no comment. He gave gold to the priest attendants. But those who followed him to Siwah declared afterward that the oracle had pronounced him the son of Ammon-Zeus.

For some reason, either because he wanted to explore a new route or because the guides told him it was impossible, he returned to the Nile at Memphis the shortest way. This route took him around the southern edge of the terrible Kattara, over the clay plateau to the stagnant Fayum. But he got back.

This was the beginning of his long and incredible journey east.

Two things were happening in Egypt, hardly perceptible at first. There Alexander had been separated from the bulk of his army, which—now that the Mediterranean campaign was over—extended in numerous settlements, shipyards, trading centers as far back as Tarsus. Some of the Macedonian farmers were experimenting with crops along this coast; the scientists were gathering specimens; the physicians had set up hospitals at the likeliest spots. Alexander, necessarily, had absented himself from the mass of the army. No longer could the phalanx-men see him going in and out of the adjoining quarters of the Agema. The guard had to move elsewhere, escorting Alexander.

So when he did appear at a settlement on the big black horse, with a few Companions following, the men rushed to greet him, to touch his knee, to ask what was doing next. Whenever he rode through the palm-shaded streets of Memphis the crowds drew back, inclining their heads and sometimes kneeling.

For Alexander was now the Pharaoh of the Egyptians.

He had not been able to escape that. Egypt might be modern in its commerce and rice and grain agriculture, and in its shipping; yet it harked back to the tradition of the Pharaoh, the Great House of despots ruling when science had advanced with such tremendous strides, harnessing the Nile waters by irrigation, calculating time itself by the movement of the constellations, raising those monumental buildings—temples and tombs more than palaces—which became the pride of the modern people and visible evidence of the existence of life after death. Whoever ruled Egypt had to be a Pharaoh, and a Pharaoh was kin to the immortal gods. Alexander, as Pharaoh might move among the crowds —at a decent interval—or climb the stones of a pyramid to gaze at the gray, shining ribbon of the river, but he was indubitably a despot and divine. Otherwise the Egyptians, especially the all-powerful priesthood, would have had to change their concept of their Pharaoh.

This gave Ptolemy, son of Lagus, and the others who kept records food for thought. It pointed to something both incredible and absurd but nevertheless true.

They compared their journals. All records agreed on this point. Alexander had been king of the Macedonians —tribal head, as chosen by the council—and protector of the Delphi shrine. Simultaneously he had become captain-general of the Hellenes, and then overlord of the Ionian cities, military ruler of Tyre and the Syrian coast, as well as the islands. Now, in Egypt, he had become a Pharaoh and a god.

"It may be easy to say, and explain away," Ptolemy observed to Anaxarchus, the Greek sophist. "But when you write it down, it doesn't make sense."

"There is little enough of sense," Anaxarchus pointed out, "in this expedition."

With this Ptolemy agreed inwardly. The Macedonian commanders were intelligent and realistic individuals, quick to turn a profit or seize an opportunity. This sight-seeing and discussion and building in Egypt seemed to them to be a waste of time, when so much spoil was to be had for the taking. Instead they had to treat the Egyptians more respectfully than the Ionians, who at least could speak Greek.

"What doesn't make sense is Alexander himself. Try writing down his titles sometime."

"Well? He accomplished a miracle in three years."

"Did he?"

Ptolemy did not think that. Miracles were for the poets. The Macedonians had performed the nearly impossible by taking this eastern end of the Mediterranean within three years. Yet it had been accomplished not by Alexander but *because* of Alexander.

Writing a few words on parchment, the general showed them to the sophist. *Alexandros III, Strategos Tyrant Demagogue Pharaoh*. And after a second's hesitation, while Anaxarchus read, he added the word *Deos*. "His titles, as from today. In their simplest form. If he can live up to all those it *will* be a miracle."

Whereupon he rubbed out the written words with sand.

When Hephaestion invited the two to a feast, announcing that he had received a gift for his table from Alexander, the Greek sophist was disappointed in discovering that the gift consisted only of a basket of fish from the river. "You who have accomplished great deeds, like to those of the immemorial heroes, should have greater reward than headless fish," he said sonorously.

"It's as much as his table ever has," Hephaestion defended.

"Do you think Alexander is altogether human?"

Ptolemy washed down his fish with wine, and Hephaestion answered.

At Gaza, he said, Alexander had been warned by Aristander that he would be severely injured if he joined in the attack. For some time after that the king kept back from the danger zone. But when the men were involved in hot action on the causeway he plunged into it and was carried out with the wall of his chest broken through. Bleeding and in pain, he had said to the Companions around him, "You see, that is human blood and no ichor of the immortal gods."

"Blood, yes." The sophist studied Ptolemy delicately. "But did he say from what father his lifeblood came? Did he ever say?"

When Hephaestion repeated this conversation to Alexander, the Greek sophist was summoned to the commander's tent. He found Alexander occupied with a writing board, by a chest of record rolls. The one lamp shed a faint light on the board, but Alexander had not troubled to move the lamp closer. In one corner stood the dark shield that was supposed to have been the shield of Achilles. It bore no mark of having been used in battle. "Carry my greeting to the Athenians," said Alexander, "and this."

Scrawling his signature on the square of parchment, he held a stub of wax over the lamp flame for a minute. Pressing the soft wax down at the end of the signature, he waited a second, then licked the surface of his seal ring, impressed it in the wax, and gave the sophist the parchment.

Anaxarchus had to hold it close to the lamp to read it. It was a grant of the island of Samos to the city of Athens. The signature—*Alexandros, Strategos*. The grant, then, was from the captain-general of the Hellenes.

Startled, Anaxarchus muttered something about a royal gift.

"It is not my gift. It is the gift of my lord and father, Philip of Macedon." Alexander waited, but the sophist made no comment on that. "I heard him say, once, that Samos should belong to the Athenians."

The sophist began to say that the Athenians knew how to be grateful. After a moment he felt that the Macedonian was only half listening. His head on one side, his long legs stretched out toward the shield, he waited patiently, as if for something he did not hear. Then he stirred restlessly and asked, "What is Demosthenes doing?"

Anaxarchus did not think he meant this to be an insinuation. He simply asked the question. Actually Demosthenes, in favor again, was still speaking against the Macedonian tyranny, and Anaxarchus suspected that Alexander knew this well enough. He only said: "The orator is not as young as he was. Few people share his opinion now."

This last was a lie. Alexander nodded, as if satisfied.

And the sophist took the nod as a sign to leave. On his journey home across the sea he thought often and carefully about his own remark concerning the fish, suspecting that Alexander had been testing him in some way. But Alexander had done no more than give him the deed to Samos and ask about Demosthenes.

When Parmenio came down from Tyre, Perdiccas told him that he had no army now. Instead he had *taxis* of military settlers, breeding children on these eastern women and raising strange fruits and grains. They were even planting wine grapes here, that they had got somehow from home!

Parmenio, however, had other worries. Harpalus, a calculating miser, had absconded from Sardis with the treasury, taking refuge like a fool on an island. Then, when he had been brought back after some trouble, Alexander had not only refused to punish him but had reinstated him as treasurer, saying that he did not think Harpalus would make the same mistake again, while another man might.

"There's no discipline outside the army camps." Ptolemy was petulant. "Every peasant and caravan broker does as he feels like. He washes his backside in a fountain while a Macedonian soldier waits to fill a water jug. If a Phoenician girl wants to fill her jug a soldier can't even touch her, and if you want a horse you have to pay for one. You even pay a horse thief. And with what? We have plenty of good Asiatic gold coins for once. But they are not so good. Alexander's made the Athenian owls standard, so our gold isn't worth its weight, as coinage. The dealers here weigh our gold coins and give us no more than eleven for one."

It seemed to Parmenio and to most of the officers that Alexander was disciplining the military, in order to let the inhabitants do exactly as they pleased. He took pains not to change their native ways. In Memphis he offered sacrifice to Ammon-Re, as he had sacrificed to Zeus at Pella. He had not shifted one palm tree or horse block in the broad streets of Memphis—he had only bridged the Nile here at this city. Instead he had laid down a great new metropolis, Alexandria, upon sand and marsh and a lighthouse island.

Alexander granted all the requests of the emissaries who now flocked to his tent like eagles sighting food to be picked up. He released the last of the war prisoners and settled them in Gaza and Tyre. When the Arabian tribes of the interior asked for a governor he named an eastern Greek, and warned him: "Don't make any change in their customs."

In fact, from Troy to Memphis, Alexander had made no change in the local governments. Although supposedly Pharaoh of the rich land of the Nile, he left it in charge of two Egyptians, attaching only two Macedonian officers and a sea captain to this Memphis administration as advisers—security officers. In Libya he posted a fiscal officer.

Studying Alexander's measures of control for this great Mediterranean area, the astute and experienced Parmenio could detect only one new departure. In each land tribute collectors had been appointed who were independent of military control. The moderate payments these treasurers gathered in were used for road and bridge building, for hospital equipment, and even for new water clocks. So all along the coast the garrison officers had no control over the money; if they wanted funds they had to send a request to Sardis. With this unusual measure Parmenio had no quarrel; but he foresaw that it would lead to trouble if ever Alexander should be absent from the coast for long.

He recalled Aristotle's saying: *It is more difficult to organize peace than to win a war; but the fruits of victory in war will be lost if the peace is not well organized.*

But the organization, such as it was, of Alexander's new Mediterranean world resembled no rule or government hitherto known. To be certain of that, Parmenio noted down all the types of government known to the Greek world, as Aristotle had listed them. And the list showed:

187

Polis (city-state): rule by representation of all educated citizens.

Democracy: rule by the propertyless masses.

Aristocracy: rule by the small minority of the best men.

Oligarchy: rule by the small minority of the privileged and the owners of wealth.

Monarchy: rule by the one most gifted individual.

Tyranny: rule by the one individual who has seized military power.

Study this list as he might, the chief of staff could not fit Alexander's imperium into any of its variations. He recalled that Aristotle had believed that the most workable form of government lay somewhere between an oligarchy and democracy. Then, too, he remembered vaguely that Aristotle had believed it to be useless to set up an ideal form of government. You had to start with the best workable form, improving it not by statute but by improving the conditions by which it was shaped. With this thesis Parmenio agreed; yet it seemed to him too difficult to put into practice. Philip, he thought, would not have attempted it. Philip had wrestled tangible benefits for the Macedonians—silver mines, seaports, military control.

What frightened Parmenio was that Alexander's imperium appeared nameless, and his actions certainly seemed aimless. For nearly three years he had drawn one half the young manpower of Macedon out of the land; in that time he had sent back only letters and trophies and enough bullion to pay Antipater's expenses. Here, on the east coast, he was building roads, shipyards, pouring medicines into hospitals, designing academies, gymnasiums, theaters for the future. He was working with the strange peoples here, apparently to improve the conditions shaping their lives. So far as it made sense, this was the sense of his conduct. *He was shaping the whole Mediterranean world by changing the conditions in which it existed. . . .*

And that, to Parmenio's thinking, was not sense but absurdity. It was worse than setting up a Platonic republic, in which men cultivated virtue by the process of acquiring knowledge. Parmenio knew well enough by experience that human beings did not cultivate virtue when they acquired more knowledge. They were more apt to cultivate vices. Alexander knew this.

Weary of trying to visualize a plan in what they were doing, Parmenio went as always to Alexander. He asked about a tangible point, something that could be grasped and held to.

Why did Alexander continue to sign orders as captain-general of the Hellenic league, when the project of the Hellenic League had broken down almost as soon as they crossed the Hellespont?

Alexander signed as captain-general because he was that, officially, still.

But even the Greeks themselves did not believe in the Hellenic League idea and never spoke of it. Instead they made orations about their civic liberties.

Yes, Alexander knew that.

Then why hold to pretense instead of reality? Philip had planned something real, a Macedonian monarchy superimposed upon a united Greece. Macedonian rule could unite Greece.

Not without sacrificing the independence of the individual cities. Of the *polis*. If you united Greece you put an end to the city-state. The weakness of the city-state was that it could not extend itself to protect Greece. It had tried to do this by forming leagues which soon broke down. Given protection from outside, the individual city-state could continue to exist. Athens, for example. And it would torture him if Athens should cease to be Athens in order to become a city of a united Greece.

"Torture? Torture whom?" the chief of staff demanded, puzzled. "You? Philip's ghost?"

"Demosthenes."

Parmenio gave up his exploration of this dangerous level of inquiry into Alexander's mentality. "Demosthenes," he said curtly, "has abandoned his Philippics only because he now has Alexander as the object of

189

his hatred. If you want to be an individualist you will find that Demosthenes will keep you company." And when Alexander did not respond to this touch of irony Parmenio tried ridicule.

"A few days ago you gave an order, after consulting me. It directed the commander of the Cyprus fleet of galleys to proceed with a hundred ships toward the southern coast of Greece and to cruise off Spartan territory, ostensibly to watch for pirates, actually to observe any attempt of the Spartans who are still allied to the Great King to assemble a fleet. You gave this order, and I heard it, as captain-general—which you are not—of the Hellenic League—which you have just admitted does not and cannot exist. Why?"

Alexander answered at once, seriously: "Because the Spartans are stupidly proud. If they thought the fleet was sent against them they would stand to arms indefinitely along their coast. Do you think there is a better way to work it?"

Parmenio gave up his probing. It seemed to him that Alexander had no plan and that they were all drifting from opportunity to opportunity, doing whatever seemed to work out best at the time.

This suited unthinking men like Nearchus perfectly. But Ptolemy had an opinion of his own. He thought Alexander was going through a process of self-mortification, perhaps to atone for Philip's death. Imitating Heracles, their commander labored for the sake of laboring. Certainly he did not bear himself like an offspring of the gods. Worse than that, he seemed to think himself now as an *agent* of something—but of what, only the gods knew.

The men in the ranks had no such misgiving. Whenever Alexander appeared among them, they raised a shout: *"Enyalios."*

Ptolemy turned his back on Memphis reluctantly. When he rode across the new bridge he looked over often at the soaring pylons and the pyramid tips rising from the plain. Memphis seemed to him calm as a lovely, sleeping woman. In Memphis he had found

Thais, who somehow combined the innocent appearance of a girl with the spiritual savor of a priestess, in her skill as a prostitute.

Early that spring the Macedonian army was gathering by order at the new base of Tyre, and at Tyre occurred the first bitter quarrel between Alexander and Parmenio and many of the staff.

That winter the Great King had offered terms of peace simple enough and apparently sincere. He would ransom his wife and family from the Macedonians for ten thousand talents; he would cement friendship between Alexander and himself by offering one of his daughters in marriage; he would surrender all the territory between the boundary river Euphrates and the Greek seas.

The quarrel between commander and chief of staff on this issue is handed down through the historians by this passage:

PARMENIO: "If I were Alexander, I would accept peace on those terms."

ALEXANDER: "So would I, if I were Parmenio."

Reading beyond these words, it is clear that a decisive conflict of opinion divided the Macedonian planners in this spring of 331 at Tyre. Conservative counsel pointed out that they had fulfilled all Philip's plan— and Isocrates's—and more. Including the Balkans, the Macedonians had taken over about nine times the extent of their original territory. They had no further reservoir of manpower at home upon which to draw. They were, on the contrary, fairly secure along this coast where they had the desert at their backs, except for the fertile northern belt around the headwaters of the Euphrates. They had enough; why risk what they had to gain more?

The risk-takers felt that nothing remained secure so long as the main Persian army existed inland. Until that army was eliminated they could only hold the coast on sufferance.

What Alexander said is not known. What he did was

191

to order an advance eastward. This decision marked a change in Macedonian affairs. Alexander had imposed his will on the veteran generals and Companion nobles. The army moved henceforth as he directed.

After that conference at Tyre a change is noticeable in Parmenio's behavior. He merely carried out tactical orders, as directed. And before another year ended he was left behind in command of a base. From that time on Alexander depended more upon the advice of the younger minds, Hephaestion's, Ptolemy's—even upon Perdiccas's and Nearchus's.

At Tyre Alexander could have had no conception of how far he would need to journey into the east, nor of all that lay beyond the Euphrates and Babylon. For one thing, he had no maps to show him the true size and configuration of the continental mass ahead—for another, he was leaving the area known to Greek traders and settlers. In the way of texts he had only Herodotus's colorful narrative, the *Anabasis* of Xenophon, the world plan of Hecataeus.

Moving inland around Mount Hermon, passing through Damascus, he angled sharply north, to keep to the fringe of good grazing and to avoid the heat of the central Syrian plain. So he crossed the Euphrates, on bridges already prepared, where it was little more than a sluggish stream near its source.

Here he found himself on the broad prepared King's Way, leading to Babylon. And here he noticed—as the army brigades which had marched separately assembled to cross the bridges—how the army had been swelled by the arrival of another year's recruits from home. And how the wagon trains had grown, carrying more of the engineers' machines and even a few women. Some new units had been added—interpreters, ship-builders, technicians from Sidon, and mathematicians from Memphis. Perhaps thirty-five thousand in all now followed the patrols feeling their way across the plain between the Two Rivers—the Euphrates and Tigris.

XII. LADY OF THE BEASTS

Upon that plain even in the north the grass had been burned by the intense summer heat. Harvests were being gathered near the villages. For days the columns marched across land as level as the sea. They pushed forward into a hot, dry wind. When this wind blew, the horizon danced hazily and white streaks of water appeared on it, vanishing into dry clay as the columns came up to the mirage. They were pushing forward into space.

The Greek historians say that at this point the marchers made a sacrifice to a new god and that the name of the new god was Fear. The men in the ranks had not been afraid when they had marched down the seacoast two years before along the highway threaded with ancient cities. But here they were moving across the sea of dead grass, toward unknown Powers. Some of the new Greek recruits began to complain, asking what purpose drove the commander in this direction and what he sought—this man who had forsaken his own land and disowned his father. The Macedonian veterans jeered at the recruits. They said they knew Alexander's purpose: to gain a treasure and to end the war.

Still, it was undeniably a new kind of earth lying before them. No one had beheld such a plain as this. No intelligence service here could acquaint the marchers with what lay ahead of them. They had seen a few Asiatic horsemen along the Euphrates. And captives had informed them that the Asiatic army was gathering somewhere behind the next river. From the stories of the captives, the veterans judged that this new army would be larger than the masses they had met at Issus, and that gave them food for thought. They wondered how Alexander could cope with still greater masses of horsemen on a plain such as this. They were not yet afraid, but they wondered.

Instead of striking due east toward the second of the Two Rivers, Alexander led them northeast, until the earth turned red again and the flat-roofed villages changed to clusters of clay cones, like beehives. He led them up to the mountains again, climbing into fir-clad foothills and gray rock ravines before turning east again. Here the air was cooler and water flowed swiftly down from the heights, and they could march with the comfortable feeling that no enemy was in these mountains above them. Some of the veterans who had gossiped with the surveyors guessed that these mountains led back to the Gordium plateau land, and they spoke of them as the Gordyene Mountains. Being on the shoulders of these mountains gave them confidence. When they crossed a rushing gray river in a long valley they became more confident, because the surveyors said this must be the headwater of the Tigris itself, and so the army had crossed the Tigris, the second of the Two Rivers, without being sighted by the Asiatic army.

Yet while they forded the Tigris the moon had darkened in a total eclipse that was surely a sign of a crisis approaching. Phoenicians among the engineers argued that the darkening of the moon foreshadowed the approach of the Lady of the Underworld, who was also called Astarte, who held great power over this land of the Two Rivers. This Lady was served by the beasts of the three worlds—the sky, the earth, and the underworld. So she might appear mounted upon a dragon or a lion or a great serpent. In any event her advent would be ominous or evil. These Phoenicians, far from their seaports, became very much afraid.

Having passed the Tigris safely, the columns united for a while, turning south along the river and then leaving it to follow an open valley where clouds and mist hid the heights around them.

When they dropped down out of the cloud level they encountered gray buffalo, which resembled oxen only in their passivity and strength. They might have been oxen transformed by Circe or this Lady of the Beasts. When they sighted a dark gray plain far beneath them the outermost scouts came in with tales of fresh wonders. The scouts had stumbled on giant stone beasts with wings and roofs and the heads of kings. These winged monsters had been standing on either side the gate of an empty city, where armed men and eunuchs also stood, lifeless, partially projecting from the tiled walls, all facing the same way, as if waiting.

Also the scouts had seen a dry aquaduct, raised upon a stone causeway, disappearing into the mountains. The next day the columns passed the face of a cliff upon which the giant figures of kings or gods had been carved. The experienced Phoenicians made little of such rock carvings, only saying that they were Assyrian kings and gods, a long time dead, and so plainly without power to harm or to aid.

When the scouts sighted the first force of strange cavalry moving on the plain beneath, a mounted regiment stiffened by troops of Companions and guards were dispatched to bring back informants. They learned from the few captives they took that the Army of the Great King had assembled directly below them, where the foothills merged into the open plain. And this army now had the corps of Persian Guards, the spearmen called the Immortals, as well as new contingents of armored cavalry and horse archers from the inner reaches of Asia—Scythians and Bactrians. It had more horsemen than infantry.

Alexander was now faced by a greatly superior force of horsemen, on open ground. For three days he camped in the lower foothills, resting the men and perhaps hoping that the Persian host would advance to attack him on the higher ground.

Then he broke camp after dark and made a rapid night march down through the rolling grassland, coming over a ridge into full view of the enemy at sunup. The Macedonians in the ranks had expected to be deployed and led on into action, in phalanx formation, that dawn. Instead they were halted, once the battle line was formed, and rested. The engineers fortified a camp enclosure behind them, and the officers spent the day riding out to study the ground and the enemy's formation.

Because no Macedonian had ever seen as many horsemen as were gathered there, near the village of Gaugamela, confronting them.

The fear that had been in the minds of the Macedonians during the marches grew greater that day and increased at evening, when torches and oil-fed fires blazed in a long line, cutting the nights in front of them, marking out unmistakably the vast extent of the enemy's masses.

When the waning moon rose, marking shadows on the earth, and a night wind stirred the brush around them, it seemed to the watching men as if hostile forces were in motion over the ground. The night touched them with horror. The officers felt this fear. They took measures against it. They had fortified the camp in the rear, but that would be a flimsy defense if the Macedonian formations were broken through. To guard against encirclement staff officers divided the infantry phalanx, ordering the rear half to be prepared to face about.

Fear touched the mind of Parmenio and the elder staff officers. They urged Alexander to get the ranks into motion and to make a night attack. Under cover of darkness infantry might move against cavalry, and the Macedonians might have a better chance against four to five times their number. Against this inhuman multitude waiting to destroy them.

Alexander would not order a night attack. He would not trust to a movement in darkness, with torchlight in the eyes of his men. After observing that the Asiatics were standing armed in battle order, with lights, he told the officers to rest the men where they were and to get what sleep they could. The conflict of the next day, he said, would be the last battle, because it would decide who would rule Asia, the Macedonians or the Persians. And he warned the officers to be careful to carry out orders quickly—it would be dangerous to delay.

He felt the fear around him, like a tangible pressure coming out of the darkness into the minds of his men. But he showed no signs of nervousness. When his officers kept arguing and talking about the next day he turned back into his small sleeping tent and lay down.

He was still sleeping when those who could not sleep gathered around the tent in the chill before the first light. When Parmenio came up Alexander had not stirred. He had overslept.

Parmenio ordered breakfast to be served in the ranks when light touched the line of hills to the east. When he could see a veil of mist below the hills he went in to wake Alexander and had to call him twice by name. Alexander got up and looked out, and put on a light quilted jacket that had been captured at Issus, with a light helmet of thin polished iron.

The black war horse Bucephalus had been led to the tent. But the men around him noticed that Alexander mounted another horse, although now he always rode Bucephalus in a close action. He seemed to be putting off that final moment of engagement, for which every preparation had been made during the spring and summer now past. . . . The Macedonians were afraid as men are always afraid when they move forward into the space between themselves and other men in which they may be killed or broken or blinded. They go forward because an order has been given, because they have always done so, and because it is unthinkable to turn back alone when the others are moving forward, until the danger in front of them ceases to be there in that ever-narrowing space, or until it gains force, controlling their physical actions and drives them back and away from the danger. . . . Late in the morning Alexander was riding Bucephalus, moving forward at a walk with the regiments of the heavy cavalry, as he had been accustomed to do and as the cavalry had been trained to do. There was no opening for them as yet in the insane confusion ahead of them.

Twice messengers had come to Alexander, asking for support. The enemy had broken through and held the Macedonian camp behind them. The left of the army had been broken apart, and Parmenio sent a personal plea for support. The Companion cavalry waited, moved on a few paces, waited. They waited while the units on their right were enveloped, twisted, and flung about. They could not do anything now but wait, while the advanced end of the Macedonian phalanx edged, step by step, deep into the masses of the enemy, and the Agrianians and the Thracian cavalry pushed forward the other side of the wedge.

Then there was a shifting of the masses in front of them. A body of Asiatic horsemen had swung out of position, to circle out to the right.

Into this opening between the forward edge of the phalanx and the struggling Thracians charged the heavy companion cavalry. It burst out of the tip of the wedge into the space vacated by the Asiatic horsemen, it angled past other units, and struck at full gallop into the rear of the close-packed Persian Guard, the Immortals, so called. The thrust bit deep into the guard.

Directly in front of them the fear within the body of the Great King Darius mounted beyond his control. Physically he was a coward, and he could not wait there in his chariot in the path of these oncoming horsemen.

For the second time Darius ran away too soon from a battle. His chariot raced back, out of the path of the Companions, and the chariot horses ran away. His flight at first did not affect the greater part of the masses that obeyed him. It caused no more than a drifting back of the escort and guards around him; a drifting that gradually became a pull exerted outward, drawing back the center of the army.

That army had assembled upon the plain of Gaugamela because it obeyed the personal command of an emperor. Its parts had assembled from Babylon, from the Kurdish and Armenian mountains, and far Bactria and Soghd and Scythia, because an order had been given to the satraps who themselves gave orders in the provinces. Except for the Armenians and Kurds, these portions of a warlike host, met together for the first time, had come far from their own lands. No hatred or defiance of the strange Macedonians drove them into action near this village of Gaugamela. They had merely followed their own officers hither.

But when the news that Darius himself had run away passed from unit to unit the army of the Persian Empire was held together by nothing, and it broke apart, as different units followed their officers away from danger. This army had not been defeated. It had ceased to exist.

Alexander, at the moment of the first breaking up, had led the cavalry around to Parmenio's beaten troops, where he joined the fine Thessalian horse, still holding its own. By then the Persians were leaving the field, and, being mounted, they went quickly.

This battle of Gaugamela (for a long time identified by the name of "Arbela" or Irbil, the citadel toward the mountains, sixty miles away) was recorded in all its details by the Roman historians much later. They describe it as an extraordinary example of how an inferior force, mainly of infantry, advanced to attack a far superior force, mainly of cavalry, upon an open plain, and succeeded. They take notice of the superior discipline of the Macedonians that held them together under stress, and the superiority in leadership of Alexander when opposed to Darius. But they make no mention of the fear that drove the Macedonians forward against the levies of the Great King, which had much less to fear.

For the Macedonians could not retreat from Gaugamela. They had to scatter and to drive to a distance that much greater strength of horsemen in order to survive themselves.[1] Whereas the Asiatic horse could re-

[1]Four Roman armies at various times offered proof, later, of the hopelessness of fighting a losing action against Persian

tire with little harm. The Macedonians had no alternative but to break the opposing ranks, terribly and completely. This controlling force of fear was added to the cohesive force of their discipline and training, and the driving impulse of Alexander's personality. It was true of the Macedonians, as a Roman pointed out later concerning his own legions, that *they were never so much to be feared as when they had most to fear.*

In the vast confusion of the plain that afternoon the Macedonians gathered in strange and rich spoil, including armored elephants and scores of chariots equipped with scythe blades, and the gilded spears of the Immortals, and regiments of dour mountain men who spoke a strange tongue—Armenian—and skilled horsemen who wore loose trousers and flowing turbans—Kurds. These captives indicated that they came from the mountain wall to the east.

As soon as Parmenio's shattered command had been disengaged Alexander assembled the least-wearied mounted units and launched a headlong pursuit down the main highway to the south, where he knew great cities lay, and where he suspected Darius had fled. Parmenio followed within a few hours with the main command, pausing only to load the wounded and most

---

horsemen on this Syrian plain. Marcus Antonius ("Mark Antony" of Cleopatra notoriety) saved a portion of his command by retreating into the mountains. A Roman army was almost annihilated at Carrhae, where the Emperor Crassus was killed, much closer to the coast than Gaugamela. Another was destroyed near Edessa and its emperor, Valerian, taken captive. (At least two cliff carvings by Persian artists still survive, showing Valerian kneeling before Shapur, mounted.) The fourth was led by the Emperor Julian as far as Ctesiphon, and suffered severely in a long retreat up the Tigris, Julian dying on the way and one wing of his command disappearing entirely.

Xenophon's retreat with the famous ten thousand out of this valley, north to the sea, was accomplished without opposition from any unified command; the Greek mercenaries simply fought their way through and lived off the country, and they had a hard time doing it. At least they wept with joy when they beheld the sea again.

valuable loot—weapons, instruments, and bullion—into carts.

This time there could be no celebration or delay. Alexander called a halt at a stream after sunset and allowed his pursuit force to rest for five hours, then took the road again. Within forty hours he covered the sixty miles to the rock citadel of Irbil almost at the mountains' edge. From this height he could observe the plain where dust layers marked the routes taken by the retreating units of Darius's command. Apparently they were fanning out southward and eastward into the mountains.

And again, this time at Irbil, he found Darius' gold-adorned chariot and bow case. But this chariot seemed to have been left for him to find. Darius, he learned, had headed east along a mountain road with the fine Bactrian horsemen and nuclei of the Greek hoplites and Immortals. Into those mountains Alexander dared not follow as yet.

Because at Irbil he realized the dilemma into which he had fallen by entering his eastern Mesopotamian plain. The battle at Gaugamlea had decided nothing, militarily. He was still leading some thirty thousand wearied men across ever-widening space. Hostile forces still lay south and east of him. He had scattered those vastly superior forces at Gaugamela. He had not crushed them.

Thinking back, he recalled that, except for some cavalry officers, the forces at Issus had not been the same as at the affair on the river Granicus. Except for some Greek mercenaries and Babylonian units, the Asiatic army at Gaugamela had contained none of the commands he had faced at Issus.

The lesson to be drawn from this was unmistakable. He was leading his thirty thousand against a manpower of many millions. A manpower scattered over plains, mountain heights, and desert areas that dwarfed the Mediterranean coast. Provided new armies could be assembled against him as he advanced, he would meet inevitable defeat in the end. Each engagement would reduce the strength of the Macedonians, while the Asiatics could recruit fresh armed forces from new territory. It was evident already that these lands of Asia could breed new contingents of well-armed and dangerous horsemen. Also each day's march was now moving the Macedonians farther from their base on the Mediterranean.

"It's like fighting a Chimera," Hephaestion pointed out. "When you cut off one head of a Chimera, another one bites you. You can kill a beast with many heads until the last head is cut off."

"No, not a Chimera," Ptolemy corrected. "This is a new kind of monster, with one head—the Great King—and many bodies. No ancient hero faced a monster like that. It's really unnatural."

Nothing, however, could be unnatural. Once a situation was understood, it ceased to have hidden potentialities for evil. With his young leaders Alexander studied the situation to determine what advantages it might have.

It had this in his favor. He could gain, as he advanced, fairly accurate information about the forces ahead of him; they could not know what reserves he had behind him. The tale of his victories had not lost in the telling. Certainly no contingent of Asiatics that had faced the terrible Macedonian attack cared to run that risk a second time. Evidenlty the Asiatic peoples understood by now that they were facing no force of hired Greeks, who made a profession of military service, on one side or the other. The miracle of the overthrow at Gaugamela laid a paralysis on all this countryside. That happy effect might endure for a month or two. After that he would have to produce a new miracle or retreat like Xenophon's ten thousand to the coast.

Then the Macedonians possessed the inestimable advantage of Darius. This commander in chief of the immense forces of Asia was not only a coward, little respected by the generals serving under him, but a coward whose hesitation hindered any united move against the Macedonians.

The Asiatics, it seemed, obeyed Darius not because they respected him but because they reverenced the person of the Great King, the King of the Lands of the Earth, successor to the first Darius, and the mighty Xerxes, who had in turn grasped the imperium of the Assyrian monarchs, whose likeness appeared carved in stone upon palace and cliff walls. They gave loyalty to the human being who was emperor, the incarnation of divine power. So the Macedonians were opposed not so much by the human Darius—who had actually been of great advantage to them—as by the concept, in Asiatic minds, of the ruler who was destined to sit upon the throne.

So much being clear, Alexander acted upon it at once. He had only a small margin of time to en-compass vast space. Therefore he moved with the utmost speed down the plain, keeping between the Tigris and the mountain wall—not daring to divide his forces now—in march columns, prepared for action, himself riding in the newly captured chariot, wearing his plumed helmet and white floss cloak, followed by a host of captives. This made an impressive pageant.

Meanwhile he sent ahead at utmost speed two officer-messengers, to the two nearest capitals, Babylon and Susa. These officers announced the approach not of an enemy but of the new ruler of Mesopotamia, destined to succeed the fugitive Darius. They summoned Babylon and Susa not to submit but to welcome the new Great King who would grant freedom of worship to all temples, who would disturb no provincial government nor exact tribute of any personal property.

Yet Alexander approached Babylon cautiously, deploying the head of his column. He passed through dark fertile gardens, over wide canals fed by water pumped up from the river, under groves of date palms and citrus-bearing trees, along wide roadways where the dust was laid by sprinkling carts.

And he was met by a procession of priests and officials, welcoming him to Babylon with gifts of shining metal and gems and embroidered cloth. He barely

203

paused for their greeting but pushed on, across the great canal, seeing immense walls rising from an embankment, and above the walls the pinnacles of ziggurats and palace summits, of terraced gardens towering over the immensity of roofs.

In full procession he traversed the long avenue leading to the tiled Ishtar Gate, passing between towers so massive that they dwarfed the temples of Memphis. He rode up the ramp of the palace, looking out over summits of buildings, above the green of trees, where the brilliant sunlight flashed on the gold and black and turquoise blue of the temple towers. And he dismounted where the spear-bearing Immortals stood at the palace entrance.

So Alexander of Macedon came to Babylon, his capital city.

Babylon had an effect of shock upon the Macedonians, who found here a creation of strange hands, immense and permanent. There was nothing Greek about it. The sculptor Lysippus walked through corridors without a single statue, yet glowing with tiles and enlivened by processions of fantastic animals within the tiles. The sign of the Lady of the Beasts, the crescent moon, rested upon the lintels of towering gateways. Space, outlined by walls stretching to the horizon, gained new meaning here. A human figure, walking up a ramp toward a pinnacle, was dwarfed by the structure upon which it stood.

Yet a little investigation convinced Lysippus that these gigantic walls and summits were built out of clay, molded by the hands of slaves and baked in ovens or dried in the sun. Even the ornamental tiles were no more than this earth, cleverly glazed. Learned Chaldeans showed him libraries of tablets and thin squares of clay, stamped with wedges and then dried so that they never yielded to age. Such tablets recorded marriages, loans, and gifts made centuries before. The bricks of the lower walls carried the stamp of Nebuchadnezzar.

Building out of the earth itself, the Babylonians had tried to escape the earth's surface by raising their edifices in step-back pyramids to the upper levels of cooler air. Such a structure had been called the Tower of Bab-El—the Gate of the Lord—in the time when the wandering Hebrews had lived by the waters of Babylon, waiting to journey on to their Mount of Sion.

Aristotle might have wondered at the fertility of this soil, impregnated by the heat of the sun and the constant moisture from the canals, so that plant life covered every exposed portion and human life, sustained by an abundance of food, multiplied itself swiftly. The Macedonians marveled briefly at these waters of life. They considered that these hanging gardens of Babylon were a greater wonder of the world than the Mausoleum at Halicarnassus or the other pyramid graves along the Nile.

As quickly as possible Alexander arranged for the government of the Babylonian province. Keeping his promise, he reopened the great temple of Bel, and that of Marduk, and attended the opening himself. In the palace he installed the hostage family of Darius. The handsome wife of that Persian monarch had died in childbirth during the journey—being pregnant when she was captured at Issus. Alexander had taken pains to give her a ceremonious burial.

While he inspected the shipping along the narrow canal that bisected Babylon, connecting the metropolis with the Tigris, he sat late at night with his surveyors, hearing the account of the Babylonian revenue agents who told him of lands stretching south to a great gulf or inland sea, and of roads that penetrated the mountain wall to the east.

Beyond those mountains, the Babylonians said, he would find the other three capital cities of the empire, where the *gazaphylakia,* or imperial treasures, were kept, in Susa, Persepolis, and Ecbatana—so his Greek secretary wrote down the names.

The treasure in Babylon he confiscated. With a few words he disposed of the administration, leaving the viceroy of Darius, Mazai, in charge, with a Macedonian officer and a small garrison. The schools, the temples, the tithes, and the charities of the metropolis were to remain as they had been before, until his return.

And in Babylon, with a touch of malice, he left the women, the heavier baggage of the army, and the loot that had been collected at Gaugamela. He left here his own favorite actors who had staged plays on the journey and the Athenian lady Thais who belonged to Ptolmey. He gave orders sharply, hurrying preparations for the road, playing the new part of despot of the east.

At the end of work in the hot nights he stripped and went swimming in the river. After drying off he liked to sit out on one of the lofty terraces, watching the lights in the tall buildings and listening to his interpreters explaining how the Chaldeans had completed their tables of the known stars. He drank a little wine while his officers drank much—the were not so keen as Alexander for the long mountain marches ahead, with winter closing in on them. They did not care that somewhere to the east lay the greater barrier of the Parapanisades, marking the edge of the known world.

Always the dark-eyed Mazai watched his new lord, who had arrived in Darius's chariot and had occupied the royal palace. He heard the Macedonian officers jest about that, saying how Alexander was making himself into a Great King.

"Instead of one Darius," Mazai said once, "he may be making himself into many Alexanders."

When they marched from Babylon through the Ishtar Gate and turned east along the highway, up into the mountains, they met a messenger bearing a letter from the officer who had hurried on in advance to Susa. He reported that Susa welcomed Alexander and that all the imperial revenues and stores within that city would be kept sealed against his arrival.

Susa projected from the hills like the Acropolis that Athens, with the main citadel surrounded by hillside suburbs straggling up from the river. It had been the favorite resort of the Great Kings during spring and fall, as Babylon had been their winter residence. The treasure there amounted to fifty thousand talents—equal to the yield of the Macedonian mines for fifty years.

There also they found statues that Xerxes had carried off from Athens generations before. Among them were the bronze figures of Harmodius and Aristogeiton. Alexander sent them back to Athens.

It seemed to the Macedonians to be a good omen, to find these statues, which rejoiced Lysippus, so far with the eastern mountains. And when Alexander allowed them to celebrate with field sports and a torch race they were more than willing to push on in winter, not caring that they were leaving behind them the escape route to the now distant coast.

Even in autumn it was too hot in Susa to please the Macedonian highlanders. (Susa stood not far above the modern Ahwaz.)

"Here the sun fries everything not in the shade," they complained. "When lizards cross the stones of the street they are fried before they can get across. We don't have to cook meat here—we only lay it out on the stones."

XIII. PERSEPOLIS

The four capital cities of the Great Kings had been capitals of different nationalities in the past. Susa, perhaps the oldest, had been the vital center of Elam; Ecbatana [modern Hamadan] had been the great city of the tribal Medes; Babylon had been the metropolis of the neo-Babylonians, who had risen—along with the Medes—upon the ruins of Assyrian power. Only Persepolis, "City of the Persians," had been built by the Great Kings in their homeland, upon the Persian plateau itself.

The Macedonians were now marching against time toward this heart of Persia itself, hoping to arrive there before Darius could mobilize new manpower to meet them. Leaving the foothills around Susa, they struck into the first of the long valleys that threaded through the mountain wall. They were heading southeast as they climbed.

And immediately they ran into a bit of comedy. The independent tribes of these highlands, living upon sheep and cattle, had been accustomed to exact a toll from dignitaries using the highway. These Huzha (the Greeks called them *Uxii*) tribesmen, very much like those in the same regions today, were poorly informed about political changes in the outer world, while they clung steadfastly to their own ancient privileges. They sent word to Alexander that he would not be allowed to pass through with his forces unless he paid to the Huzha the toll customarily paid by the Great King.

Alexander sent back word for them to come down into the defiles to receive this prescribed toll. Complacently the tribal warriors thronged down toward the road to get their fee. They had no conception of what a Macedonian army in the field and in a hurry might do. The next sunrise they awoke to find Macedonian units posted along the road, while others were occupying the nearest Huzha village—having encircled them by a night march.

The confusion that ensued caused more panic than bloodshed. It ended with the Huzha perched on distant summits with the remnants of their cattle, having received, as Arrian relates, *these gifts of honor from Alexander*. At this point the mother of Darius, who had come to be a friendly counselor to the young Macedonian, interceded for the tribal folk and explained their psychology. Alexander agreed to allow the Huzha to return to possession of their lands and to pay for that privilege a yearly tribute of one hundred horses, five hundred cattle, and thirty thousand sheep. He had observed that the tribes had no money, nor did they till the land, so he asked for the animals and left the Huzha to wonder ruefully how it had happened that instead of gaining money they were forfeiting cattle to this demoniac Great King.

The Macedonians noticed that Alexander was taking pains to restore order in this eastern limbo. After consulting with the guides from Susa and the chastened Huzha, he divided his forces, sending the baggage with Parmenio over the winding wagon road and taking the better troops with him over a high level trail that led straight toward Persepolis.

The second stoppage was more serious, but again the Macedonians had to get through in a hurry.

It was Alexander's column that met the obstacle. The trail they followed led through a narrow defile to the summit of a pass. This defile had been walled up and was defended in force. The Macedonians attacked the wall itself, made of rocks roughly fitted together. They were thrown back the first day and went into camp to consider the situation.

They had taken a few prisoners. From these they

209

learned that a trail led over the mountains on the right to the river beyond the pass.

Over this trail Alexander started with the Macedonians of the phalanx and the Agrianians and other picked units. With the prisoners as guides they worked their way up at night and covered a distance of twelve miles. The camp in the valley had been left in command of Craterus, a new leader whose persuasive magnetism made him a favorite with the men. Craterus, slender and elegant as a Corinthian, could get more miles out of a marching column than the others. He seldom gave orders, usually contenting himself with advice, smiling when he promised his command that no other brigade of Macedonians would earn so much glory as they. Alexander did not object to this theatrical pose. Now he left only a small force with Craterus, believing that the Persians in the defile would not venture to attack the main Macedonian camp.

High on the shoulders of the mountains Alexander's command had to wait out the day before they could move again without being seen by the Persians. At evening he sent Philotas and Coenus with cavalry and engineers ahead to rejoin the main route at the river and begin the construction of bridges across the river.

They could see now on either side of them, above the cloud level, giant snow peaks standing sentinel-like as if to mark an invisible gateway. The soldiers christened the one above them Olympus-in-Asia and the pass itself the Persian Gates. All in all, they believed the apparition to be a favorable omen, especially as the name of their chief guide turned out to be the Wolf, and they remembered that it had been predicted that a wolf would lead Alexander to success.

When they worked their way down toward the pass they did have success. They managed to capture or drive uphill three separate cordons of sentries without alarming the Persian camp below. Before full light they poured down in the rear of the camp. When they sounded the trumpets—the signal agreed on with Craterus—the Macedonians in the valley attacked the wall.

Outnumbered and attacked from front and rear, the Persians broke out of the valley. When they ran into more Macedonians holding the river they scattered in panic. *The flight became terrible,* Arrian relates, *when men threw themselves over the cliffs.*

Alexander marched on without rest to the river, where the bridges were being finished. Without stopping at the river, he started the forty-five miles of descent toward Persepolis, dropping down from the cliffs into dense forests and emerging upon fields of grain where villages hugged the streams. Pushing on with the cavalry, he came out on a plain as level as a temple floor, where slaves plowed the earth with buffalo. Against the hills at the edge of this garden valley the Macedonians sighted the gleaming limestone of Persepolis.

They had outstripped the news of their coming.

Of the four *gazaphylakia,* the treasure cities of the Great King, the Macedonians anticipated most from this, his innermost dwelling place. They ended their hard march down from the heights, as if coming in to the finish of a Marathon. The best mounted of the Companion horsemen streamed across the garden plain, with scouts and archers straining to keep up with the wearied horses. They leaped water channels, cut through cherry orchards, rode the horses up the massive stone stairway to this hidden acropolis of the Persians. They raced in, to secure the treasure of gold coin and gold leaf, and purple dye and perfumes, and solid plates of precious metal, before the Persian officials could make off with the treasure.

Half drunk with fatigue, muddied, laughing, joyous, they smashed through the fragment of Immortals—the celebrated bowmen—mustering at the stairhead. They pushed between the winged *daimons* of the Xerxes Gate before the massive doors could be closed. They battered in the portals of the Hall of the Hundred Columns, herding before them a frightened mob of servants. They scattered through palaces where gigantic

211

wooden pillars supported roofs gleaming with solid silver plate.

Like hunting hounds in a rabbit warren, they nosed through the palaces of Darius, the small edifice of Artaxerxes. Realizing that they had won the race and gained the mighty wealth of Persepolis intact, they drank heavily of the wine standing in porous jars in the cooling chambers.

When torches were lighted and the wild search penetrated the corners of this palace height, the *apadana,* or throne room, of Xerxes caught fire. The flames spread to the adjoining barrack and women's quarters. By the time the officers could organize fire fighters the apadana was a blazing torch, the flames climbing the woven hangings and carved, gilded woodwork. The silver plating melted, running down in streams, spattering through the embers.

Alexander, moving through the fire fighters, saw where a stone slab bearing a likeness of Xerxes on the throne had been overturned. Abruptly he stopped, asking what it was. For a moment he studied it, while the men watched him—all of them conscious that this was the portrait of the Great King who had destroyed Athens generations before. Alexander said, "Shall we set him up again?" Then he went on, leaving Xerxes where he lay.

When he received the satrap of Persia the next day he seated himself with ceremony on the throne of Artaxerxes, which had been used by the last Darius. Some of the veteran Macedonians wept with relief and joy—perhaps with the fumes of wine still strong in them. One, Demarath the Corinthian, an old man, wiped away his tears, muttering that he grieved for all the Macedonians and Greeks who had died before they could see their commander on the throne of Persia. To such veterans this was the end of the war and the unceasing marching. . . .

The tradition persists that Alexander of Macedon burned Persepolis. If you travel through Iran today you will hear that tradition; authorities repeat it, and by repetition it has come to be the single circumstance universally connected with his life. But it is dangerous to assume that whatever happened in Alexander's presence happened because of his presence.

If Alexander ordered the Persepolis palaces to be burned, why did he order it? Certainly he did nothing of the kind at Babylon or Susa or later at Ecbatana. (Although he did order such destruction still later and still farther to the east, especially in what is now Turkestan and India.)

The Greek and in consequence the Roman narrators give many versions of this burning. The romantic version, featuring Thais, is well given by that able writer Plutarch, who was more interested in the working of human souls than in the account of battles.

Before taking the road again to go after Darius, Plutarch relates, *Alexander entertained his officers at drinking, even allowing everyone's mistress to sit by him. The most celebrated of these was Thais, an Athenian, mistress of Ptolemy who was afterward King of Egypt. At this feast she spoke up daringly, although excusably—being an Athenian. She said it was some compensation for her toils in following the army over Asia to sit here drinking in the palace of the Persian kings. But it would be much more fun if she could take a torch and set fire to this hall of Xerxes, who had burned Athens in his time. Everyone applauded this whim of hers. The king himself put a garland on his head and took a torch in his hand. So he led them around the hall, while they danced and sang and set fire to the hangings. When the Macedonians outside saw what was doing, they also ran in with torches. They did so with huge delight, for they saw in this destruction a sign that the king had no desire to stay among these barbarians and was inclined to go home.*

This scene fascinated poets and playwrights for centuries. Yet it is not probable that Thais, if she was ever present at Persepolis, had made the march with Alexander's column over the heights. And if Alexander destroyed a palace to please her, he never did the like again in his career.

Other explanations, rationalizing after the event, have it that he wished to avenge the destruction in Greece more than a century before, that he burned Persepolis for the moral effect on the Asiatics, or to emphasize that the old Persian dynasty was gone and that the Asiatics were dealing with a new king. Arrian has Parmenio argue that it would be a mistake to burn Persepolis if Alexander planned to remain inland in Asia. Yet Parmenio is known to have favored, with his faction of the staff, occupation of the western coast rather than the inland region.

Against this there are clear indications that the apadana of Xerxes burned in the confusion after the inrush of the Macedonians. The fire destroyed much of the gold and silver ornamentation of this hall, and apparently Alexander, or his officers, ordered it put out. At any rate it destroyed only the central portion of the palaces, not all the palace height. And certainly later on Alexander took pains to seal up and preserve intact the tomb of Cyrus, not far away.

In all probability the fire started accidentally and was put out as soon as possible.

The Macedonians rested at Persepolis for a month or two, until winter ended and snow cleared from the roads over the passes around them. In this time Parmenio's slower-moving column came in, and supplies were got from the countryside. They could afford to take this time to rest, because they heard that Darius was pretty well snowed in among the mountains of the Medes and that he was having trouble assembling a fourth army.

To the Macedonians in the ranks this seemed to be no more than a necessary pause before the last move and the end of the campaign. The wealth taken in at Persepolis staggered their imagination—enlarged though their concepts had been after listing the spoil of Susa.

214

On the charts of the military surveyors something equally amazing showed. In the last ten months the army had passed through or around a huge area—some three hundred and sixty thousand square miles. To this immense space in the east, of course, were added the territories taken over earlier, the Ionian coast, the islands, Egypt, Libya. A dozen Macedons could be fitted inside these new additions. The surveyors were no longer certain of their exact position on the earth; they had no familiar landmarks to work from; already they were making corrections in the world plan of Hecataeus.

Those officers like Ptolemy, son of Lagus, who still kept connected journals, had similar worries. The army controlled this new area because it had confiscated the public wealth, arranged for tribute to be paid, policed the roads, garrisoned the great cities and trading points. It had assumed responsibility, for what?

Already the mere task of administration overtaxed the staff, experienced as it was. Insensibly the body of the army had grown. Women, who had been ordered to remain at Babylon, appeared mysteriously again out of the baggage trains. The popular actor Thessalus turned up again and gave performances on the moonlit hillside above Persepolis. The contingents of servants increased. Wrestlers, musicians, and even the beloved roots of the wine grapes somehow made the journey after the army. The Macedonian farmers hurried to get the roots into the ground while it was still cold and wet. No one person had ordered all this. It simply happened, at Persepolis as at Memphis. The army, it seemed, had tangible appendages that could not be severed from it. Only now these appendages had grown. Money, for instance. The soldiers disliked leaving it behind, no matter how safely it might be stored in their names.

Once on a route march Alexander had noticed a transport driver. This man had shouldered heavy bales that had been loaded on a mule, when the mule went

215

down. The weight was too much for a man, and Alexander asked him what he was trying to carry.

"It's your property," the Macedonian growled. "Valuables."

"Then get it into camp if you can."

Alexander said nothing more then, but at camp he ordered the contents of the bales to be given to the man who had carried them in. He seemed to be indifferent to the new wealth, so far as it concerned him personally. He gave decisions about funds without thought, except to make gifts. Already there was more than enough for everybody.

The men noticed that their commander liked to be asked for gifts. An actor extemporized a plea for cash for deserving thespians during an evening's performance, and Alexander laughed and gave it. One young officer, however, made no such request although his duty kept him close to the king. After a time Alexander became aware of this. "Why don't you ask for anything?" he demanded.

The officer did not explain, but at the games soon afterward when they were tossing a ball from hand to hand he made a point of throwing the ball to everyone except Alexander, who stopped the game to inquire why he was being left out of it.

"Because you haven't asked for it," the officer told him.

Alexander laughed and presented him with a gift. While he seemed to grow more indifferent to the value of money, he did not relax discipline in Persia. As much as possible he gave judgment himself, and the men said he kept a finger on one ear at such times to remind himself to listen to justice, not to arguments. When he heard that a local culprit had been pursued into a shrine that was a Persian sanctuary, and that the Macedonians were going in to arrest the man, he advised them to stay outside and try to trick the man into coming out of the sanctuary.

The Macedonians thought this reverence for local

customs unnecessary, and they blamed the wings and the Achaemenians for it.

These wings were a pair of eagle's wings, carved in the stone over the entrances to the tombs. Such wings had been seen in Egypt, where they formed the emblem of Osiris, the sun god. They had also been found in Babylon, attached to the shoulders of the bas-reliefs of the grotesque god Marduk. Here they supported only a head, the head of Ahura, the Lord of Wisdom, who also shared in the power of the sun. If Ahura, within his disk of the sun, supported himself on the pinions of an imaginary eagle, it was all one to the soldiers, who had seen many images of strange gods by now. But it interested Alexander greatly. He wanted to know why the rulers of Persia were related to the sun and to the wings of the eagle.

When he discovered that the only temples of this land were stone altars on high places where fire burned at night, he questioned the Zarathustrians—the Greeks called them Zoroastrians—who attended these fire altars. They said that the eagle, the great bird dwelling nearest the sun, formed a link between men and the sky. They believed that the *Si-murg,* the spirit of the eagles, descended to the hilltops to aid men.

These Zarathustrians thought that human fate was not preordained, to be interpreted by the circling of the stars as the Babylonians claimed. Instead the human spirit endured through eternity, struggling to raise itself out of darkness to light, losing strength when it came under the power of evil, gaining strength when it progressed toward good.

Unlike the Yahweh of the Semites, or the Lord [Bel] of the intelligent Babylonians, the god Ahura took no share in war, being involved only in the struggle with evil, as such. In this Ahura differed also from the Father-God Zeus of the Greeks.

"The sky is their Zeus," the soldiers said of these Zarathustrians.

Yet they had a legend that the deity of the sky who descended to earth, Mithra, had been born in the night of the winter solstice in a cavern that was the grotto of the world between the star constellation of the ox and that of the ass. This had come to pass at the time of the ascendency of the sign of the virgin in the night sky.

So, precisely, had the divine Dionysos been born. Mithra was a very twin to Dionysos. And it seemed to Alexander that the Persian Zarathustrians—his men called them Magians, or magicians—had drawn their knowledge from the same source as the ancient Greeks. Only the names differed—and he discovered that the Zend, the ancient speech of the Persians, did resemble Greek. The family of their Great Kings, the Kings of the Lands of the Earth, was Achaemenian, not Achaean.

At some time in the past, then, the Greeks and Persians had been related. But where had the Persians come from?

From the north and east, the Zarathustrians said. From ancient Iran-venj, their lost paradise. There, far off in the limbo of the steppes, they had been close to the divine Powers. Emerging, they had bred horses and ridden horses—they called the ancient breed the splendid Nisaean herd—and they had worked metals. These early Iranian tribes had migrated out of the lost paradise through the land of Soghd, through Bactria and Parthia, around the waters of the clear inland sea. The Iranian tribe called *Parsa* had given their name to Persia, to the great plateau where the good grass grew that fed their horse herds. The Achaemenian clan had been leaders of this Parsa tribe.

The foremost of the Achaemenian clan, Kurush[1]—

---

[1] In this book proper names are given in their most familiar form, whether of Greek or Latin origin. Modern usage has clung to Alexander instead of Alexandros and to Hephaestion, Ptolemy, and Thais. Nearchus appears most often in Latin guise. In the case of oriental names an attempt has been made to give them as they were actually pronounced. The early Persians wrote "Kurush" and "Cyrus" as the name of their first emperor, and "Rushanak," not "Roxana," as the name of Alexander's bride.

called Cyrus by the Greeks—had gained supremacy over the Medes of the mountains and had swept with his horsemen westward as far as the Mediterranean Sea. Only two centuries before, Kurush had reined in at the waters of the sea. He had united the different peoples under his rule. He had laughed at the gold stored up by Croesus of Lydia, on that coast. With his horsemen and his camels he had ridden over Lydia.

This Kurush had mocked at the Greeks of the cities who had to get their food, he said, by gathering together in a place called the market place, to dispute and pay money for what they ate. Among his peoples, Kurush had said, food was given and not sold.

The tomb of this Kurush stood back in the hills under bare trees by the thread of a stream. It was built of simple blocks of limestone, worn and burned to a golden hue by the sun. The name Kurush meant the Sun.

Alexander visited the tomb of Kurush, whom he had begun to admire. Climbing up the pedestal and sitting on the top tier against the sarcophagus chamber that had a pointed roof like a house, he could see the wide steps across the fields leading up to the hall and the few buildings of the first town Kurush had built, called Pasargadae.

Going over to Pasargadae, he found no inhabitants there. The space of the hall had been leveled off against the slope of a small hill, and it had no fortification. You climbed easily up the broad steps and sat in the shade, looking out over the fields now turning green. It was good country for horses. Only a few Zarathustrians attended the tomb of Kurush, who had formed the western Asiatic world into one, joining the people under him but allowing them to have freedom in their lives. Alexander told the Zarathustrians to keep on with their guard. He did not want the tomb molested.

It seemed to him that there was a meaning in this solitary white tomb among grazing herds. He did not know what meaning the tomb had for him, but he felt it.

219

At the bend of the road going back to Persepolis he saw the rock tombs of the later Achaemenians, of Darius the Great and Ahasuerus, whom the Greeks called Xerxes. They all had the eagle wings and the disk the sun above the threshold. But no city was near them. Only a single fire altar, tended by priests.

He thought that Persepolis itself had been built not as a city but as a palace home. The columns were shaped like the trees of the vast forest, the open halls were like pavilions pitched by wanderers for a night's shelter. At first the Achaemenians had tried to dwell within this place, then the administration of their immense domain made up of kingdoms had drawn them farther and farther afield, so that they returned only at rare intervals to the homesite by the tombs. They had become lords of the first world empire.

Around here, the Zarathustrians said, there had been no war for two centuries. The Achaemenians, in that respect, had made their home like the ancient Iran-venj, of the first Aryans.

Alexander recalled that Iran-venj, the lost sanctuary, must lie toward the east, beyond the knowledge of the Greeks, beyond Parthia and Bactria and Soghd, and the beginning of the steppes. And he remembered that route clearly, as he remembered such things. For in his imagination that easternmost point had been the dwelling place of the gods.

There was so much he could not understand in this that he sent a message west to Aristotle, asking for someone of his school to travel out to this new region, if he could not come himself.

Aristotle did not come, but he sent a nephew, Callisthenes by name.

When snow melted along the heights in that spring of the year 330 B.C. the Macedonian army took up its pursuit of the elusive manpower of the Great King Darius.

It headed directly northwest along the higher ridges past the cliffs where Alexander had inspected the

Achaemenian tombs, moving at about cloud level where the horses could graze on fresh grass. So it almost doubled back on the line of march of the autumn before—only keeping east of the summits of the Zardeh Kuh, or Yellow Mountains, among tribal people where food abounded. Alexander arranged for the future government of these uplands as he marched through, quickening the pace of the army as it circled through the valley leading to Ecbatana some six hundred miles distant from the starting point at Persepolis.

As they neared Ecbatana the Macedonians found the situation changing. The warlike mountain folk, who had tasted Macedonian power at Gaugamela, showed no further inclination to support their overlord Darius; instead the chieftains of the Medes and Kurds came in to discuss terms with Alexander. So the Macedonians were able to parade into the last of the four capital cities, Ecbatana, while their commander took over the responsibility of all of the western half of what had been the Persian Empire.

The last Darius had escaped again, but this time with no more than a couple of thousand Greek mercenaries and some light cavalry following him. He headed down across the Iranian plateau to take refuge, and to recruit new forces, in the east.

Thus at Ecbatana Alexander began the last stage of the pursuit of Darius, starting east with the nucleus of his army, the Companions, Macedonian phalanx, the archers and light cavalry and the ever-present Agrianians.

The pursuit at this point became a test of endurance and speed. Swinging down from the Ecbatana hills, Alexander pushed the army nearly three hundred miles in eleven days.

Magians with the army told him that he was now tracing the path of the Iranian migration of long ago. The Nisaean horses had bred on the rolling pastureland. Soon they sighted the solitary snow peak in the north that the Magians called the Blue Mountain

[Mount Demavend]. From the summit of this peak a plume of wind-driven snow swung up and vanished in the clear sky.

Within the walls of ancient Ray, hugging the foothills of the Blue Mountain, Alexander halted. Information reached him that Darius had passed on, several days before, through the narrow defile called the Caspian Gates. Coenus was sent out from Ray to forage for supplies, while Alexander waited for laggard units, left behind on the march, to catch up. Before they could do so and before Coenus could return, new intelligence came in. Darius had been arrested by his own satraps, who held the Great King prisoner as they pushed east.

At once Alexander took the road with the cavalry and the toughest of the infantry, carrying rations for two days. Craterus was left to maintain liaison at Ray.

The pursuit force kept going that night, passing through the dark walls of the Caspian Gates after daybreak—stopping at noon at a stream to rest and sleep for a few hours. They marched all night, wearied men dropping out and horses dying. They reached the campsite that the Persians had vacated only a day and a half before.

Here they heard that the satraps now in command of the resistance force planned to push due east with their royal prisoner, to raise a new army in Bactria.

After three or four hours' sleep Alexander marched without halting for a night and a day, coming on the camp the fugitives had left some twenty hours before.

Until now they had been following the caravan road skirting the foothills, keeping the open desert on their right. Now Alexander learned that there was a way straight across the desert, but without water. Inspecting the units that had kept up with him, he dismounted five hundred of the most weary cavalry, replacing them with the same number of infantry in the best condition. Leaving the remainder of the foot behind, he struck across the desert by moonlight.

This time he did not stop. Through the day the

mounted column began to thin out. In the noon heat the men went on like automatons, because Alexander kept on. They were out of water. Some scouts came in with a small skin or a helmet filled with water that they had scooped up from rocks. This they offered to Alexander.

"Who are you bringing this to?" he asked.

"To you."

Around the water hundreds of men were gathered, their eyes on it. No one said anything. Alexander emptied the water out into the sand. "It does no good for one to drink alone," he said.

Toward the end of the afternoon they sighted the dust of the fugitives, on the road close to the hills. The desert march had lasted for forty-seven miles.

The men were in no condition to go into action, but Alexander led them on, past Persian stragglers and abandoned carts. (The Greek mercenaries had turned off into the hills long since.) The satraps had escaped into a ravine. The exhausted survivors made only a semblance of resistance, throwing themselves down as the leading Macedonians came up.

There was no sign of Darius. One cart, apparently without a human occupant, was being dragged away by a pair of mules. The thirsty animals had smelled water, and were moving toward a spring. In this cart, just before daybreak, the pursuers found the body of Darius, murdered by his own officers. With one of his theatrical gestures, the Macedonian threw his white cloak over the body of the Great King.

XIV. THE WINGS, THE SUN,
AND THE EMPIRE

This ignominious death by a knife in the hand of a follower, in a cart, was of little importance. This man who wore the high tiara and shawl robe of a King of Kings had ceased to be a leader—Darius himself had assassinated his predecessor, the last of the true Achaemenians. Since Persepolis, Alexander of Macedon had held the mastery in these lands, and since entering Ecbatana he had assumed the responsibility of a ruler.

Ecbatana itself had met him with an almost physical impact. Its seven walls rising by the caravan route gleamed with seven colors. Its citadel shone with gold. Wind-swept, cold as his native Pella but infinitely more majestic, Ecbatana had been shaped in the semblance of Greek architecture. It rose before Alexander like a Thebes restored.

More than that, it commanded the chains of mountains that dwarfed the knobby heights of Greece. Unseen in the north lay the snow peak of Urartu, or Ararat. Armenians from Ararat told him of mountain lakes as vast as inland seas, and mines still unexploited. These Armenians had submitted to the rule of the Great Kings, which outlawed warfare, owing to the mild influence of Zarathustra, who had lived in a hut by those lakes. The mountain folk—Armenians and Kurdish tribes—had accepted the faith of Zarathustra, building fire altars in the cold air of the highest places.

This must have brought back to Alexander the lessons of Mieza, where Aristotle had laid down a challenge to superstition, claiming that particles of the human race could shape themselves by their environment, and in this struggle could attain nobility of soul. These

Zarathustrians believed themselves to be engaged in such a conflict, in which they bowed down to the image of no god. Often when these Aryans spoke of simple things such as fire and water and life, Alexander could understand their words, which were similar to Greek. In their folk memory they had survived a flooding of the waters of the earth in these mountains around Ararat. They expected to survive the last catastrophe of fire when a comet should strike the earth, ending the agelong conflict between light and darkness, good and evil, so that some would perish in the fire while some passed over into the tranquility of everlasting paradise.

They introduced Alexander to everlasting fire. A dark liquid bubbled out of clefts in the earth and flowed down like water to a pool that burned without cessation. Such fires smoked and gleamed in the depths between rocks. It seemed to the Macedonian scientists that here was a new element—although it resembled both naphtha and bitumen. It kindled instantly when a burning stick was held in the air over it. With this inflammable mixture of liquid and vapor the Macedonians experimented, thereby perhaps making the first recorded examination of petroleum.

The barbarian people showed them the power of it by sprinkling the street leading to the king's dwelling with drops of it. When night came, they stood at the far end of the street with torches. When the first torch was applied to the moist ground, the flame leaped along the ground more quickly than a man could think of it. The whole street blazed instantly.

Another experiment, in which a Greek bath tender, who thought himself stronger than the marvelous flame, rubbed himself with the new liquid and let the Macedonians ignite him, did not end so happily. This human torch was doused with the water from the bath jars, but he had plenty of burns to show for his test of strength with the new power.

Deiades and the engineers were fascinated by the peculiarities of the new power.

In his own thought Alexander had sensed dimly at

Persepolis and clearly at Ecbatana a new power of a different kind in the rule of the Achaemenians—the descendants of Kurush, whom he now admired. Like the Macedonians, the Iranians of Kurush had been a horse-riding and freedom-loving people, uncouth, even their women going about and doing work in public. But these *Shahinshahs,* these Great Kings, had accomplished something that had never been done before. They had a genius for ruling. They had made a commonwealth of the peoples of their world.

His new informants—Persians, Kurds, Armenians, Magians—told him how government had existed before then. The Babylonians, for instance, had formed a city-state—a mighty one, but still the rule of one city over the others. The Assyrians had conquered other peoples, superimposing a kingdom of Assyrians over others as subjects. The Persian Achaemenians, however, had managed to govern other nations, *preserving them as nations.* They had made a whole by preserving the parts.

Over each part they had set a governor, a *kshattra,* or warrior, whom the Greeks called satrap. They had built canals to link rivers to the sea, and roads to link the cities closer together. They had conveyed over these roads the silver from the Taurus mines to roof the buildings in Persepolis, and frankincense from Arabia to sweeten the air of the rooms. These Shahinshahs, or Great Kings, who had made themselves truly Kings of the Lands of the Earth, had laid upon these lands the law of the Achaemenian peace. At first, with their splendid horse archers, they had been able to enforce this peace, from the Dardanelles to the river in the east that they called the Indus.

Obviously something had happened to the Achaemenians from the time of Kurush to that of the last Darius. Just what had happened the wise men of the east could not explain satisfactorily. At first Kurush, for example, had paid no attention to the temples in Babylon. When he discovered that the Babylonians believed that he, the Shah, ruled only by power of their

226

god Marduk, he had closed the temples of Ammon-Re in Egypt.

Gradually, it seemed, the Achaemenians and the Persian people had changed. At first they had gone about the task of government, moving from city to city as need arose. Then, becoming owners of vast lands, their descendants had remained more on the land, to attend to it. They had gained wealth. At this stage they depended for protection on that perpetual guard, the Immortals—and at need upon a levy of the nobility. Then they had found it more convenient to hire mercenaries such as the Greeks and the Phoenican fleets. Instead of ministering to the different nations of their whole, the later Shahs had merely been supported by the different nations as a kind of movable fugurehead, around which centered intrigue. But still the plan of Kurush had endured, because internal peace was preserved. Until the coming of the Macedonians no outside people had ventured to challenge the rule of the Great Kings.

Meditating upon the plan of Kurush in the mountains of Ecbatana, Alexander's quick imagination could visualize its tremendous significance. This commonwealth of nations, once attempted, could be carried out on a scale to include all the western world. He had the old system of satraps and advisers to work with. Already he had made one change—to limit the powers of the satraps to political administration, and to install independent treasurers for the public funds. He had summoned Harpalus to Ecbatana, and set up a strong guard there, under Parmenio. (And when the ailing Harpalus came, he brought seeds and cuttings of all the plants of Macedon. Only the ivy failed to grow in this eastern soil.)

Alexander already posssesed, ready to hand, a mobile police power in the veteran Macedonian army. He had road surveys, rough plans of the different lands. And charts made by Nearchus of the coasts.

In such a commonwealth Athens could be independent of Sparta, and Sparta could continue to follow its own strange way of life. Perhaps under this rule of the whole, the age-old, murderous Greek partisanship could be ended, by rendering it futile. The plague of civil wars might cease if no tangible gain could be derived from such wars.

How much of this Alexander reasoned out for himself at this point, and how much he learned from hearing of the early Persian imperium of Kurush, may never be made clear. What is certain is that he visualized the possibility of a world state, a universe of men—in which women might share—that could preserve a balance of freedom within its parts.

The Oikoumene, the habitable world, could be formed into one whole.

Already the Macedonians had revised upward their concepts of time and distance. For here couriers speeded message along the Persian post roads by changing horses at the relay stations. The highways themselves, like the great King's Way, ran through from frontier to frontier, and were kept in order. Many of these highways connected with the sea-borne traffic at the Gates of the Sea. They also tapped the desert regions. (The roads within Macedon had been no more than cart tracks winding from village to village, as the villagers themselves happened to use them. In the last eight months the Macedonians had marched more than ten times the width of their homeland.)

Moreover they now held what Kurush had never had: control of the sea and its shipping. That is, of the Mediterranean and the Red seas. And Alexander had brought along with him the technical tools of navigation upon seas still to be explored, in his shipbuilders, mariners, and pilots. He was eager to come within sight of these unknown seas.

Already he possessed the means of communication between peoples, the Greek language which, with the universal trade slang of the *koiné*, was understood as far east as Babylon. From Babylon eastward Persian, the language of courts and trading centers, was the general medium of communication. And scholars accompanying the army had discovered the resemblance between the two. By now the Macedonian leaders used Greek in their daily talk. Some younger officers like Peucestas had mastered Persian quickly. They could read the *avestas*, the sacred writing of the *Zend* or ancient Persian, that told of the cosmic battle between the dual forces of good and evil, in which each individual had to struggle toward salvation. . . .

At Ecbatana, Alexander had with him a nucleus of human minds capable of creating a new state. Greek scholars now consulted with Chaldean mathematicians and with Magian wise men. The vast knowledge of these easterners made even the philosophic Greeks appear provincial. In fact, measured by the new standard of intelligence, they *were* provincials. But they did not feel inclined to admit that.

At Ecbatana for the first time Alexander allowed himself to be addressed by the easterners as "Great King, One King among Many—King of the Lands of the Earth." Someone told him that that title had been carved upon the yellow cliff not far from Ecbatana by order of the first Darius, written down there at Behistun in the world language of Zend.

Men like Ptolemy, son of Lagus, objected instantly to this new title. Alexander was king of the Macedonians, and hence neither Pharaoh nor despot of Asia. He ruled, of course, *in* Egypt; he was now *in* Asia, but he had not ceased to be Alexander of Macedon, and Ptolemy's half brother.

"If I write home about Great Kings, people will laugh, and they will have reason to laugh," Ptolemy complained.

Old men like Aristander the soothsayer, who still corresponded with the priesthood of Delphi, grumbled because the temples of Bel and Marduk had been reopened in Babylon. "Now those people will bow down in public to the power of that winged monster Marduk."

"What of it—if they want to?" Alexander wondered.

"What of it? The Babylonians think you have attained supremacy through the will of Marduk."

And Alexander burst out impatiently. In what respect did the thoughts of crowds in Babylon affect him? They could not change his nature by their thinking.

"What men think matters much."

"They have thanked us and given praise."

"In words, yes. The unspoken thoughts hold deepest meaning."

Irritably Alexander sent the old man away. Aristander felt that his king no longer paid close attention to the significance of the omens, which indicated the will of the divine Powers. He merely kept Aristander to satisfy the superstition of the men. Hephaestion smiled, and took the sting out of this sharp disputation by calling Alexander "Despot." In common with most of the Companions, he knew Alexander's enthusiams and eagerness to experiment with new tools and forms. He knew that at Mieza Alexander had heard Aristotle demonstrate how an ideal state, a republic such as Plato conceived, never had existed, and so could not exist. Wishful thinking could not create such a government. It had to grow out of human needs. In another month or so Alexander would occupy his mind with new hospitalization, or medical purges and fever baths, or perhaps the construction of a fleet, if they could find him a sea somewhere.

In reasoning thus Hephaestion was both right and wrong. Alexander did find such things to occupy him, but he never lost his new conviction that the peoples of the Oikoumene could be fused together.

Lysippus, who was modeling heads of Alexander to be used for the new coinage of silver tetradrachmas, bemoaned the absence of statuary in these eastern lands. The Persians, he complained, showed no ability to mold an image of the human form. They did no more than carve decorative or legendary scenes—upon cliffs or stone slabs. They used animal shapes repeated in a pattern for ornament. Whole strings of stylized running deer or flying eagles . . .

Alexander did not feel mournful about that. The artists here, he thought, were more like artisans—they ornamented walls to make a building pleasing to the eye. They designed a building to fit into a hillside, where it belonged, with open porticoes where people could gather and be cool—not simply to supply the building with a pretty front.

"But it's inhuman! They make people into things, into processions of spirits or slaves under those everlasting wings—as if humans were only shapes actuated by divine power."

"Well, what actuates the horsemen of Phidias—the desire to kill Amazons?"

Lysippus threw down his wooden shaper, howling. "Amazons! At least you can look at them. Do you know what these folk see in you? The head of a lion. And why? Because you have a mop of hair like a lion's mane, and because one of their hero-spirits wore a lion's-head mask and rode around on that *Si-murg* eagle thing. So they say your head looks like the legendary lion's head."

Instead of laughing as usual, Alexander thought about that. And the sculptor, noticing this, went on to say quickly, "If you'd get a haircut and stop shaving your chin they wouldn't think that."

When it was finished, the head of Alexander modeled by Lysippus had a long-mane resembling a lion's skull, and to point up this striking resemblance, a lion's paw appeared beneath the chin. Alexander had wanted it like that. But when Lysippus brought him the finished model he studied it for a long time and decided that he did not want it on the new coins yet.

A more serious problem had to be met at Ecbatana: the length of service of the men in the ranks. Four years had passed since the mobilization on the Macedonian coast. Moreover their commander had promised that Gaugamela would be the last battle. What was he to say to the men in the ranks now?

Probably not more than half of those who waited on his decision at Ecbatana had crossed the Dardanelles with him. Deaths, wounds, sickness, had made gaps in the ranks, and many companies had been left along the line of communication. And then the third yearly levy from home had joined the field army at Susa. Besides, many eastern units had been enlisted. Still, there was his promise to the veterans—and Alexander never shirked his responsibility to them. At Ecbatana they had taken over the last of the four capitals of the former Great King, and the men in the ranks knew as well as the officers that their war was won.

Alexander's solution was this: any organization that voted as a whole to return home could do so, while men of that organization who chose to stay on in Asia could do so by joining other units. (Apparently, here, he gave the older Macedonian units no choice, or else their decision was never in question.) Those who voted to leave were the Thessalian horse and other allied Greeks.

They were paid in full and arrangements made for them to sell their horses at the coast and embark in the new shipping under escort for Greece. Alexander added two thousand talents (worth perhaps twenty million dollars in purchasing power today) out of his personal account, as a bonus. Other organizations were allowed to remain at the base in Ecbatana. But Alexander had decided on the new move to the east by then, because he sent orders to Black Cleitus, who had been left behind ill at Persepolis, to rejoin with his squadron of Companions, in Parthia.

A few men muttered that to go on now, without reason, was the act of a madman. But they were hooted down by those who had followed Alexander to ever-increasing success. Some officers complained that the Macedonian army had been changed over into military settlers. Philotas, the brilliant Companion brigadier, went about in such state, magnificently uniformed, that he was cautioned by his father, Parmenio. "You are making more display than Alexander himself."

232

Not even the staff had expected the total of public treasure to be as great as it proved to be after tabulation—some hundred and eighty thousand talents in coin, bullion, and precious stuff, including the plating of the palaces of Persepolis. Such wealth could not have been imagined in Macedon four years before. Transported home now, intact, it could support all the six hundred thousand-odd Macedonians for a couple of generations. Every family would be wealthy.

If it could have been so transported and used as money, that is. For this treasure was the greater part of the wealth of the Oikoumene, as the Macedonians knew it. Even a portion minted into money would have flooded the markets of the west and bankrupted among others the Greek merchant cities. It was vastly too great to use as a whole.

Here in the east it had served as the reserve of the decadent Persian imperium, and Alexander meant to keep it here, to reconstruct the fabric of that imperium. The war bonus he paid out, the gifts to distinguished officers and to veterans, took no more than a trickle from this vast reservoir of wealth. The bulk of it was left with Parmenio and the garrison troops, in the treasury of the citadel at Ecbatana.

Actually Alexander had taken only a few days to make all these rapid arrangements at this city.

There were many intangible threads pulling him east, toward the rising sun. The richest part of the treasure trove had been gold dust marked "from the lands of the Indus." Those lands, he knew now, lay at the eastern end of the habitable world, where the river Indus flowed out of the mountains called Parapanisades.

There lay the goal of his imagination, the unknown region beyond the last mountain barrier, much vaster than the Yellow Mountains he had just passed.

Along this river the Magians said that other Aryans dwelt.

On the way thither stretched the Inland Sea, above the Caspian Gates. And beyond, at some point unknown to men, lay Ocean itself, encircling the continental mass.

Those threads all joined together, to pull Alexander on to explore. Already some of the minds close to him fed his eagerness deliberately. It suited them more to have Alexander off ransacking new territory than for him to remain and complete his organization. For he left Ecbatana so hastily that the fabric of his new imperium, administered by Macedonian officers and Persian officials, was no more than half shaped and not yet put into working order. His departure at that time was a signal for growing disturbance and trouble.

He had started after Darius in that spring of 330, no doubt intending to return within a year or two. He did not return for more than seven years.

THREE

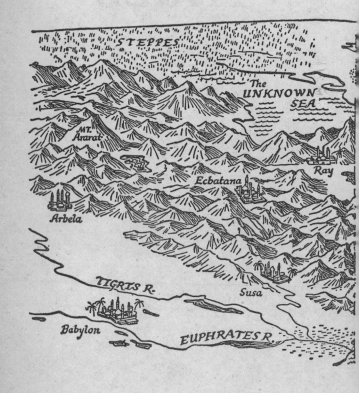

XV. THE BLIGHT OF LUXURY

It began with little things, with personal luxuries, hobbies, and servants. It grew imperceptibly into a conflict of personalities. Probably it had begun long before, during the campaigning, but it became more evident during these months of occupation of western Asia.

The Macedonians, from phalanxmen to commanders, were experienced campaigners, which meant that they knew very well how to make themselves comfortable. Moreover, compared to the eastern Greeks—the Ionians—and noble-born Egyptians and Persians, they were barbarians. They had learned only the two sciences of warfare and agriculture; now they were learning new methods of trade and commerce. Only in exceptional cases—those of Alexander and Peucestas, and Hephaestion—did they try to understand the mentality of the Asiatics. But almost all of them were greatly impressed by the conveniences and luxuries available at every stage. Farming here involved no such toil as in the Macedonian hills—harvests grew as if by magic out of a seed supply, irrigation canals, and the plentiful slave labor.

Alexander's generosity had made even squadron leaders wealthy, by Macedonian standards. A regimental commander could buy a village or a fleet of river barges, and Alexander openly encouraged this form of investment in the new lands. He was not so pleased with some other ideas of the soldiers.

They had developed a taste for oriental perfumes and bath scents. They liked to be rubbed down with Egyptian ointment instead of plain oil. They had acquired, somehow, silver basins—Alexander noticed one officer who would have only silver nails in his sandals—and skilled Syrian masseurs. Another officer had arrangement for a special rubdown powder to be shipped regularly by camel load from Memphis.

Philotas liked to go off hunting with his private coterie of secretaries and attendants. He had special nets made, which, when set up, covered a half mile of ground. By driving gazelles, boar, and lions against these nets he could bring in a huge haul of game. On such occasion he gave banquets on a royal scale, serving imported wine cooled with snow. Alexander's own mess had grown, with his new staff of Magians, interpreters, and geographers. But he kept on serving simple food and limited his stewards' budget.

In one of her incessant letters Olympias complained bitterly that he was limiting his own resources while giving his lieutenants wealth enough to create followings of their own. "You will find yourself destitute in the end, when you will have made them equal to kings."

Alexander paid no attention to such advice, but he did dress down non-coms who had taken on servants to clean their equipment and groom their horses.

"If a soldier can't attend to the needs of his body with his own hand, is he fit to be called a soldier?"

So long as they were quartered in towns it was not easy to separate his veterans from this immense throng of servants. During such halts the army had a way of multiplying itself like a cattle herd penned in good pasturage. Women produced offspring; interpreters appeared with aged fathers who had to be cared for; guides developed brothers. Moreover the new Persian coworkers had large staffs of technical assistants. When the satraps of Parthia and Hyrcania came in to make formal obeisance to the new Great King they brought with them trains of councilors, physicians, stable managers, accountants, and a whole regiment of couriers. They also had wives, who also had entourages.

For several centuries these people of Asia had

flocked to the person of the Great King, and they did so now, because Alexander was making himself both feared and respected. They called him *Iskander Shah* and Divinely Sent, and unless prevented they prostrated themselves when he stepped among them. This pressing of the head to the earth before the presence of the Great King was not so much an act of servility as an act of reverence to the divine Power invested in the person of their new ruler. They were bowing down to the memory of Kurush, and the splendor of Ahura, Lord of the Sun. It was not easy to prevent them from doing this. Philotas made fun of such prostration.

Alexander tried to ridicule his followers out of a desire for so many attendants. Did they, he asked, expect others to do their thinking for them, as well as run their errands? Did they expect to keep as fit and sleep as sound as formerly, if they delegated their work routine to other men? Such admonitions had little effect—partly because Alexander's own mess had grown in the same way, what with his new Persian teachers and Hephaestion's Magians. For Hephaestion, like Alexander, cultivated the friendship of the Persians, eating with them and trying to learn from them. While commanders like Philotas and Craterus conducted themselves as Macedonian overlords in a subjected land.[1]

---

[1] It is important to remember always that Alexander of Macedon was not setting up a Greek system in Asia. His new imperium can best be called Macedonian-Persian—a world state fashioned out of Macedonian leadership, upon Persian concepts. More than that, it was something new under the sun.

Some modern histories have inadvertently left the impression that Alexander established a state upon the Greek model, thereby extending Greek culture eastward. There is little truth in that.

Alexander had studied the defects as well as the advantages of the Greek political system at Mieza, and in the treatise of Isocrates, as well as in Philip's counseling. After his own experience at the two councils of Corinth, and in trying to establish Greek nationality upon the Ionian coast, he seemed to abandon

The brilliant and restless Craterus jeered at the philosophic Hephaestion, calling him Persian-lover and thespian. Alexander refused to be bothered by this personal quarrel. "Hephaestion," he said, "is Alexander's friend. Craterus is the king's friend. Both are equally loyal." He said nothing, at this point, about Philotas.

Only when he set the divisions marching into new territories could he inspect the personnel now accumulated around his commands. Disliking to order his men to rid themselves of their new appendages, he made a practice of leaving as much as possible behind at bases along the roads. Also he threw the regiments with him into arduous route marches, cutting through mountain ranges and making wide circuits to explore the country. But the army knew as well as he that there was no military necessity for such marches.

Then Alexander encouraged the officers to go after the more dangerous kind of game. The Asiatics shared in this love of hazardous hunting. Alexander often dismounted to go after lions on foot with a short spear,

---

any hope of carrying Greece with him into Asia. Lysippus and the other Greek artists who accompanied him had the specific duty of designing coins and engraving gems, and painting his own portraits. Aristander was not a Greek. Most of the Greeks he appointed as officials in his new provincial administration were from the Asiatic cities. He designed Alexandria in Egypt more on the plan of Memphis or Sidon than Corinth. At Ecbatana he sent home, or allowed to go home, most of the Greek allied forces. The famous lighthouse at Alexandria was designed on the model of the tower at Halicarnassus, which seems to have impressed Alexander greatly.

He was influenced even more profoundly by the magnificent Persian art. He sent home continually, to Mieza, Pella, and Athens, exhibits and specimens of all that was new in Asia. After Babylon, Magians, Zarathustrians, Indian Aryans like Kalynas were asked to accompany him. Only today is the significance and importance of Persian and western Asiatic culture being recognized, as Alexander recognized it. The influence of Aristotle upon Alexander has been assumed to be great; the influence of Alexander and of his discoveries upon Arisotle and the Hellenic world has not been estimated correctly.

which was far from being a safe pastime. A Spartan hostage—he had been an envoy to the former Great King—watching Alexander in one of these encounters, remarked sarcastically, "I find it hard to say which of the two is the more majestic brute."

Craterus, who was suffering from fever, ridiculed the lion-hunting project more subtly. He summoned Lysippus, after one lion had been killed, to make a quick model of the group, with the lion going for Alexander and Craterus killing the lion. "Cast it in life-size bronze," he urged the sculptor, "and set it up on a pedestal, to mark the spot where Alexander slew the king of beasts."

(This was in Hyrcania—on the shore of the Caspian—where lions, tigers, and wild buffalo abounded in the forest. The Macedonians had set up such statues of soldiers as memorials after the early battles.)

"No," Alexander corrected, "send the group back to the Delphic shrine as a thank offering."

Craterus had nothing to say to that. Again, Alexander heard in the general table talk that Peucestas—one of the Persian-favorers—had been badly bitten by a bear during a hunt. At once he dictated a sharp remonstrance to that officer, asking why Peucestas had not informed him of the wound and giving him advice how to treat it, with a purge of hellebore.

He realized that he was losing touch with the personal problems of his officers. Except for the regiments actually serving under the king, the Macedonian units were now scattered along the communications of an area of more than six hundred and fifty thousand square miles. Even with the new courier-post system, over the fine imperial roads such as the King's Way, it took nearly two months for a letter from Alexander's advanced headquarters to reach Alexandria in Egypt. Staff officers were widely separated, at bases like Tyre, Babylon, Ecbatana, and Ray. With them the Macedonian leader tried to keep in touch by courier dispatch. But sheer distance made it impossible to maintain liaison now with the coast region. He had to draw his active commands eastward as he advanced.

The full weight of responsibility fell on one man. To the great problems of supply—in meeting these, he had to calculate the seasonal yield of harvests, grazing, ahead as well as behind him—were now added the nagging perplexities of a dual administration of these vast provinces. Since he had appointed Macedonian officers to work with the Persian satraps, he had to smooth out inevitable differences between them. Philotas, for example, saw only catastrophe in trying to put the civil administration in the rear areas on the same authority as the military. As commander of the Macedonian cavalry spearhead, he refused point-blank to co-operate with a civil governor in guarding merchants' caravans. "Are we rulers of these lands or servants of these people?" he asked his intimates contemptuously.

Alexander was obdurate on the point of protecting civilians. He went out of his way to make clear that this was not a conquest but a reconstruction of the world state of the Great Kings. He had ordered in detail the ceremonious funeral for the body of Darius at Persepolis. The young sons of Darius he kept with him, supervising their education, with the help of the mother of Darius, teaching them Greek as well as military discipline.

To even read the mass of travel orders and routine reports coming in from the new base camps required many hours of the night, but Alexander tried to do it. In one order, for an overage veteran, Eurylochus of Aegae, to be enrolled as physically disabled and sent home, he questioned the reason for it.

He was told Eurylochus did not appear to be disabled but he wanted to go back. Alexander sent for the soldier.

The veteran Eurylochus admitted he was well enough—admitted that his real reason for putting in for a sick leave was that he had left a girl back in a coast port, a girl named Telesippa.

"You left her? Then who does she belong to?"

"Nobody. She's a free prostitute. She'll go home with me, Telesippa will."

The commander wrote a few words on the order. *"If the girl Telesippa will accompany the veteran Eurylochus of her free will, permit the two to return to Macedon. If not, return the veteran to duty."*

Only officers like Hephaestion and Peucestas had any sympathy with Alexander's insistence that the women of the Asiatics should be treated like the wives of the Macedonians. The Macedonians had understood well enough the Greek code affecting women—that wives should be secluded and do the work, while the prostitute class were the free companions of all comers. But here the only promiscuous women were in the lower slave class; other women, although only partially secluded, were to be treated as wives and daughters, and could make complaints, even against Macedonian officers, if abused.

Alexander insisted on it. If his Macedonians were to live with the Asiatics the women would have to be treated as they were treated before the invasion.

By now he was showing more strain under the labor of administration than during the campaigns. Sleeping less than before, he formed the habit of sitting over wine with his intimates during the early hours of the morning, and still waking for the sunrise sacrifice and breakfast consultation. When he overslept now he would lie unconscious for thirty-six hours. He drank more heavily, often bathing afterward, before turning in. Moreover, in his anxiety to get through routine which he refused to neglect, he showed increasing impatience. Statements to him had to be hurried through; he snapped at objections. *Those around him developed the habit of saying only what might please him, for to disagree with him would rouse his anger. It was not that he relished flattery, but he listened most readily to praise of his actions, and those who had honest censorship to voice often remained silent, to his disadvantage.*

245

By this time, too, Alexander suffered from the loss of Parmenio's services and the breakup of the old staff. Hephaestion was no more than a very gifted viceroy—the Persians called him a *wazir*—and the magnetic Craterus a fine divisional commander. Such officers could not replace the old general staff of Philip's forming, that had advanced the army so smoothly all the way to Tyre. But under Alexander's new concept of government there was no place for such a military staff.

Many stories are told about the execution of Philotas. It seems that as far back as Damascus he had picked up a prostitute, one Antigone of Pydna, and as long before as the residence in Memphis she had gossiped about Philotas, who had told her the Macedonian success had been won by his father and himself, and not by the youthful and inexperienced Alexander. The king appears to have summoned Antigone and questioned her, without taking any further notice of the talk.

Unquestionably Philotas had been insubordinate and arrogant—recklessly giving away money and garments as lavishly as Alexander, and opposing his commander stupidly in personal matters. As commanding officer of the elite Companions, Philotas enjoyed prestige with the troops almost equal to Alexander's.

The incident that enraged Alexander seems to have been a vague report by a stripling boy attached to an officer: a report of a conspiracy to kill the king, which the boy claimed to have related in fright to Philotas. Philotas certainly made no mention of it to Alexander, and when charged with neglect in reporting it, only said that he had not believed it.

The fact is that Alexander, in a blind rage, ordered soldiers of the Agema to kill Philotas with their javelins. Immediately afterward he sent three officers at urgent speed to Ecbatana with orders to replace Parmenio in command there, and kill him without hearing or trial. This was done as he ordered. Arrian says that after slaying Philotas Alexander must have feared to leave Parmenio in command over the treasure and the troops at that important base. Parmenio had lost his other sons in the wars.

This merciless liquidation of his former chief of staff and the leader of the Companions drew no explanation, apparently, from Alexander. He acted in rage but only after long brooding. It raised a wraith of dread among the other officers.

Having thus divided the important command at Ecbatana between two officers, Alexander now gave dual command to the Companions, forming them into two regiments under Hephaestion and Black Cleitus, who was now recovered from his illness. These two stalwarts would carry out any order from him without question. They had no thoughts apart from Alexander's wishes.

Not content with this, he formed another cavalry regiment on the Asiatic model, lightly armed with a sheaf of javelins instead of the inconvenient Macedonian lance. Those Thessalians who had volunteered to stay made up the nucleus of this Asiatic light horse, but Persian officers were added. By this measure he also whittled down the bloc of the military council itself, made up formerly of Companion officers and nobles. Insensibly the feudal Macedonian army was being altered into a police force of an allied military occupation, subject to the single command of the Great King.

At the same time all of the soldiery came into dependence on one man, Alexander. No one else could lead them back now to the safety of familiar lands.

Meanwhile the Macedonian army, or at least the column advancing with Alexander, had got itself lost. It happened in a curious way. The army knew where it was, on the earth's surface, but it no longer knew where that point on the earth's surface might be. It had marched off the map—off the only available Greek maps.

The surveyors, directed by Baeton and Diognetes,

had kept up their calculations of the distance covered each day, even during the race across the desert. They had kept themselves pretty well oriented. Probably they had used a shadow stick—an upright pointer casting a shadow on a smooth field of sand or marble; by marking the points of this shadow's end each half hour they could distinguish the shortest shadow, cast at noon—the line of which would cut the horizon at the north.

Their own rough calculations would have been rendered much more exact by the skill of the Egyptian and Chaldean astronomers now accompanying the army. These easterners had tabulated the movement of the star sphere; they could estimate latitude very closely. So by now the Macedonian surveyors knew their position in relation to Persepolis or Ecbatana, or the Blue Mount towering into the ether above ancient Ray.

But the last true landmarks of the Greek world chart had been left behind at Babylon and the Twin Rivers, Tigris and Euphrates. That had been the eastern limit of the Oikoumene known even by hearsay to Aristotle and the Greeks. The Macedonians could no longer calculate where they were in relation to such old landmarks as Tyre or Mount Hermon or the mouths of the Nile: nor could the Persian scientists enlighten them as to that. During the race after Darius they had had neither time nor occasion to worry about where they were.

Following the death of that unhappy Great King, the Macedonians looked around to see where they were and found themselves straddling the great east-west caravan route, with villages sprinkled along it at intervals of a day's pack-animal march. Southward stretched the shimmering desert plain, where ghostly towns took shape in the midday heat, vanishing toward sunset. To the north stretched the familiar mountain wall dominated by the Blue Mount—the same barrier, they thought, that they had overlooked at Ecbatana and had left behind them at the Cilician Gates when they first dropped into the heat of this red plain. At those Cilician Gates they had known this barrier range as the Taurus Mountains, and they assumed that they were camped now outside the same Taurus—although the Persians knew nothing of the name. It was a natural mistake.

Furthermore they had found themselves outside a winding ravine, temptingly cool and wooded. (Actually they were probably on the stream that flows by the village now called Chash Giran, and not at Damaghan—the ancient *"Hecatompylae,"* or Hundred Gates—as has been assumed.) By turning north into that ravine, the country people assured them, they could cross the barrier range and find themselves on the shore of the great Inland Sea that stretched for an unknown distance to the north. It was only four marches or so to the shore of this mighty sea.

Naturally Alexander turned off the caravan route immediately, to explore that unknown sea. They came out through pine forests, where wild folk thronged the heights to stare amazed at the passing army, upon a cool gray beach where the water tasted fresh because of the many streams rushing into it. They found swarms of waterfowl and only a few small fishing craft upon this unexplored shore.

It was actually the southern shore of the Caspian, but the Macedonians had no way of knowing that. The fisherfolk called it the Sea of Birds, or of Ghilan, or even Parth. That did not help any. A mild swell beat along this dark, fertile beach, and unquestionably the sea was great in size. A hot argument began between the readers of the Greek maps and the surveyors.

The map readers pointed to the world chart which revealed a symmetrical string of seas stretching eastward—the great Mediterranean, the lesser Euxine, the small Cimmerian [modern Sea or Gulf of Azov]. This last was also thought to be the Fetid Sea, wherein serpent life crawled through stagnant water and salt beds. The river Tanais [the Don] flowed into it, and around and beyond it lay the Cimmerian steppes where Amazons roamed, up to the edge of the Land of

Darkness [Russia]. This was indeed the last sea on the map, the last of the neatly connected bodies of inland water on the map. Beyond it, to the east, only a lake had been sketched vaguely on the map. So these map readers thought the army had crossed the Caucasus and stood now on the edge of the Fetid Sea, with the river Tanais almost within reach. Only the water of this surf tasted fresh, and no serpents could be seen swimming offshore.

The surveyors and Persians did not agree to this. They thought the army had crossed the main barrier range, the Taurus midriff of the earth, to the shore of the half-mythical eastern sea that opened into the surrounding Ocean in the north.

Apparently Alexander agreed at first with the map readers, but soon became convinced that the surveyors were right. If so, they had advanced much farther to the east than they had supposed; and the Oikoumene must extend, accordingly, a greater distance toward the rising sun than the Greeks and Aristotle had estimated.

This thought intrigued him greatly, but it worried most of the army. They had heard that against the heights of the Caucasus the Titan Prometheus had been chained, and there or thereabouts even the reckless Argonauts had turned back, even though they had had the hero-god Heracles to fight for them, and the enchantress Medea to lay convenient spells for them. Yes, even the dumbest Thracian horse tender knew that the Argonauts had grabbed the golden fleece while they could and had fled up the river Tanais. If, indeed, the army had left the Caucasus behind—if it was actually skirting an unknown eastern sea—then it must be approaching the *edge of the world*, beyond which lay darkness or antagonistic spirit life. Perhaps the Amazons were here.

Aristander would take no side in the argument, believing himself descredited. Nearchus and those who knew the lore of seacraft pointed out that only shore smacks had been found on this strange sea.

Ptolemy said that after meeting successfully all other

250

armies they should not be afraid of Amazons. The officers who still had Greek texts with them read up on the adventure of the Argonauts and pointed out how this dark sea did resemble the terrain at world's end— *shadowed around by circling trees where silence may never rest, above the ceaseless moaning wave, stirred by the wind that breathes above the river Acheron, falling into an eastern sea.*

Presently they discovered a city. Here simple folk made fine red pottery and cups of thin gold. These people had never seen an army before. This city the Macedonians called Zadracarta [modern Asterbad, or Gurgan], and they marveled at the fertility of the land, sloping away to a river winding through limitless grassy plains. No wine grapes were cultivated here, but the Macedonian farmers knew the soil would be good for such grapes.

They rode out a little, to explore the prairies, reveling in the high lush grass that changed color as the wind blew. Still, they thought such vast plains to be unnatural, after the narrow valleys of Macedon. On one of these excursions some wandering barbarians stole a horse, with its keepers, and nearly precipitated an attack by the whole Macedonian army. For the horse was Bucephalus.

Alexander sent messengers out to the prairies, with warning that if the black horse were not returned he would burn the tents of the nomads. Bucephalus was brought back and peace restored. But the commander stationed a permanent mounted guard along the river, to guard against future raids of the nomads. (A wall, built along the mountain ridge by the site of Zadracarta, in later times, was still called Alexander's Wall—although the Turkmen tribes today call it the Red Snake, because, built of reddish stone, it winds over the slopes south of the Turkmen steppe. Curiosly enough, another wall built by other hands on the far side of the Caspian near the town of Darband is also known as Alexander's Wall—the story goes that he built it to keep out the destructive tribes of Gog and Magog.)

While Alexander rested his men he gathered information about the lands to the east. And what he heard excited him immediately.

Here the people knew nothing of the western regions of the Mediterranean. (They called the Macedonians *Yunnani*.) They faced east, as it were, toward the Ashkenazis, the great Scythian horse-breeding tribes, toward the eastern pasturelands of the mighty Nisaean horses.

If Alexander kept on to the east, they said, he would be on the track of the ancient Aryan migration from the land of the Sun, the land of Kurush. If he continued on he would reach twin rivers flowing out of Paradise, the River of Sand and the River of the Sea. Just as he had passed the twin Tigris and Euphrates, by passing these rivers he would come within sight—if he endured so long—of the greatest of the mountain ranges, towering above the timber line, above the level of bird life, dwarfing these hills around Zadracarta.

Those mountains were the Parapanisades.

Promptly the Macedonian started toward this goal, beyond the horizon. Yet every consideration of strategy and caution should have led him back to Ecbatana, to organize his immense imperium. The Greek scholars put away their maps, and the scientists settled down to the task of orienting themselves in an unknown region— for the Persian officers had only a vague concept of what lay beyond Zadracarta.

And couriers speeding back to Ray and the base at Ecbatana, with orders for routing reinforcements eastward, brought word that Alexander had started east into the limbo of the world. It was, they whispered, the act of a madman.

These common soldiers understood much that was never taught in the schools of the philosophers. They could see no good reason for going on. It seemed to them that Alexander felt within himself a mastery of circumstances that no human leader could control—as if he were driven on by a fixed idea. Here frontiers had vanished. At no point did they find themselves, as in Greece, at the established limit of a land. The caravan road passed ever eastward, twisting among the bare red hills that they called the Taurus. This Taurus itself led ever upward toward heights so vast that in a day's march the men could not see that they had come any nearer. They looked around them now not for familiar landmarks but for a sign of anything homelike and natural—an abandoned shrine or a bit of ivy growing. Pushing forward against icy winds, they tried to determine where Alexander might be in advance of them, and toward what destination he was struggling. The cold bit deeper than the winter chill of the Aegean lands.

"He's building more Alexandrias," said the couriers.

Back came odd specimens, to be transported to the coast—the *terebinth* tree from which aromatic juice flowed when an incision was made in the bark (turpentine) and *silphium* that smelled even stronger (asafetida). Out of these juices, the physicians said, balm could be made. Back also came sheets of thin, transparent stone that you could tear in your fingers, and goats with silky hair. What, the guards along the caravan road asked the couriers, was Alexander doing?

He was lying down to eat on a couch of gold. On his helmet, instead of the plumes, he had put two white birds' wings, resembling eagle wings. He had paid honor to a masterless tribe for no other reason than that it had aided a former Great King, Kurush. When he was alone he burned incense in the tent.

Climbing the gigantic ramp toward the Earth's Top, as the soldiers christened the heights ahead, they began to run short of supplies, because in winter—this was the winter of 330–329—these heights offered little sustenance. They had to piece out their barley and goat's cheese with mule meat and silphium. It was the first time they had suffered from hunger. (They were within what is now Afghanistan, near the northern frontier.)

253

While they burned tamarisk, taking shelter behind rocks from the ever-buffeting wind, they watched the crescent moon disconsolately as it passed over bare summits. The Lady of the Beasts might be riding the moon chariot in that sky, transparent, without clouds. Dust and dried dung swirled around them, as if evil daimons were dancing. They did not like it. They saw no men. The towns and the people, the cattle and the dogs were hidden away somewhere in the maw of the Earth's Top. At times lights flickered as if spirits were mocking them; but when they ran out to pursue the torches they fell into gorges they had not seen.

Evil omens manifested themselves up and down the line. Craterus was wounded by a javelin through his thigh while he hunted a giant lizard on foot. Some of the witnesses of this accident related that the lizard was actually more like a dragon, and it may well have been a servitor of the Lady of the Beasts, because after the javelin had hit Craterus this semblance of a dragon had disappeared into the sheer face of a cliff. The soldiers sulked over this bit of news because Craterus had become their favorite.

Insensibly Alexander had begun to use the dynamic Craterus more often in contacts with his veterans, because he himself saw less of them now, and the older soldiers liked Craterus because he kept all his Macedonian habits, refusing to consort with Asiatics. Hephaestion, on the other hand, absorbed Iranian ways and talk eagerly, and Alexander used him now in dealing with the growing Asiatic elements.

This had the natural result of setting the brilliant Craterus in conflict with the good-natured Hephaestion. Their protégés disagreed sharply and inevitably on matters of camp routine and foraging. Moreover many of the Iranians would eat no flesh of a dead animal, whereas the Macedonians by now could find little to eat except the flesh of sheep and lambs, eked out with the pungent medical silphium roots. When rations ran short tempers flared, and once the two Companion commanders clashed openly. Alexander arrived on the scene, gave Hephaestion a dressing down, called Craterus aside to argue with him, and then brought his lieutenants together to embrace and pledge friendship.

"I swear by Ammon-Re," Alexander assured them, "that if there is one more quarrel before the phalanx-men both of you will be executed—or at least," he added cautiously, "the one who starts the quarrel."

After that the two commanders were careful to be civil in all they said to each other. But by then commanders and men had other troubles to think about, because the attacks had begun.

Like the winds of the Earth's Top, these attacks were sharper than anything the Macedonians had experienced in the west. Horsemen raided out of ravines and vanished as quickly as they had appeared. Guard posts along the road were stalked and wiped out at night. Yet when regiments advanced into the hills to retaliate they could find no enemy nor sign of cattle and sheep herds—except tracks in the ground. It seemed to the men that the mountains themselves were arming against them.

Actually they were meeting for the first time with the resistance of the land itself. The nations here were against them. These Aryan mountain peoples, like the Macedonians themselves, had known no military yoke. They regarded the Macedonians as European invaders, aliens, and infidels. By now, Baeton and Diognetes said, the Macedonians had put nearly a thousand miles by the road between them and Ray, the last great city of Persian officialdom.

Alexander could not make use of this great persuasive powers upon these tribes, because he could neither assemble them nor talk to them. On the other hand, two of the *khsatrapas*, the satraps who had killed Darius, had escaped hither, into their own lands, in advance of him, to organize resistance. One of them was caught presently in a village, and Alexander, driving through in his chariot, stopped to question him. Why had he slain the Great King, the descendant of Kurush, and his own blood kin?

"I was not the only one to slay him."

Alexander hesitated, then ordered the prisoner to be stripped and a wooden ox yoke to be fastened on his shoulders. Thus paraded, the captive satrap was to be scourged. He was not killed until later, when his companion-officer was flayed alive.

By now the column had reached a muddy rushing river. The guides called it the River of Birds and believed it flowed northward to the Mother of Cities [Merv]. Beyond this rushing water stretched the mass of the central Earth's Top. Even at the water's edge the ground was under deep snow. Tracks crisscrossed the snow, where men and horses and cattle had moved away, but no living thing was visible.

Alexander turned back here. He dared not advance the column into the ravines ahead of him, across the torrential river, while his line of march was under attack by partisans. They had been advancing nearly due east; now he almost retraced his tracks. In this way he avoided the main ridges under winter snow.

At first he might have intended only to explore southward and to find a region where the army could supply itself. Here the horses were underfed and dying off rapidly. To preserve the animals they had to reach stocks of fodder or grazing. But then or later the Macedonians hit upon the answer to the new warfare of attrition by the Aryan highlanders. They would penetrate and subjugate the country section by section, thus driving the tribes from the valleys into the upper ridges; they would found cities at strategic points. These cities would be colonized, garrisoned, and walled in for defense. Out of the chain of new cities task forces could make sallies when necessary. Meanwhile the colonists in the cities, under military protection, would cultivate the surrounding countryside and set up depots of supplies.

The colonists—and this Alexander did not see fit to explain at first—would be recruited from overage or

256

sick soldiers, from merchants who were now following in the track of the army, and the most reliable of the subjected people. So although under command of Macedonian officers aided by Iranian civilians, the new colonies would become mixed or international centers of population.

This was a rigorous and thoroughgoing plan of occupation. It evidenced two things: first, that the Macedonians could not rely here in the east upon a preservation of the local government—as in Egypt—and had to follow a plan of conquest; second, that Alexander insisted upon a permanent government over these restless, independent peoples. Only Kurush had attempted such a full subjection before him, and Kurush, as he knew now, had been killed in the attempt to do so, by the Ashkenazis, or Scythians, far inside Asia, to the north and east.

It is easy to say that the imaginative and reckless Alexander wished to imitate Kurush and to round out the former limits of the Iranian Empire. Actually he seemed determined to establish his own Eurasian commonwealth of peoples and to make it last—following the example set by Kurush of the Achaemenian tolerance and peace and combination of peoples. He had not tried to reach the limits of Iranian rule in Asia Minor; he exceeded such boundaries in the Scythian lands and in northern India. Instead of availing himself here in the east of the existing populated centers he laid down new cities where he thought they would be necessary and peopled them in a new fashion. He never forgot his early experience with the intractable and prosperous cities of Greece proper. He wanted to construct Asiatic Athens in these fertile lands, but he did not want to duplicate here the actual Pella or Athens or—especially—Sparta. In all he ordered more than seventy cities built.

When he began to edge south around the heights he selected the site of the first of these easternmost Alexandrias on the shoulder of a valley, opposite an ancient caravan city called Harai [Herat] where

Magians and merchants were quartered. Here he left most of his disabled men, with Semitic traders, Persian artisans, and a varied assortment of women, money-changers, and a physician to look after their health. Earth walls were thrown up for temporary protection, enclosing a city of tents and stone and thatch huts.

Then, with the melting of the snows, he moved south, to the shore of a great salt lake, the Helmand, where new horse herds were rounded up. Here the Macedonians discovered they were on a caravan route from the river Indus back to Persepolis. Alexander did not try to follow out this southern transcontinental road, but he did not forget it. Years later he sent Craterus over this route of the Helmand.

Instead, with the good grass of spring, Alexander turned back toward the heart of the mountain masses, setting up his colonies and beating off resistance.

This self-appointed task of subjection occupied him for two years and involved him in the most dangerous kind of conflict. He had not anticipated the immensity of his Parapanisades nor the number of people therein. (Actually his course now led from the northern frontier of modern Baluchistan, through most of Afghanistan, across the Turkmen Soviet Republic, and the Uzbek Republic, into a region still unnamed. Before he had done with it his main army had marched more than thirty-nine hundred miles from his first sight of the Parapanisades to the point where he crossed the Khyber Pass later, into the Indus valley.)

XVI. RIVER OF THE SEA, AND RIVER OF THE SANDS

The trouble with Callisthenes was that he had wit. This nephew of Aristotle, this academician from home, had been eagerly awaited by Alexander. He proved to be a dry young-old man, relishing jests, but with a taciturn intellectual honesty. As gifts he brought copies of Aristotle's latest writings on metaphysics and the natural world; as a companion, he brought an amateur philosopher, Anaxarchus.

The coterie of Macedonians now around Alexander had lost their way of jesting. For five years they had been dealing with realities and had abandoned any attempt to follow philosophical opinion. When Callisthenes repeated the latest quips of the Lyceum—smiling when he admitted that the worthy Athenians were designing a golden crown for the stubborn Demosthenes—these Macedonians were not amused. They could not decide whether the new arrival were a sophist or cynic, but they finally began to call him the Sophist. (Aristotle himself said later of the Callisthenes affair that the man had a keen intellect, spoke well, but lacked judgment.)

Alexander read eagerly the newest texts of his master, finding in them discussion of many problems, such as the existence of the Immovable Mover, which Aristotle had treated as Mysteries aforetime—as matters of higher understanding, only to be discussed with a chosen few. Perhaps the Macedonian commander felt let down at seeing what he had been taught secretly spread upon written pages for every school clerk to ponder.

"But Aristotle writes so badly," Callisthenes grinned, "there is no danger of such people understanding him."

Still, Alexander dictated a letter to his master. *Alexander to Aristotle, greeting. You do ill to write for anyone to read what should be reserved for discerning minds.*

Five years had made a difference in their viewpoints. The philosopher desired now to teach an ever-widening circle; the ruler had become jealous of his privileges.

But he was delighted with what Callisthenes reported about his journey out. Shiploads of artisans, sculptors, gem cutters, vasemakers, music and language teachers were embarking for the ports of the new world in the east. Ships were already docking at the new Alexandria-in-Egypt, bringing Greek wines and oils. The slave trade with the islands had doubled with the end of the fighting there. Greek farmers in the land of the Two Rivers now owned their homes, and a Greek theater was under construction within walking distance of the Ishtar Gate of Babylon. Even caravaneers jingled as they walked, with newly-minted coins. People performed public worship in the temple square before a statue of Alexander, executed by Lysippus.

The Macedonians were not so pleased. This Sophist, who was so close to the commander, did not get drunk; he kept silence at meals as if he disapproved of them. They did not realize how much of their argument was strange to Callisthenes, nor how much they argued the same points over. When they jawed about the old question—was the winter here colder than in Greece?—Callisthenes only smiled and said he thought it was. "Because in Macedon one threadbare cloak sufficed a man, whereas here I see you need three costly fur mantles."

Callisthenes indeed wore a simple cloak, and Black Cleitus, beside him, had on a double mantles trimmed with black lambskin that had become popular here. Once, after the Sophist had praised the glorious deeds of the Macedonians, Alexander interrupted him irritably, to quote from Euripides: *"No wonder your words turn out so well—when on good subjects you choose to dwell!*

"Now tell us," he demanded, "what you really think!"

The Sophist took the commander at his word. He said that the Macedonians had taken advantage of opportunities amazingly—but they had moved so rapidly from place to place that they had left, as yet, only uncertainty behind them. *"In civil strife,"* he quoted, *"a peasant may look like a king."*

"I hate lies!" Alexander burst out unreasonably. "If that is so, why are you here, with the *peasants?* What did you come out for?"

Callisthenes might have answered that he had come because Alexander had sent for one of Aristotle's staff. Instead he was silent a moment, studying the question.

"I have come because my country was depopulated, and I wish to help the exiles back to their homes," he answered simply.

Alexander shook his head angrily. "Exiles—exiles! Who do you mean? I've allowed all prisoners to go home, even the Athenian mercenaries. What exiles are there?"

"The Macedonians."

Alexander stared at him, then left the table without speaking or drinking his wine. No one else spoke. Big Cleitus slipped off his fur mantle stealthily and sat there in his tunic, scowling. Hephaestion told the Sophist quietly afterward that Alexander would never forget a slighting word, whether it was the truth or not. That word "exiles" should not have been uttered where he could hear it.

Apparently Alexander did not think of it again. At times Callisthenes caught the commander watching him intently. Once when he was discoursing—and he spoke eloquently—on Demosthenes's defense of Athenian liberty, Alexander smashed his drinking cup down on the table, crying out, "You cannot extend a city-state beyond the bounds of city feeling! Athens has committed suicide. Athens has made herself into a prostitute, bedecked with baubles, plying her trade with all comers, extending her kingdom as far as men have

261

desires. A prostitute must have protection—you cannot give her virtue!" He checked himself, adding thoughtfully, "Of the Athens of Pericles what remains?"

"Perhaps," Callisthenes said, "only the consciousness of what should be."

But either because the Sophist could not grasp the problems of the east or because Alexander disliked his advice, he was not consulted about Macedonian plans. Before long he began to write a book about their journey, calling it *Alexander's Anabasis*.

Their conquest of the eastern mountains was not going well. After founding a third Alexandria [which may be Kandahar today] and a fourth [near modern Kabul] they struck far into the north. In good summer going they came upon the first of the two rivers which they believed had sources in the heights of the Earth's Top. Flowing swiftly in flood, broader than the Nile, it could not be crossed by swimming. Alexander was dissuaded from having men attempt to swim it on their shields. Stakes driven in near shore were carried downstream by the current, and, besides, timber lacked to make a bridge. A crossing was made finally, on rafts of skin stuffed with straw, but not before a large foraging force had been cut off and killed by the unseen enemy. When a cavalry regiment went in pursuit the Macedonians were beaten off and Alexander himself wounded by an arrow that broke the fibula of his leg. For long after that he limped.

Then came the terror of the *Branchidae*.

It happened after crossing this first River of the Sea—called the Oxus by Greek geographers, and Amu Darya by the Asiatics—and it took the Macedonians completely by surprise. They had little information now of what lay ahead. The vanguard of the advance blundered into a mob of savages waving branches and garlands of green leaves and shouting out greetings in broken, stammering Greek.

They shouted that they were the *Branchidae*—the Exiles. Shaggy as beasts, clad in skins and homespun wool, they danced madly, trying to articulate, like idiots. Exiles, they yelped, Greek—the same people—captives. Alexander, riding up, stared at them and ordered them killed. The Macedonians massacred this colony of descendants of Greek prisoners, taken during the old war at Marathon and Salamis.

Whether it was done in one of the sudden fits of rage that seized him more and more often now, or whether he feared to allow these animal-like survivors to join his troops, no one can say now. It was a display of stark cruelty, more merciless than the murder of Philotas and Parmenio. (Arrian does not report it, but Quintus Curtius Rufus does.) Eulogists who wrote about it made the excuse that since these Greeks had joined the enemy in Asia they merited such punishment. But under the circumstances this was a poor excuse.

Callisthenes for once kept silence.

What the army as a whole thought of the massacre is recorded by no one. But it is noticeable that this year Alexander had to order the forces into action several times, and had to lead the way himself more than once. At the city of Kurush, where a high stone wall defied the engines, he and Craterus led an assault along the bed of a river, shallow in the midsummer heat, that traversed the city. And here he was badly wounded in the head by a heavy stone, so that for some time afterward he could not see well. Craterus also was laid out by an arrow.

For here in the north the Macedonians found themselves in more open country, along the caravan route that led back to the Caspian. They also found themselves operating against the fine horse archers, the Parthians of Bactria and Soghd. And here for many months the Macedonians could make no progress.

This was no orderly campaigning, like that of the Mediterranean coast. It was merciless conflict, for survival. The horsemen of northern Asia proved to be too swift for the westerners to overtake in pursuit. The Macedonians fell back on feinting and maneuvering—

staging a siege of one city while they struck at another strong point elsewhere at night. It helped them to pinch off the towns—where several times Alexander ordered execution of all the men taken inside—but it did not help them to hold the towns, once taken. Alexander's scheme of strengthening colonies with garrisons did not work out against organized resistance. It was necessary to destroy the armored forces opposing him.

By degrees he identified the head of this successful resistance. A high-born Mede, Spitama, an officer of the former Iranian army, had rallied the forces of the steppes around him. More than that, he seemed to be drawing in the formidable Scythian horsemen from the further north. And for a while Spitama outmatched the Macedonians at their own maneuvering.

Apparently Alexander tried to change the equipment of his cavalry, lightening it, to cope with the splendid Bactrians. He accomplished little by this. Then he began to induce the plains dwellers to settle in his new colonies. When he appeared among these northerners he put on the long, robelike coat, the scarf, and wide-sleeved jacket of the Persian Great Kings. Informers told him that Spitama had been seen wearing the royal tiara—which might have been the real one, taken from Darius.

"He has raised his cap on high," they laughed. (The tiara was the high conical headgear, imitated from the cylindrical headdress of the last Babylonian kings.)

Whatever the Macedonians did, Spitama seemed able to do better. Until Alexander, recovering from his wound, determined to end the frittering away of the Macedonian strength and advanced into the north toward the oncoming Scythians.

His column circled the desert of Black Sands, striking into the open loess region, where the red conglomerate stood in treeless masses as if carved by the hands of men. From this loess a haze of dust arose at the wind's touch. At sunset the whole land was the color of blood, and Aristander did not like the looks of that.

To avoid the horsemen of the plain, Alexander moved eastward into the foothills to a small river lined by groves of fruit trees. Here at the city of Maracand [modern Samarkand] he left a strong garrison occupying the stone citadel and pushed on, feeling for the Scythians. He went on in spite of the tradition that Kurush had gone from Maracand to his death at the hands of the Scythians.

So they came to the second river they had been searching for, the River of the Sands. They were now slightly north of the main mass of the Earth's Top that the people here named the Hind-i-Kuh or Mount of India. In the clear atmosphere they could make out the highest peaks behind them and to their right.

Here beside the River of the Sands [the Syr Darya] they started work on the northernmost Alexandria. They had to fortify the site, being under attack the while. The water was bad in the muddy river. Across it appeared the outposts of the dreaded Scythians—horsemen armed with long swords and strangely curved bows, who jeered at the Macedonians from across the water barrier while they grazed their horses. Masses of them began to arrive.

It did not seem to the Macedonians that this could be the hoped-for river, flowing out of Paradise. To make the situation worse, couriers brought up word that the large garrison at Maracand had been driven into the citadel, which Spitama—who seemed to be everywhere Alexander was not—had begun to besiege.

To retreat south would be an invitation to the assembling Scythians to cross the river and follow. To cross this River of the Sands themselves would be to leave the vast area in their rear to Spitama's tender mercy. They were fairly caught between two horns of a dilemma, as the philosophers pointed out.

The brigadiers began to ponder that network of communications behind them, defended only by isolated garrisons and task forces. The more they pondered the more disconsolate they became. It was as if they had wound their way through a labyrinth, unwinding a thread as a guide behind them. If that thread should be broken . . .

These staff officers had no illusions about the Minotaurs now waiting to rush upon them in this labyrinth of mountains and deserts. They recalled that the *Skuthai,* the Scythians, were reputed to be the strongest of all the peoples of Asia. As far west as the steppes of black earth near the Balkans, these Scythians roamed and bought gold jewelry for their wives from the Greek artisans of the Euxine Sea. Darius I had been humbled by them and driven out before he had invaded Greece. Somewhere around this river the mighty Kurush had been slain by them. With their long, braided hair and baggy trousers, these barbarians looked like beasts, atop their shaggy horses. No aspect of the situation encouraged the staff officers, and they took pains to let the aging Aristander, the omen taker, hear their discussions.

And Alexander, they knew, was in no condition to lead an army just now. That stone crushing against the base of his skull had numbed his mind for many days. Although he could see clearly again, he had agonizing headaches, which he tried to relieve by drinking the last of the supply of wine. Either this wine or the muddy river water had weakened him with dysentery.

Alexander himself said little to them, except to urge haste in fortifying the new outpost city. He said it would serve as a bridgehead into these steppes—as a protection against the nomadic peoples. Obviously, however, he was disappointed. He had reached, by a tremendous effort, the River of the Sands near its headwaters, hoping as usual to orient the army by tracing the sources of the river back into the mountains, the mass of the Hind-i-Kuh. But these sources lay at unguessed heights above him.

He felt no friendly aspect in this northern land. The sun itself made its arc across the sky far behind him. No one around him could recall a legend that even

Heracles or Dionysos had penetrated this region before them. They all knew that the limits reached by the exploring Argonauts lay far back toward the setting sun.

Meanwhile the masses of Scythians across the water grew greater daily, the stone wall of the newest Alexandria rose slowly, in spite of the efforts of Deiade's engineers, and something had to be done to relieve Maracand [Samarkand].

Alexander detached a strong column—a squadron of Companions, with two regiments of allied horse and foot, about twenty-four hundred men in all under command of a brigadier named Caranus. And he ordered the glum Aristander to take the omens for a crossing of the river. If there was nothing encouraging in the situation he might be able to show the men a good sign from the taking of the omens.

Aristander obeyed, and reported that the liver of the slain sheep showed clear marking of ill fortune if the army advanced over an obstacle. Hearing this, Alexander turned away, angered and silent. He sent back word for the soothsayer to repeat the test.

"If you have no faith in me," Aristander replied, "find another to do your bidding."

"Take the omens again," Alexander ordered.

A second sheep was opened and its liver examined. Having had opportunity to ponder the crisis, Aristander reported this time that the army might cross safely, but misfortunate would come to Alexander.

"I'd rather meet with whatever it is," the commander retorted, "than stay here longer to be made a laughingstock by the barbarians."

"Take care," the old man cried, "to heed the portents of the gods. They will not change their intentions because of your wishes."

The army was not reassured by this argument between the diviner and the commander.

But the Scythians were puzzled by what the Macedonians did next. As soon as the defenses of the city could be considered adequate the sick and those who had served their time were quartered inside, with the farmers of the countryside, while the engineers turned to building rafts and floats. Also series of *gastraphetes,* the new oversize mechanical crossbows, were set up along the river bank. They were not operated until the hour of the crossing. Meanwhile Scythian archers had amused themselves trying to shoot across—an extreme range for a handbow. To this dropping fire the Macedonians paid no attention. Then either to encourage his troops or to bewilder the Scythians, Alexander staged one of his eccentric shows—pouring libations into the River of the Sands and holding field sports and horse races between the new Alexandria and the river, to the accompaniment of music. Naturally the Scythians crowded closer to the far bank to watch and jeer at the extraordinary performance.

At this point, with the rafts ready and the regiments lined up to advance, Alexander gave order to loose the barrage of crossbow javelins. These heavy missiles flashed far across the water, doing not much execution but amazing the steppe riders by the force with which they penetrated wicker shields and leather body coating. The Scythians cleared the river bank promptly. And Alexander ordered the first rafts into the water.

Arrian gives a clear picture of this crossing.

Seeing the Scythians confused by the discharge of his missiles, Alexander ordered the trumpets to sound and keep on sounding. He led the first wave of the crossing. After the leading archers, javelin throwers, and slingers had got to land, he ordered them to advance a little and harass the Scythians with missiles, to keep the horse archers from charging the first ranks of the infantry phalanx stepping out of the water, until all the cavalry had got across.

Probably at no time, before then or later, did the Macedonians manage to get themselves into such a dangerous position. Alexander had had no experience with the tactics of the formidable horse archers of central Asia. He got that experience now, and quickly.

A skirmish line sent inland from the bank—about

two thousand light-armed, mixed formations, probably the ones who had first served as a screen—was quickly enveloped and shot to pieces by the Scythians, who merely rode around it. When the main line advanced more cautiously the Scythians repeated the maneuver. Clan groups, stronger than the individual Macedonian regiments, circled close in, losing flights of arrows, and passed quickly out of range. The Macedonians halted.

There was no possibility of carrying out their customary attack, of the wedge to the right followed by the thrust of the Companion cavalry, because the Scythians were not there to be attacked. They were circling already to the rear, riding around at a pace the Macedonian cavalry could not match. And it would be sheer folly for the mass of the phalanx to advance in a square. The phalanx itself was helpless on open ground before the Scythians.

Alexander had to devise a new tactic immediately. He had only one advantage—his disciplined troops, sensing the danger, were now keyed up for rapid action. What Alexander tried was improvised on the spur of the moment, but it worked.

Halting the phalanx, he immobilized it. Throwing together a column of allied and miscellaneous horsemen, he started it out on one flank, hurrying the mobile Hypaspists after it to keep it from being encircled. This thrusting, fast-moving arm could not come to grips with the Scythians, but it penetrated their sweep. Then Alexander plunged back, took command of his column of Companions, and circled with it inward, opposite the other moving arm.

So the Macedonians struck left and right, inward, breaking up the clockwise sweep of the steppe cavalry. The Scythians drew back rapidly. The two Macedonian columns, leaving the phalanx up in the air, drove after in pursuit. Close-pressed now by disciplined troops, the Scythians turned and ran for it. At headlong speed flight and pursuit swept away from the river and kept on going.

That was the end of it. Arrian says the Scythians

lost a thousand, including a chieftain the Macedonians identified by name, and left one hundred and fifty prisoners. Obviously the Macedonian losses had been greater than that. But the moral victory was decisive. The Scythians had been puzzled by the building of the fortified city, and amazed by the swift crossing of the river. They wanted no further encounter with the Macedonians, and had, besides, no incentive to keep up a conflict with these impressive westerners—except their alliance with Spitama. So when Alexander later on led his columns farther, along the ridges to the caravan terminus of the Stone City [modern Tashkent, on the new transcontinental railroad], they realized that he meant to stay. And they sent envoys to agree on a peace.

But after the racing pursuit that day Alexander, weakened by dysentery, broke down and had to be carried back to the river in a litter. So Aristander pointed out that the omens had been justified: the army had crossed the river successfully, while the commander had suffered by it.

On their return from the thrust to the Stone City, and before the Scythian envoys arrived, the Macedonians heard more bad news. The relief column under Caranus, hurrying to reach Maracand, had been trapped at a small river crossing and wiped out entirely. Spitama had been responsible for this, aided by a contingent of Scythians. Evidently the officers of the column had been unable to meet the tactic of the horse archers.

At once Alexander got together a flying column of the best of the cavalry and the hardy Agrianians, and started for Maracand. He pushed his relief force grimly, so that Arrian says they covered one hundred and thirty-five miles in three days and nights. At dawn on the fourth day they descended the valley and sighted the citadel of Maracand rising from its gardens. But the besiegers under Spitama had heard of their coming and had drawn off to safety. Alexander relieved Maracand, yet had to content himself with burying the dead of the massacred column.

Another winter closed in on the Macedonians. Snow blocked the higher passes, and the troops forsook their tents to take shelter in the stone hillside huts. This was the winter of 329–28.

Completely checkmated by Spitama's tactics and the resistance of the wild horsemen who could not be overtaken, Alexander hung on in the uplands, resorting to extermination methods—laying waste a countryside, forcing the inhabitants farther up the slopes into snow where their beasts had no fodder. During the winter, too, animal life came down to the lower slopes, so the Macedonian hunters could get at this ample source of meat, while the fugitives above them starved. By gathering in the cattle herds and keeping them under guard at the settlements, the Macedonians deprived the inhabitants of their chief stock of food.

Meanwhile it is clear that Alexander summoned very large reinforcements into this new mountain frontier zone. The yearly quota of recruits from Pella arrived as usual, bringing mercenaries with them, after the long march to these Alexandrias in the east. Two years before, Alexander had enlisted no such mercenaries, but here he had need of colonists trained also as soldiers. In fact the settlements throughout Bactria and Soghd became populated by Greeks, in the main. By Exiles.

Nearchus and other officers turned up with a mysterious reinforcement brought, the historians say, *from the sea*. Since Alexander had opened up no sea route as yet, this seafaring contingent must have been drawn from Semitic mariners along the Mediterranean coast. To these were added reserve regiments from the pleasant base at Zadracarta. And allies—fifteen hundred of them—appeared unexpectedly from an eastern lake into which they insisted both the River of the Sea and the River of the Sands emptied [the modern Aralsk Sea]. Their chieftains enlisted voluntarily with the victorious Macedonian, and they called themselves Kharismians, which the Greek scholars noted down as *Corasmians*. Their stories of the northern steppes bewildered the Greek geographers but interested Alexander. Their chieftain offered to guide Alexander to his great lake and supply the army on the way, and by way of further inducement to show him the Amazons—those women riders who were expert as men with bows. (The Macedonians had heard much about Amazons but had not been able, so far, to come upon any living specimens.) More, the Kharismian promised to get Alexander a royal Scythian bride, if he wanted such a woman. Alexander may have been tempted, but he thanked the chieftain and said he wanted no Scythian marriage.

He now disposed of from a hundred to a hundred and fifty thousand souls, including the mercenaries and servants, in this limbo of central Asia.

And he was winning over Spitama not by superior military skill but by creating fear. The inhabitants were discovering that they could only expect to die, hunted down or starved, unless they joined the colonists. The settlements offered them life and food, even if it meant a different way of life. Two years before, Alexander had had the country against him, now he turned the country against Spitama, his ablest antagonist. It was an amazing feat to accomplish in that time and place.[1]

Why Alexander persisted in doing it is difficult to know. His persistence could have been due neither to glory hunting nor to craving for merely geographical conquest. For one thing, he did not enter the Scythian steppes again, or try to match his power with the great Scythian clans, already pushed from behind by the Hunnic clans. Nor did he seem to feel here that he was

---

[1]The Roman Empire extended its frontiers thereafter by much the same method of leapfrogging armed camps with settlements, which were in turn stiffened by discharged veterans. But the Roman legions were never able to push farther east than the middle Euxine and the general boundary of the Euphrates. Accordingly they extended west into Spain, Africa, France, and even England.

carrying out a dictate of his destiny. It is more the thought of his journalists than his own thought that he tried to emulate the deeds of Heracles and Semiramis and the heroes of tradition. At times he did speak of such legendary achievements, but apparently he did so more to encourage the troops than to inspirit himself.

Alexander was always inclined to worry at difficulties until he mastered them—he hated failure or retreat. But it is probable that he had determined already to push on, through the Parapanisades-Hind-i-Kuh into the lands of the Indus. If so, full control of the Bactria-Soghd highlands had to be gained. Already he had discovered the danger of pushing on, when rebellion could stir up behind him. Then, too, he had shown a disposition to match the characteristics of the people he encountered. At Persepolis he had taken pride in doing as the Persians did. Here he shared the wild life of the steppes, with the folk moving ever on horseback over vast distances, dancing to the music of their pipes and drums. They had a proverb that only a man who sat in the saddle was free—the one who sat in a house was a slave. They had saddles too. Alexander showed a naïve eagerness to emulate the Bactrian-Scythian warrior.

This total war of two years took its toll from the army, not only in wounds and suffering. The ordeal embittered the men, hardening them to other suffering, and those who emerged on the far side of the Parapanisades had gained a capacity to hate as well as to endure.

They had been divided up also into five commands, under Hephaestion, Ptolemy, Perdiccas, Coenus—with a Persian associate—and Alexander himself. During the winter those five armies had hunted Spitama through the heights, giving him no chance to rest or recruit followers.

It was Coenus's command that cornered the brilliant rebel, after Spitama had surprised and devasted one of the new settlements. Spitama was killed by his own men and his head sent down as a peace offering. His men had heard that Alexander was hurrying up, and they were afraid.

This did not end the resistance. *These barbarians go willingly from war to war,* Arrian relates, *because they are ever troubled by poverty, and having no cities or fixed homesites, they are held back by nothing that they cherish and fear for.*

After ridding themselves of Spitama, however, the Macedonians made efforts to conciliate the stubborn folk. One town on a cliff held out because the inhabitants believed no human beings could manage to cross the ravine that led to it. Yet the Macedonian engineers drove pegs in the cliffsides and built up a trestle from the bottom during snow and sleet storms. When the trestle reached as high as the town wall the inhabitants gave up.

XVII. ROXANA

It was this winter and in such a quest that Alexander met his wife.

His division had tracked down a resistance force to a rocky height shaped like a tower and called the Rock of Soghd. The defenders had withdrawn to the summit, well supplied with food. Their first inspection convinced the Macedonians that this natural tower could not be stormed nor broken down. Deep snow supplied the Bactrians with water in plenty.

Alexander had them hailed and offered them full amnesty, to return to their dwellings. The Bactrians laughed at the summons.

"Go back," they yelled at Alexander, "and get yourself soldiers with wings! Then perhaps you can fly to this place of ours."

Alexander had heard that the family of Uxiart, a Bactrian chief, had taken refuge on the Rock of Soghd, which was thought to be impregnable. The challenge of the defenders nettled him and gave him an idea at the same time. Calling for the Agrianians and men experienced in cliff work, he made them an offer.

A purse would be made up, starting at twelve talents for the winner, and ending with a few gold darics for the last man. They were to climb the rock at night, not along the easier face but up the chimney formation, across ice surfaces, where apparently it could not be climbed. They were to reach the summit above the defenders by morning. This part of the cliff was not guarded because it seemed to be unscalable.

Some three hundred experienced climbers volunteered. They studied the rock face, while they provided themselves with iron tent pegs and pliable ropes made out of flax. By Alexander's order each man also took a flag, wrapped around his body.

During the long winter night the climbers worked upward, driving in their iron pegs and slinging ropes where they could. Some thirty of them fell, disappearing into such deep drifts that their bodies were not found the next day. The survivors reached the summit after sunrise and signaled down to the officers, who sent out a herald to shout to the Bactrians.

"Look!" he shouted. "Look up, ye men of the mountain. *We have found the soldiers with wings.* They are there. Look for yourselves."

And the Bactrians beheld, poised behind them against the sky, armed men waving banners that might have been wings—poised in full sight of them. Alexander had rehearsed this denouement with the climbers the evening before. The trick succeeded and the Rock of Soghd was surrendered.

It was the last refuge of the mountain folk, and Alexander climbed the approach to inspect it. The Bactrian officers made way for him reluctantly, and he went to the one house of size, at the cliff's edge.

A girl came out of the door, not prostrating herself before him. Standing there alone, she waited for him to speak. She had long braids light as new wheat twisted back from her head, and she was lovely to watch, afraid but not going away. Her head glowed in the sunlight, and when he asked her name they told him it was Rushanak ["Roxana"], the Daughter of Light.

This barbarian, child of a Bactrian lord, knowing no Greek, stirred some memory in Alexander. He might have wished to take a wife from the Bactrians, but he seemed to desire Rushanak. He took her hand, and she did not pull away, because she was now the chattel of the victor, to dispose of as he pleased.

Taking a bracelet from his wrist, he glanced at it and put it on her arm. "Keep it," he said, "for you will be my wife."

Rushanak went with him to India and bore him a son. Lacking Barsine's education, her thoughts centered upon two matters: her religion and her husband. She became in every sense Alexander's wife.

The army did not approve of this marriage to the Bactrian.

Onesicritus, one of the new arrivals, enjoyed the title of pilot in chief. Apparently, with Nearchus, he belonged to the staff of navigators who had little to do as yet. Certainly at this stage he conformed to the prevailing fashion and began to keep a journal—a plotting of their daily position upon terra firma. But since Onesicritus had an ear for marvels, he began to embroider his pilot's journal with sensational events. Alexander and the older Macedonians remarked that his title should have been liar in chief.

Out of Alexander's journey into the steppes, the encounter with the chieftain of the wild Kharismians, and the marriage to the barbarian Rushanak, Onesicritus fashioned a juicy marvel. It seemed—as he finally wrote the tale—that Alexander's renown had spread through the vast steppes of Asia until it reached the ears of the queen of the Amazons, of those fierce and warlike maidens who lived without benefit of men. Whereupon the haughty queen, no less, sent messengers to Alexander to inform him that she would meet with him at the edge of her grassland frontier, to sleep with him one night in order to have a child by him.

This was perhaps the first of many such tales of marvels—of the Alexander legend.

On their part the imaginative Persians, who had a fondness for hero tales and eulogy, had begun to associate Alexander's deeds with their own folk memory of Kurush and the *Niakan,* the great ancestors. They traced this resemblance so that their own descendants would believe they had served not a barbarian invader but an Iranian hero. So in their writings the journey into the steppes became a venture of the heroic Iskander, who bore the twin eagles' wings on his helmet, into the Land of Darkness which took thirty days to traverse, under the beneficent guardianship of the

277

Niakan, to the sun-illumined Mount of Paradise. This mount, in later versions, Iskander climbed to converse with the spirit of Ahura-Mazda, in the best Iranian tradition. Then another purple patch was added. That Iskander had labored in this journey to build a great wall, saturated with oil and then set aflame. By the construction of this fiery wall their Iskander had penned into the north the destructive powers of the tribes of Gog and Magog. (Much later, when the Iranians became converted after a fashion to Islam, the guardian ancestor-spirit changed to the prophet Khidr, in the newer *Iskander nameh* or *Alexander Tale*. And Ahura became the Angel Gabriel.)

Actually, during the stay in Bactria Alexander did strike oil again. That is, his tent was found one morning to have been pitched beside a pool of translucent vapor oil that seeped from the ground like a spring of water. Both the Iranians and the diviners took this to be a favorable sign.

For nearly three years of incessant hardship, aggravated by wounds, the king of the Macedonians had shown no evidence of mental exhaustion. But when, at the end of the third winter, Bactria and Soghd and the northern frontiers were subjected, the new cities built and communications established, the strain showed in him. He did not sleep as well as when he had been on the march; he spent most of the night in hearing all the multitudinous reports of his new administration. When he did make an end of this he wanted to lie at the table with fruit and wine, in company with his entourage, to listen to talk and often to talk himself, when drunk, until sunrise. After such a heavy drinking bout now he fell often into a stupor, watched over by the physicians and the royal bodyguards.

Since the defter, more politic Iranians knew how to praise and please him in such a stage of mental fatigue, he began to favor them openly over the dogmatic and blunt Macedonians. They in turn noticed that whoever had been closest to Alexander in the past irritated him the most in his new mood.

It was not that Alexander had changed. His instincts had intensified; he seemed to be more aware of danger, and at the same time threw himself bodily where the danger was greatest; his anger had become deadly.

He liked to confide in new personalities who—not understanding him—were careful to treat him with reverence. He even developed a fondness for the new Greek mercenaries, and Asiatics who had never been associated with his early campaigns.

He hardly spoke to Callisthenes, who usually remained silent at table. He no longer wanted to reason about what should be done or to be reminded of affairs at home. In a strange way Macedonians at home had become antagonists, in his imagination—although he wrote to Antipater and the others constantly, as if to justify himself. It was as if, the elder Macedonians said, his friends had become his enemies and his enemies his friends.

Black Cleitus, now a regimental commander, was the brother of Lanice, who had been Alexander's nurse in childhood. So this burly Companion had been a kind of foster brother to Alexander, who knew, besides, that all of Lanice's own sons had been killed during his early campaigns. Black Cleitus moreover had saved his life in the charge at the river Granicus—as all the army knew. Black Cleitus was dumb in the head and disliked the new fashion of Persian dress and manners. Black Cleitus had been heard to say that Alexander was no more than the son of Philip, King of the Macedonians.

One evening, or rather morning, Alexander had been pleased to order sacrifice made to the sons of Zeus, aiders of human beings. The group of flatterers around him had seized the chance to whisper that their king was himself equal to the hero-sons of Zeus. Callisthenes looked down into his empty wine cup. Some drunken soul struck up a ditty: *"West is bad and east is best."*

279

Some newly arrived Greeks remarked that the old-style Macedonian commanders had done well enough in the west but had been thrashed by the Bactrians here. Alexander smiled on them and looked around for Black Cleitus. That officer was not to be seen at the table, and the bodyguards explained that he was preparing the two lambs for sacrifice to the sons of Zeus as ordered.

Alexander, however, was pleased to call for Cleitus. The Companion veteran appeared after a few minutes in haste, with two lambs crowding at his heels, their heads dripping with sacrificial unguents. Black Cleitus had been too mellow with wine himself to notice that the lambs had followed him. "Here is Cleitus, Alexander!" he shouted.

It made a restless stir at the table, this apparition of the victims of sacrifice, which should have been left at the shrine. Angered, Alexander motioned for Cleitus to take his place at the table. *"West is bad and east is best!"* echoed again. And Cleitus, drinking, heard for the first time the laughter over the Macedonians who had run from the Bactrians. He crashed his cup down, furious.

"They who died yonder in the hills were better men than you who laugh at them!"

"Be careful," shouted someone, "whom you speak of."

Filling his cup and drinking again, the big Companion kept on muttering. He had room for no more than one idea in his head at a time. "I speak of the best men—I speak of those men who won victories for Philip. Ay, for the old army. Ay, at Chaeronea, at Thebes." Glaring around, he looked at Alexander. "Speak up, do you call them cowards?"

"Be still!" Alexander shouted.

The outcry and the babbling ceased, except for Cleitus's hoarse voice. "Now . . . we freeborn may not speak our minds. Now we can't speak to Philip's son—"

The older men got around Cleitus, shaking him, and

he lurched to his feet, stripping back the sleeve from his scarred arm. "Get back!" he howled, and shook his arm toward Alexander, who was rigid with rage. "That arm was good enough to save the life of Philip's son in the river Granicus. Now Cleitus can't speak to him—"

"Speak," Alexander snapped. "You won't be punished—"

Warily Cleitus shook his head, shoving the other officers away. "Oh, we Macedonians can't do that, without leave from the Per-sian of-fic-ials. We can't possible without bowing down to your shining white Per-sian girdle. No—no. And you can't punish us any more—than we've been punished."

Jumping up, Alexander reached behind him for his sword. But his sword-bearer had been led from the pavilion by Ptolemy. "Trumpets!" the king shouted, not in Greek but in the old Macedonian speech. The trumpeter of the guard remained motionless behind him, and Alexander crashed his fist into the man's face.

The men around Cleitus seized this chance to hurry him out of the pavilion entrance into the darkness. But they all heard Alexander's shout: "Cleitus!"

Hearing that, the big Companion lurched back, swinging the curtain aside. Dead drunk, he had heard the king's voice. "Here is Cleitus, Alexander."

And Alexander, catching a spear from a guard, leaped to meet him, thrusting the spear through him.

When Cleitus lay on the mat, gripping at the spear's haft, choking, the officers came around, not speaking. When Alexander stared down at his friend, and kneeled, trying to pull out the spear, the officers gripped the weapon, afraid that the king might kill himself with it. After a moment Alexander got to his feet and went out, lurching through the curtain. He went to his tent and flung himself on the ground.

For a long time no one dared go near him, nor would he send for food or drink. When Anaxarchus, frightened by his silence, went in with Aristander the next day, they found Alexander sitting in the robe he had worn at the supper, his eyes inflamed as if he had been weeping. They brought in water and food, to which he paid no attention. Aristander ventured to speak, saying that all things happened by the will of the gods, not by human will, and so had the death of Cleitus occurred.

Alexander lookde up. "Lanice had no sons. Now she has no brother.... There was a woman at Thebes ..."

Anaxarchus struck his hands together sharply. "Alexander, King of the Macedonians and Lord of Asia," he said in a sharp voice to the old diviner, "sits there crying like a slave."

The caustic natural voice cut through Alexander's self-torment, and after a while he went to sleep, his head dropping over his arms, locked together as if holding desperately to support.

When a man is most alone, he holds most closely to myth. During spells of deep depression, like the one following the slaying of Black Cleitus, Alexander felt an overpowering sense of guilt. He had murdered those who had been closest to him; he had torn down and burned Thebes. It was not so much an obsession as it was the phantasmagoria of violence and death that tortured his imagination. At such times he saw himself and his actions not in a blur of self-pity but in the terrible clarity of memory. When these ghosts of the past marched on him and overcame him his mind could not summon up a defense. Drinking brought no nepenthe.

At such times the souls of Rushanak and Hephaestion could not stand between him and the phantasmagoria. He was, as Aristotle had seen, alone.

Some understanding of Alexander's self-torment is apparent in the dry words of the Roman Arrian, who was a Stoic. *I do not think it strange that Alexander committed great errors either from impetuosity or from wrath. He was young, and he had risen to a great height by the impulse of Fortune. Nor is it strange that he was led to conduct himself like the Persian kings, immoderately.*

As for the associates he grouped around him, kings

will always have such associates and such associates will always work on them to do wrong—without thought of their vital interests.

But I am certain Alexander was the only one of the ancient kings to repent so greatly the wrongs he did. Most men, then as now, when they have committed a sin, make the mistake of concealing it by defending it as a just action. Alexander was singular in not doing so.

Arrian is apologizing here, as a Stoic, but he has caught the significance of something strange in Alexander's self-abasement.

Apparently Alexander did not feel that ritual sacrifice could wipe out the bloodstain that lay upon him. (The two lambs that had been anointed by Black Cleitus were sacrificed afterward as planned, only to Dionysos the hero-god, not to the sons of Zeus.)

By this time also he had given up hope of finding the way to the lost paradise of the Iranians, to Iranvenj—the height in the northeast corner of the Oikoumene from which Kurush had set out. He had back-tracked Kurush as far as Maracand where Cleitus was probably killed.

Now he was crossing the Parapanisades without discovering anything more remarkable than ranges of extremely high mountains populated by barbaric folk. But at the same time he was enlarging his concept of the Oikoumene. It stretched farther east than his geographers had supposed. Up at the northernmost Alexandria [where the new town of Leninabad may stand today, under the Alaisky Khrebet Range] he had heard Scythians tell of a land unknown to the Greeks—Sin or Tsin, beyond the steppes. And he knew now that the river Indus lay long marches east of the Parapanisades passes.

But what lay beyond Sin and the great valley of the Indus? There must be the limit of the Oikoumene, the edge of the Eurasian continent—Ocean itself.

There also might be found the mysterious source of the great river Nile, and the Indus. Greek myth assured him that *from the springs of the Sun in the utmost east flows the river Ethiop, to empty into the cataracts of the Nile.*

For neither Alexander nor his surveyors knew the shape of the land mass south and east of him, under the Pleiades. Aristotle had believed that the mass of land in the south stretched from southern Egypt to India. And that the Nile actually had its source close to the Indus, in this limbo of the farthest east.

The Macedonians, of course, had seen for themselves—some of them—the northern tips of the Red Sea and the Persian Sea, but they did not know as yet whether these were arms of the outer encircling Ocean or inland seas. Alexander suspected they were arms of the great Ocean; but most of the men believed them to be inland waters. If that was the case the land must extend all the way from the upper Nile to the Indus— probably the Nile itself dipped under the surface of the earth to reappear in Egypt. They had heard much talk in Greece of such subterranean waters that might reach to Hades. There was the Styx for instance.

Meanwhile one argument had been settled. Everyone agreed now that they could not be near the Fetid Sea and the Tanais [the Sea of Azov and the Don] a point from which they might return easily to Macedon by a short circle to the east, following the course of the Argonauts. Every phalanx veteran had marched over too much ground toward the rising sun for that. They knew they were exploring unknown territory, beyond the Caspian, far east of Babylon.

The geographers reached a compromise about the actual shape of the earth. Now they assumed that the straight line of the Taurus mountains stretched due east, running south of the Caspian, to meet the mightier barrier range of the Parapanisades.

But what lay beyond this barrier they did not know, except that the river Indus was to be met there. Callisthenes told them that the land around the Indus formed only a small peninsula stretching to a point, out into Ocean itself.

So one thing appeared certain to Alexander. No

matter what might be found *upon* the earth in this next stage to the east, he would very soon reach the end of earth itself, and stand upon the dark shore of Ocean, with all mysteries resolved and all doubts set at rest.

Toward this shore of Ocean he determined to make his way.

To encourage the armies he reminded them—embroidering fables in so doing—that the hero-gods Heracles and Dionysos had both penetrated to this eastern limit and had won glory and satisfaction by so doing. They would journey where Heracles and Dionysos alone had gone before them, to gain immortal life.

Naturally some of the Macedonian faction retorted, when they heard this, that only those who were immortals could hope to get as far as that. These Macedonians disliked intensely the contingent of Persian Immortals who were kept at headquarters and sometimes did guard duty. Really archers instead of spearmen, the Persian Immortals were called golden-apple spearmen by the westerners, because their weapons had gilt balls below the iron points. New cavalry units of Bactrians and Scythians also appeared at the mobilization in the early spring of 327.

Even Alexander felt dubious about the multitude that poured into the camps. Soothsayers, priests, and money-changers had added their establishments to the military; the soldiers now had more women to follow them, and the women had more children. The armies had become moving colonies, and as for the baggage . . .

After his first inspection of the columns of pack animals and carts Alexander lectured the men on the sin of multiplying possessions and proceeded to burn the bulkier portions. The veterans caught the contagion of reducing weight by fire and set the torch to other mountains of baggage, until the roads became chains of bonfires, and the camps seethed like broken hives.

"Are you *still* to learn," Alexander cried at the veterans, "that you must win victories without taking on the infirmities of the people you subdue?"

He had set the example of discarding all impedimenta except field equipment. One high officer (Harpalus, the treasurer, is the name given in the chronicles, but Harpalus seemed to have remained at Babylon and Ecbatana) he suspected of concealing a great store of gold and silver bullion in chests within his field pavilion. This the officer denied emphatically, and after the denial Alexander was not willing to have the man's belongings searched. (For these commanding officers were still in the main freeborn Macedonians, nobles, and members of the national council—he had increased their authority and wealth without making any change in their rights as individuals and Macedonian nobles, thereby creating a dangerous anomaly, of which his mother Olympias had warned him and still warned him by letter.)

This difficulty Alexander solved as swiftly as he always met dilemmas. He ordered some of his personal guards to set fire to the pavilion of the offending officer during the baggage-burning. If the big tent began to burn, he thought the servants would haul out the chests of valuables the first thing, thereby disclosing the treasure. As it turned out, the fire did its work too well. Hangings, precious garments, perfumes, jewels, and bullion all went up in the conflagration. The treasure had indeed been hidden there, but no one could prove it. Ruefully Alexander paid the officer damages out of his own account.

Although the field armies had grown, the number of experienced Macedonian officers of the Companion type had diminished inevitably because most of them had been left behind to govern, with their Asiatic opposite numbers, the vast terrain already taken over. A commander of a *taxis* might be the military governor of a city or countryside of a half million souls. Alexander had insisted on this dual control; the embryo Eurasian state would have no dominating cult or nation. Even the military control would not be overriding because it held no authority over public funds. And such funds were to be used in the main for development projects, which included of course building Greek-type theaters and academies, as well as new highroads through the mountain regions they had explored, new hospitals, fleets, ports.

Nothing in all this was agreeable to the veteran Macedonian officers. They disliked the necessity of getting the signature—the seal stamp—of an Asiatic official to a decree, or begging an Egyptian or Semitic treasurer for ration money. The very names of the Asiatics seemed ridiculous. Why should a man call himself Lord of Rivers, or Son of the Truth, or Radiant One? And as for the cylindrical seals they carried—the Macedonians were very skeptical about the consequences of marking documents with the sign of the half-moon, or the image of the Lady of the Beasts, or even the popular Winged Head. No good, they thought, would come of that.

Alexander still tried to carry on the ever-increasing labor of administration alone. When an officer fell sick he wrote to demand why he had not been informed of it. When someone married an Asiatic woman he sent a gift and a note of approval. (He had let it be known that such marriages found great favor with him.) His new officials realized that there was no longer council or court of appeal other than Alexander's personal decision. And when the king disappeared off the map, as he did at this point by crossing the Parapanisades, this decision was hard to obtain. Very naturally the officers asked themselves, "What if he never comes back?" After the risks and hardships of Bactria and Soghd, the odds seemed to lie heavily against his coming back from India. In consequence most of the officer-governors began to prepare for such a contingency by laying aside private fortunes and setting up the cells of kingdoms of their own. In this the Macedonians sinned more than the Asiatics, who displayed great loyalty.

Alexander had won that loyalty at a price. He had been amazingly quick to understand the working of the Asiatic mind. When meeting with Orientals he claimed obedience not as a Macedonian commander but as a successor of Kurush, an instrument of divine authority. Inevitably he began to wear Persian dress at such meetings. Here in farther Asia the Macedonian riding dress, with its wide soft hat, baggy riding trousers, and boots, or the Greek style with kilt, mantle, and sandals, marked a man as a barbarian or a soldier. It had become vitally important for Alexander to keep not only the obedience but the respect of the Asiatics.

But the first time the veteran Macedonians beheld him seated on something like a throne with the awkward tiara on his head, they laughed. "What kind of a dressing-up festival is this, Alexander?" they asked.

That angered him. He used the gold couch at meals and kept incense burning around him because not to do so would puzzle and bewilder the Asiatics. Before these noble-born Orientals he could not conduct himself like a *Yavana* teamster.

Only with an effort had he managed to play the two parts successfully until now—to be at once the chosen king of freeborn westerners who hated a despot and the Shahinshah of the Orientals who knew no rule other than despotism. These two parts clashed fatally when the Orientals began to prostrate themselves on approaching him. Not to do so would have been inconceivable to the easterners who beheld in the robed and enthroned Alexander the person invested with heavenly power. They covered their mouths with their hands, they bent to their knees when they came before him.

This time the Macedonians did not laugh. And it put an end to Callisthenes. This Sophist, disciple of Aristotle, had rebuked Alexander openly before now. Anaxarchus and other adulators, knowing that Callisthenes was writing a history of the Macedonian, whispered to Alexander that the Sophist had boasted that his history would make their lord renowned for all time. (Actually Callisthenes had said publicly that Alexander was no god, no son of Zeus born of Olympias—and that only Alexander's actions throughout his life would establish his fame or ill fame.)

To Anaxarchus the Sophist may have said, *"Alexan-*

288

der not only seems to be, but is, one of the bravest of men, of kings the most kingly, of commanders, one of the most worthy."

Anaxarchus admitted that only after death were divine honors to be paid a man. "In their human lives Dionysos was a Theban and Heracles an Argive. After departing from among men, certain it is that Alexander will be honored as a god, and sacrifice made to his image. Would it not be more just to honor him so, while he is still alive?"

"If another man—if one of us came forward and seated himself on Alexander's throne, would he be pleased by that?"

"Never!" the Greek cried in horror. "That man would be slain out of hand for his presumption."

"And in what manner would the gods treat Alexander if he, a mortal, should raise himself to divine honor?"

To this Anaxarchus made no response. But it was whispered in the camps afterward that Callisthenes had said the king might be slain for his presumption in appearing to be a god.

Naturally the Macedonian veterans heard the opinions of Callisthenes thankfully and supported him. For this had become more than any matter of philosophic opinion. The Macedonians, who were not too analytical, beheld Alexander departing from old customs—apparently being won over to oriental ways. By so doing, they feared that he might be changing his nature and might become in very fact a lord of Asia heedless of his old clans and countrymen. Their anger arose out of their devotion to him.

When he tried the experiment one evening of combining ceremonies, the Macedonian embrace at greeting and the Presian prostration, it had unhappy consequences. They were drinking toasts, each man coming forward to salute the king before drinking. Trying to follow the example of the Orientals, the Macedonian officers bowed in silence and then stepped forward to kiss Alexander's face.

As Callisthenes stepped forward Alexander was talking to Hephaestion and did not notice him. A Companion, watching, touched the king's arm.

"The Sophist," he said, "did not make prostration before coming to you."

Alexander glanced quickly at the silent company and merely motioned Callisthenes away without greeting him.

The conspiracy charge proved more serious. Alexander had made a real effort to combine the education of oriental and Macedonian boys. Some fifty thousand eastern youngsters now received training under army teachers, especially in the Greek language and use of weapons. The only large group of Macedonian boys were the esquires or cadets, sons of noblemen who attended upon the person of the king, in his tent, especially at night and having charge of hunting implements.

In consequence these boys who came and went within the Agema, or military guard, had convenient access to weapons. Their loyalty had never been questioned. The first hint of a conspiracy was given by an officer who had one of the cadets for a lover, and it reached Ptolemy's ears. The rumor had it that some of the boys were angered because Alexander had spoken about including Persian youths in their special training—that they planned to assassinate the king at night when they were alone with him in the pavilion.

One of the youths, Hermolaus, had been studying philosophy with Callisthenes and so had been observed often in talk with him. Ptolemy reported the talk to Alexander, who turned the boys over to a council of Companions for judgment. In this case judgment took the form of torture on the rack. Two or three boys confessed to talking about killing the king— Hermolaus explaining that they grieved over the deaths of Parmenio and Philotas and Cleitus, and the putting on of oriental dress, and the prostration. But they had planned nothing. Nor did they admit that Callisthenes had any part in their actions.

They were killed by the officers, and Callisthenes put in chains. One account has it that he was kept under guard and died later; another says he was hanged. Alexander wrote to Antipater in Macedon that the boys had been stoned to death by the Companion officers, but that he himself would attend to Callisthenes *and those who sent him out*.

After the death of the boys the ceremony of prostration was abandoned.

Callisthenes may have been thrown into chains at the city of Bactria, in that early spring of 327. Certain it is that Alexander hurried on, through his Parapanisades, burning the excess baggage as has been related. He seemed to be anxious to escape from accursed ground, and this time he did not bother to take omens or hold even the semblance of a council.

Delaying only to select a site for a new base—an easternmost Alexandria—when he reached the Kabul River and the eastern caravan route, he drove the armies on. Action dispelled the miasma of doubt and incipient conspiracy. It gave relief to Alexander's overtaxed brain. It gave his commanders occupation.

Hephaestion and Perdiccas—a politician and a good executive officer—were dispatched along the main caravan road, leading down through the Khyber Pass to the valley of the Indus. The heavier units, the larger engines and the wagon train went with them.

By now the army itself had ceased to be Macedonian, although still officered in the main by Macedonians. Iranian nobles made up a new cavalry wing, as distinguished as the Companions (who were now armed in splendor with silver shields). Some of the old formations had disappeared. Survivors of the fine Cretan bowmen were turned over to Nearchus's new naval unit. The Hypaspists, decimated by long campaigning, had been made into a guard unit, attached to headquarters. The Macedonian phalanx remained unchanged— Alexander dared not lose this pivot of his army.

But mounted men now made up at least half the army. In the eyes of the new Asiatic allies only mounted men deserved respect. The warrior caste here

291

formed the cavalry, and only servitors, tribesmen, and hired spearmen consented to trudge along on foot over the vast distances of the eastern marches. Naturally the Macedonian phalanxmen shared no such opinion of their own worth. And they grumbled at marching on foot, carrying all their weapons and kits in the dust of the Asiatic cavalry. Alexander tried to minister to their self-esteem by mounting some regiments, christening the remainder Foot Companions, and granting them the privilege of having their kits carried in carts.

Even after leaving some fifteen thousand at the last Alexandria, on the Kabul—the base for the jump-off into India—some forth thousand must have gone on with the commander, accompanied by an unknown total of civilians. In military force Alexander now disposed of three to four times the strength he had had at the Granicus. But he commanded an international not a national army.

It was more than a military triumph to have welded this tremendous force together. And he was leading it on not to subject but to conciliate the peoples ahead, the Aryans of the Indus. Already he had been in communication with them, and he knew that they were ready to greet him at the edge of the valley of the Indus with gifts of supplies and a strange monster beast called elephant. They had learned much about him during the last years and were prepared to grant him peaceful passage through the land, as overlord of Asia.

For Alexander wanted no more stress of combat such as he had undergone in the last two and a half years.

In moving east this time he had divided the command, as always. With Ptolemy as his lieutenant and Craterus as his transport officer, he turned northeast, taking with him the most experienced units, like the Agrianians, the Horse and Foot Companions, and engineers with the portable machines suitable for mountain work.

In so doing, he headed toward the higher passes where the Hind-i-Kuh meets the immense ridges of the Himalayas—where no such army could pass.

XVIII. THE ELEPHANTS
AND THE LAST RIVER

Why did Alexander turn aside toward an impassable barrier? Three times before he had detoured sharply north—into the "Gordyene" Range before Gaugamela, to the shore of the Caspian, and lastly at the River of the Sands, in Scythian territory. In each case he had left the well-known routes to strike into the unknown north.

No doubt problems of climate and foraging had something to do with this. Strabo says he followed this northern arc through the highlands into India to keep within fertile lands and to cross the great rivers of India at their headwaters, where the crossing could be made easily. And undoubtedly the Macedonians liked to keep to the north during the summer heat. Mountain climbing did not seem to bother them.

Yet Alexander seems to have been impelled by more than logistics of movement. The marches into Scythia and Himalayan India were both extremely dangerous. Apparently he was bent on exploring. He wanted to examine the inland seas, to find the limits of the steppes, to penetrate this new barrier of mountains. He was eager to trace out the shape of the earth itself, which did not conform at all to the ideas of the Greek academicians.

But at each stage he had had to climb higher, to march farther. The very rivers had increased in size. Was there, at the last horizon, overlooking Ocean and the place of the sun's rising, evidence of the divine power? Did there exist beings who were more than mortal in their wisdom, having partaken of the fruit of the Tree of Knowledge and having drunk of the Waters of Life?

It has been said that Alexander felt driven to fulfill his destiny. Perhaps he journeyed on to discover if destiny existed. Was there, in fact, upon the earth's surface evidence of the presence of the gods? Did men, in truth, carry out a will superior to their own? Or was the Immovable Mover remote and unseen—merely the source of universal energy, of atomic action? And did mankind then progress only by its own efforts, toward enlightenment or toward beastliness?

Certainly his constant probing toward the north of the Oikoumene had revealed in each instance a deterioration of mentality among the marginal inhabitants— among the wild Celts across the Danube, among the *"Dahae"* [Robbers] of the Caspian steppes, and the Scythians beyond the River of the Sands. Evidently enlightenment lay to the east rather than the north.

At the outset, that spring, Alexander had the help of a bit of luck. More exactly, he turned a chance coincidence into a happy omen that encouraged his men mightily.

They found ivy. And with the ivy a legend was connected. At the pleasant town of Nysa—so the Greeks wrote down the name—on the mountain slope, the inhabitants showed them real ivy, which they had found no place else this side the Dardanelles. Moreover these people knew the word for it—they knew many Greek words.

By degrees the story came out. The Nysaeans thought themselves to be descendants of the heroes who had followed Dionysos in his wandering as far as this. Disabled men, so the tale ran, had founded this ancient colony, to perpetuate the Bacchanals, in worship of the god.

In proof they pointed to a nearby summit, Mount Meru. This, they said, was called after Mount Meroë of the homeland. And they offered to show Alexander proof of their words.

All this, Arrian relates, *suited Alexander exactly, be-*

294

*cause he wished the legend of the wandering of Diony-
sos to be believed. So he climbed with the Companions, both cavalry and foot, up the slope of Mount
Meru and found it covered with ivy and laurel groves,
with altars shaded by groves wherein wild animals
roamed free.*

*Delighted of sight of the ivy, the Macedonians made
garlands. They crowned themselves and danced around
singing, invoking the deity by all his names. Alexander
there offered sacrifice to Dionysos, and lay down to
feast with all his companions.*

This providential appearance of the sacred vine
buoyed up the Macedonians, who reasoned that even if
divine power had not led them to Nysa, at least they
had found evidence that Greek heroes had been here
before them. As a matter of fact they found rhododen-
dron farther on, and vast forests of fir. They found a
breed of long-horned oxen so fine and powerful that
they sent back a herd to Macedon.

But they had few feasts after Nysa. As in the heights
of Asia Minor and Soghd, the inhabitants proved to be
more savage the higher they climbed. Often these hillmen retired into their *sangas*—rock fortifications—on
the summits. Just as often Alexander insisted on
climbing after them, to coax them out or to pound
them out with the demountable engines which were
carried up to the summits in parts.

At times the highlanders took refuge in cliffside
dwellings, and even Macedonian ingenuity was taxed in
getting them out again. Alexander and Ptolemy were
both wounded. And the regiments reacted with cruelty;
at least once they massacred men who had surrendered—which had not happened before.

Higher they climbed toward the stunted, wind-bent
pines and rock shoulders of the massif of the
Himalayas. When the valleys narrowed and the broad
streams became thundering rapids, Alexander left the
column behind and pushed on with picked mountaineers. When the air became thin, so that they
breathed with difficulty, they found immense ramparts

of ice in their way. When they climbed these, laboriously, they felt weak, huddling together against the wind blasts that tore at them.

Beyond the glaciers they could see ahead of them and above the cloud level still loftier barrier ranges, and a single sentinel peak of pure white. This peak, the surveyors declared after making a calculation of its height, must rise above the air of the earth, into the empyrean.

"Beyond," the guides told them, "are the heights guarded by Indra, who dwells in the upper air, amid the storms."

In spite of that Alexander could see only mountain summits, vastly greater than any he had examined before. No army could get through here. No benevolent and godlike people, seemingly, could dwell here. He turned back, heading down toward the Indus, where Hephaestion and Perdiccas were building bridges for the crossing.

He turned south of his own accord, to rejoin the main army. But by then a change was taking place in his relation to that army—a change of which Alexander was unaware, although the army was keenly conscious of it. The men understood that their leader had chosen to play the part of a despot, and they suspected, at least the Macedonians did, that he believed himself to be divine in his power to overcome all obstacles lying in his path. And that might mean that Alexander was insane.

Perhaps more than anything else, the unfinished journal of Callisthenes contributed to this belief. This manuscript of the Sophist's *Anabasis*, in contrast to the Sophist's words, depicted Alexander as mortal no more, inspired by the wisdom of Zeus, led by divine favor upon the path of his destiny. It reeked of flattery. It was meant to destroy a man's soul. Alexander, reading it, must have remembered that Callisthenes had boasted that his *Anabasis* would bring immortal fame to the Macedonian. After reading the manuscript, Arrian relates that the memory of Callisthenes became odious to Alexander.

But he had more than the Sophist's writing with him while he skirted the Himalayan heights. He had a copy of Aristotle's *Rhetoric to Alexander,* which—although impersonal in tone—warned against belief in false evidence. It urged the value of discovery over disputation. It attacked the elder Greek idealism which motivated even Plato in drawing up the plan of a nebulous republic, to embody an ideal good.

To this the cynical Ptolemy objected. "By now," he declared, "you should know that what is good for one man isn't good for another. Why don't you stick to what is good for you?"

"What would that be?"

"To go back. Don't stay in Ecbatana or Babylon. Go back to our sea, and to Alexandria-in-Egypt."

He did not add that Thais, his mistress, had become homesick for Egypt.

Alexander would not listen. Both men were weakened by severe wounds, and Ptolemy's insistence irritated his half brother. After their Himalayan venture Ptolemy seldom tried to advise him.

And in poring through the new *Metaphysics* of Aristotle, Alexander discovered that his teacher had advanced far in speculation as to the nature of God. Not on this earth but only in the realm of the outermost stars did the Immovable Mover exist. The power that revolved these fixed stars about the earth moved all things else. From that timeless motion earthward, life was generated and endured throughout time. Beyond that there could be no sign of the existence of the Mover ... and if this were so, Alexander could meet with nothing but natural things in his journey.

It seemed to Alexander that their roles had become, somehow, reversed. The Stagyrite, who had argued earlier for doing rather than knowing, and for discovering rather than reasoning, had become an exponent of *theoria.* While he, Alexander, was bent upon observing and discovering for himself.

297

In this quest he was alone, more alone than when he had pored over the texts at Mieza. Aristotle had become hostile, more so than Demosthenes; Ptolemy who rode at his side, thought only of a return to Egypt. At home the philosophers—after reading Callisthenes—attributed his continuing success to a whim of Fortune, to be ended by catastrophe, as soon as Fortune rejected him. And even the faithful Antipater, influenced by the feeling at home, had begun to oppose his will.

Yet nothing, even in the splendor of his imagination, could have been more impressive than his arrival at the bridge of boats over the great Indus that spring. He came in, bringing the trees of a forest for planking, the silver shields of the Companions tossing back the sun gleam, as the wild Scythian horsemen rode out to greet him, escorting Rushanak, their pipes shrilling.

They brought gifts from the rajah of northern India—cartloads of silver bars, thousands of oxen for food, and sheep for sacrifice, with a regiment of the dark Indian horsemen, and a string of thirty caparisoned elephants, to serve him.

Coming out of the foothills in this fashion, he noticed how Rushanak his wife dwelt in the splendor of an oriental court, with barricades around her pavilions and a guard of eunuchs to escort the elephant on which she rode. She looked like a jeweled statue, half concealed within the litter mounted on the elephant's back. In this country it was beneath the dignity of a queen to ride a horse, unveiled, as Rushanak had been accustomed to do.

Although Rushanak adapted herself readily to this new magnificence—and refused to ride anything except an elephant thereafter—she felt uneasy at her isolation. She had been happier with him in the upland cold, where they shared a tent during the campaigning, and she had thrown off her furs to sit by his knee at the fire, close-bound to him by physical love. Here in the camp that was like a moving city she dressed obediently in cloth of gold and strings of pearls, unhappy that she was not yet with child by him, and uncertain whither his whim would lead him.

Alexander's first whim was to go elephant hunting. Guided by the Indians, the Macedonian officer's mounted these strange land monsters and hunted a wild herd through the brush, singling out and roping new captives, which were led back between the tame beasts. The Macedonians were impressed by the power and sagacity of the monsters, which could be managed by a boy or an old man. They watched the tame elephants dance. One of them clashed a cymbal held in its trunk against two other cymbals fastened to its forelegs, while the others moved around, lifting their legs in time.

"In battle, if a driver is wounded," Seleucus Nicator explained, "his elephant will stand over him, to protect him."

Seleucus was one of the newly favored commanders—a good-natured giant, so strong that he could twist the horns of a bull and throw him. Seleucus shared the amiability of Hephaestion and Nearchus the seaman, never questioning Alexander's decision. The power of the elephants so delighted him that he determined to raise a herd by breeding.

"In how long a time?" Nearchus asked. He had been making inquiries about the land monsters on his own account.

"As soon as possible."

"Very well. A female of this kind carries her young for sixteen months, and then she brings forth only one, like a mare. This one she suckles until the eighth year. How long will it be before you breed a whole herd?"

They were all keen observers of the strange animal life of Indian, as they called the land along the mighty Indus—terming the people Indians. Nearchus had tried to catch the spotted serpents, having seen one twenty-four feet long, but had found them too quick to be caught. He had better success with parrots, which he discovered spoke like human beings, although they knew no Greek. Onesicritus swore that he had seen an ant as big as a fox, digging gold out of the ground.

Alexander found out that men bitten by the hooded serpents—those resembling the images on the heads of the Pharaohs of Egypt—all died of the bite. He assembled in a tent Indians who knew cures for snakebites and issued orders for all men bitten by the hooded snakes to hurry to this tent. He was amused by the story of Peucestas's encounter with the beautiful little men of the forest. Peucestas had been taking his command through a jungle path, when missiles were thrown at the soldiers from the treetops. Immediately the brigadier had deployed his men among the trees, only to have stones and nuts rained down on them by these little people dressed in skins in spite of the heat.

"They are not men," Nearchus explained, "but beautiful animals who have learned to imitate men. The hairy skin they wear is their own skin."

For a long time Peucestas, a stickler in little things, refused to believe that he had ordered his soldiers to give battle to monkeys and not to men. But the methodical Nearchus had taken some monkeys captive to prove his point. For Alexander had ordered the Cretan seaman and Seleucus to probe deep into the new land and to bring in specimens of all types of people and animals—especially the elephants. Nearchus had seized the opportunity to build a fleet of small galleys, some having as many as thirty oars, to navigate the Indus, because he much preferred to do his exploring by water.

(Very quietly Alexander had shifted the command of the older Macedonian units into the hands of these men who were not soldiers but would get things done for him. By now Hephaestion led the best of the Companions, Seleucus the favored Hypaspists, and Nearchus a regiment of the trusted Agrianians.)

When Alexander beheld the new fleet drawn up along the bank of the Indus he burst out irritably. Did his shipwrights expect the army to sail over this land?

The Cretan answered for the shipbuilders. No, he

300

did not expect the galleys to sail the army to the east; instead the transport wagons would carry the ships eastward, in sections. So they would always have shipping in readiness to cross deep water. And had not Alexander ordered a bridge to be built here of boats?

"A bridge over the Indus, yes."

At first the Macedonians had hoped that they had come upon the source of the great Nile at this river which resembled the other so much—even to the rushes growing along the banks and the dragonlike water monsters called crocodiles. And the Indus, like the Nile, was already rising in flood without visible cause. Callisthenes and Aristotle had believed that the Indus would prove to be the headwater of the Nile.

Herodotus had declared that the land of Egypt was the gift of the Nile, being formed out of alluvial deposits brought down from an unknown region by the yearly floods; and at first glance the soil along this river seemed to be banked up in the same manner. If so, India might be, like Egypt, a narrow tongue of land jutting out into Ocean.

But Nearchus had investigated and made a shrewd surmise. He had learned that the flooding of the Indus came from the melting of snow and heavy rainfall up in the northern mountains—the very Himalayas that Alexander had sighted. And those mountains were far, far off. (He surmised from this that the Nile might also rise among similar mountains and lakes where rain fell, in far distant Ethiopia, an unknown region.)

And the Indus did not flow in the direction of the west-east wind; it took its course along the way of the south wind, to empty into the encircling Ocean.

"And those mouths of the Indus lie toward the sun," Nearchus ended calmly, "six thousand stadia from here. Or so these barbarians say."

That meant—in spite of the rushes and crocodiles—that Indus could have no connection with the Nile. It meant that lands, deserts, and gulfs vaster than any Greeks had conceived stretched between the two rivers. And above all it meant to the mass of the army that they could not embark here and sail upon the river back to Memphis and Alexandria-in-Egypt, to the blue water of the Mediterranean for which they longed.

Nearchus and the pilots and shipwrights, discovering this, had hastened to build the transport fleet, hoping that Alexander would be content to abandon the march to the east and sail down the Indus. But Alexander would not hear of that. He agreed to let the shipmasters transport their vessels and bridge overland; eastward, however, they must go.

"Still we will need the boats and the bridge," Nearchus laughed.

Beyond the Indus, the seamen explained, four more rivers barred the way. This land mass of India could be no neck of land; it must stretch a vast distance toward the rising sun.

No one knew what lay beyond the fourth river. The seamen hoped it might be Ocean itself. Alexander, they knew, meant to find out.

The army, however, soon learned what the navigators knew. The army took no joy out of carting the ships eastward, and it moved sullenly across the Indus, it snarled when optimistic commanders observed that Heracles might have taken this way before them. Silently, in its own way, it began to fight Alexander's progress. And in the end it mutinied.

The rains came. The skies broke over the steaming earth, flooding the night camps. Not since they left Troy behind them had the men met such a deluge as this. Yet greater than the rain was their grievance against Rajah Ambhi.

This Rajah Ambhi *(Omphi* the Greek scholars called him) had been treated as a favored friend. True, he had welcomed them with gifts and had made the gesture of placing all his cities and lands at their disposal. Yet Alexander had given Ambhi more gold than the worth of the silver received from him, and had given him back his lands. Hephaestion merely built the usual fortified road towns along the line of march, in which invalid soldiers and refugees were settled.

Alexander treated the rajah like an equal, forbidding the troops to pillage this northern India. "Never before now," the men complained, "has he raised an easterner to such honor." And the army began to be jealous of the courteous rajah.

Undeniably Alexander was pleased with the Indians. At the great city of Takshacila (*Taxila* in the Greek writing) he ordered games to be held and sacrifices made to celebrate the friendship between his now heterogeneous people and these Indians. They were Aryans, he discovered, who had drifted down out of the northern plains in patriarchal clans. Like the Iranians, they had been cattle raisers, keeping only one wife, worshiping at the sacred fire, reverencing only the god of the upper air whom they had named Indra. Their noble caste as with the Macedonians was the warrior caste, the *kshatriya*. Their priests were the ascetic *brahmins* who taught—as the priests of Kurush had taught the Iranians—that it was evil to take life in any form, to deceive others, or to struggle to gain property on this earth. Both warrior and brahmin castes held themselves aloof from the darker-skinned aborigines of the land. These members of the higher castes Alexander treated as equals, enlisting Rajah Ambhi's horsemen to serve with the Companions. (On their part, the Indians accepted Alexander readily as overlord—calling him the European King of Kings— but disliked the Macedonians; terming them barbarians, *Yavanas* [herdsmen], and Balkan mountaineers.)

The allied hosts moved eastward differing inwardly and held together only by the personality of one man. Only the lashing of Alexander's will drove his Macedonians on. And at the eastern frontier they met the embattled strength of another dynasty, that of the Paurava kings, antagonistic to Ambhi. Alexander had pledged Ambhi that his Macedonians would break the power of the Pauravas.

Perhaps he did not expect that any army would

presume to stand in the field against the Macedonians at this stage; certainly he reasoned that no army could do so with success. Not in the face of the allied forces now under his command.

But this one stood its ground, in the rain, across the swift flood of the river Jhelum.[1] Among its tents appeared elephants, several hundred of them. The Macedonians had not counted on the elephants. Nor could they bridge this river, rising daily in flood.

It seemed to them that their real antagonists were the torrential water and the giant beasts. Otherwise they estimated the Paurava force to be weak, and in this they made a mistake. The crossing of the Jhelum was Alexander's last major battle. And he lost control of it.

Alexander might have waited, of course, until the rains ceased and the river dwindled to its normal channel. But he was in no mood to wait. The Macedonians went at the problem lightly, as if playing a game for stakes. They had for once more cavalry than they needed; yet they had discovered that the horses would not face elephants. Much less could horses be expected to swim a river and climb a bank under the tusks of the elephants. After their first survey of the situation Alexander's staff prepared to throw their cavalry across where the elephants were not. And in doing so, remembering Darius, they went to work on the mind of the king-leader of the Paurava forces.

It was, Arrian relates, like no experience they had undergone before. *Alexander thought best to move in every direction, to bewilder Porus* [the Paurava] *and make him uncertain what to do. Splitting up his com-*

---

[1]As usual Alexander had kept the line of march far north among the foothills of the Punjab (Five Rivers) and the Macedonians were now on the Jhelum where the Salt Range meets the first ridges of Kashmir. The Jhelum here runs in a narrow channel but with great force after the rains beak. The time must have been the end of May or beginning of June 326.

mands, he sent them under different officers to ravage the enemy's property and to look for a place where the river might be crossed. In doing so, corn was brought in from every quarter, so the Paurava king might be led to think Alexander meant to wait at the river until the rains ended and he could ford it easily.

In this fashion Paurava was given no rest, for the boats sailed up and down the bank, and the men were seen stuffing skins with dry hay to make floats. Whenever Paurava assembled his forces at one point to defend it, he was drawn somewhere else. Especially at night, he had to march with the elephants to points where the Macedonians raised the cry of "Enyalios" and raised commotions. Alexander thus gradually got him into the habit of leading his men and elephants along, across the river from the noise. After doing this often, to encounter no more than battle cries, Paurava stayed put in his camp. Still, he kept scouts posted along the bank. When Alexander felt satisfied that Paurava's mind no longer heeded the nightly excursions, he devised a stratagem to cross.

He left Craterus at the main camp with most of the forces, where nightly bonfires and tumults had been staged. He ordered Craterus not to try to cross unless Paurava moved or fled away from the point opposite him. "If Paurava takes away only a small part of the elephants, stay where you are," he advised. "But if he moves off with all the elephants, to go against me, and leaves a portion of his other troops, then cross the river with speed. For only the elephants," said he, "can hold back your horsemen."

By the night selected for the crossing Alexander had assembled picked units commanded by Hephaestion, Ptolemy, Seleucus, Coenus, and Perdiccas, eighteen miles up the river. Between this point and Craterus a cordon of sentries had been posted to pass orders along. Boats and skin rafts had been moved up overland, out of sight of the river, and concealed in brush and trees.

Here a point projects out, where the river makes a

305

*bend. It is covered by a growth of trees of every sort.
Opposite it lies a wooded island, uninhabited. This island and the woods hid the movement of Alexander's
attack column that night, while the usual fire and motion was kept up by Craterus at the camp. A heavy
rain came on, and the noise of thunder covered the
clatter of arms and the movement at the point, and the
orders given by the officers. Just before daybreak the
wind and rain quieted down.*

*The boats were launched opposite the island, and the
horses got on the rafts. The infantry pushed off in the
boats so quietly that they were not heard as they
rounded the island. Alexander himself crossed in a
thirty-oared galley, with Seleucus and Ptolemy. They
landed in silence, and Alexander took the first horsemen up the bank, to cover the landing of the infantry
following on.*

So far the operation had been perfectly planned and
carried out. Alexander was forming his guard cavalry
to advance when the first hitch occurred. They found
that they had come ashore not on the far bank but on
another island. It was a large one that had seemed to
be part of the shore but was separated from the bank
by a narrow channel through which floodwater rushed.

While they floundered along this arm of the river the
enemy pickets opposite observed them. Meanwhile the
attack column, debarking from boats and rafts, was
piling up behind them in the darkness.

They found a place where the arm of the river could
be forded. Men had to plow through the torrent up to
their armpits, and horses were submerged to their
necks.

In the gray mist of dawn Alexander got his horse
guards to the bank at last, on ground that was no more
than a sea of mud. And thereafter all the carefully laid
plan broke down.

They were still plodding through mud when the first
enemy force appeared on their front. Alexander sent
the horse archers ahead to skirmish and investigate—
only to learn that the enemy numbered no more than a

couple of thousand, chariots and horse. Belatedly he advanced with all his cavalry. The enemy column, either mired in the mud or unwilling to retreat, stood its ground and was decimated.

Delayed by this action, uncertain what the Paurava main body was doing, Alexander decided to push south with all his horsemen, leaving the phalanx units to follow at the run. In an hour he was far out of sight of the infantry laboring through the mud of the river bank.

So it happened that he came full upon the main strength of the Pauravas with only cavalry around him. And that strength was drawn up in a long line upon higher sandy ground that offered better footing. Elephants armored for battle formed the advance of the line—two hundred of them, with hundred-foot intervals between them. In the intervals were posted archers equipped with bows so powerful that the ends had to be rested on the ground to discharge an arrow. Javelin and swordsmen supported the archers.

Unable to risk his horse against such a line, Alexander halted and waited. There was no sign of Craterus (who had obeyed orders in remaining in the camp across the river, since the Paurava king had seen fit to leave some elephants there, with a holding force).

After hours, the tired Hypaspists and shieldmen of the phalanx jogged up. Alexander had to wait for the infantry to gain breath and formation. No sooner had they deployed than he swung his mass of cavalry out to the right flank, in the customary Macedonian maneuver to the right.

He had with him now the new horse archers, the fine Bactrian and Scythian cavalry. With this wealth of power he experimented brilliantly—feigning to retreat with his Companions while the newer units made a wide circle, to take the lighter Indian cavalry in the rear when it pressed after Alexander. As usual in close combat, he was riding the aged Bucephalus.

And suddenly Bucephalus went down without a wound on him. The day's straining through the mud had overtaxed the old horse, which died under Alexander.

Outmaneuvered, and penned in on two sides by the Macedonian horse, the Indian cavalry, crowding together, resisted savagely. Alexander plunged into this action on a fresh mount, paying no further attention to the phalanx he had left to face the elephants and the gigantic bows (which had the power of small engines).

Obediently the Macedonian phalanx, some six thousand strong, was advancing as it had always done at this turn in the battle, led by Seleucus and Perdiccas, who had been given no plan for dealing with the elephants. And the giant beasts advanced to meet them.

How the phalanx managed to stand its ground is unknown. But it did stand, and hold the elephants. *This action was unlike anything experienced before,* Arrian explains cryptically. *Wherever the elephants rushed, they broke into the phalanx itself of the Macedonians, dense as it was.*

In some way the Macedonian infantry managed to stop the line of elephants and turn it. Perhaps they were able to kill off the mahouts.

By now all the Macedonian cavalry had been collected in one mass, not by any command of Alexander's but being thrown together by the effect of the combat itself. The elephants, being now cooped up with the Paurava horse, injured their own people as much as their enemies in their wheeling and rushing about. For most of them no longer kept place in the battle on account of their suffering or being deprived of their keepers. But even when wearied and unable to charge they backed slowly, facing the foe like ships backing water, only giving out a shrill piping sound. . . . All the elephants which were not killed there were captured.

In this incoherent slaughter Alexander finally made his way around to the infantry and brought them into some kind of a line by an order to lock their shields together.

Then Craterus's forces—having crossed the river at last—appeared on the scene. These fresh troops took up the pursuit of the surviving enemy. Alexander's command was too exhausted to move.

After that day the Macedonian infantry was never the same.

The Paurava king had been almost the last to withdraw, on his war elephant, both man and beast badly wounded. Alexander had noticed him, and sent officers of Rajah Ambhi's command after him to urge him to surrender. This the Indian chieftain refused to do, until one of his own officers brought him a personal message from Alexander. Then he consented to leave his elephant and await Alexander.

The Macedonian came up and dismounted before speaking, struck by the size and bearing of the Paurava. The wounded man was given a drink and stepped forward of his own accord to Alexander.

"In what way do you wish to be treated?" the conqueror asked.

The Paurava seemed indifferent to what was said. "As a king," he replied.

"Yes, but what else do you wish?"

"All else is included in that."

So legend gives the speech between the kings and legend has preserved it in many languages of Asia. Pleased with the encounter, Alexander gave full amnesty to the Pauravas and their subjects. And he ordered two cities to be built by the bloodied sands of the Jhelum, one to be named Nicaea [Victory] and the other Bucephala, because the war horse which had been his companion for seventeen years was buried there.

The crossing of the Jhelum left its mark also upon single-minded Seleucus, who became convinced then and there of the necessity for elephant power. In a very few years, when he had made himself king of western Asia, he collected elephants as assiduously as Ptolemy collected gems and women—willingly bartering a province for a fine herd.

But the scars left upon the Macedonian veterans at the Jhelum could not be eradicated by celebration, by the building of still more cities, or the gift of new treasure.

The army mutinied at the fifth river. This was the Beas, the last of the five rivers of the Punjab.

From the Jhelum to the Beas the Macedonians had mastered thirty-eight hill towns; they had marched through the rains while Alexander still kept stubbornly to the fringe of the mountains of Kashmir. They had had twelve hundred wounded at the storming of the wagon fortress of Sangala. They had passed through the lands of northern India. Neither the Pauravas nor Rajah Ambhi's people knew what lay beyond. Across this last river the Macedonians could see other elephants and the ever-rising wall of the Himalayas. Ahead, the surveyors hinted, stretched the unknown lands of a river called the Ganges, mightier than the Indus or the Nile.

The Macedonian soldiery consulted in groups among the tents at the Beas and agreed to march in only one direction, toward home.

When the officers warned Alexander of the feeling of the men he called the regimental commanders to a meeting. He had broken down insubordination before and had no reason to suppose he could not do it again. If he won over the regimental officers the men would follow, no matter how they grumbled.

"The men see no end to this war," he was told.

"There is no end of labor for a brave man," Alexander responded, "but the end of the labors themselves. Do you fear that our advance will be stopped by other barbarians? If we go back now we will have reason to fear, because these nations held in subjection may be stirred to revolt by those not yet subdued. If any one of you wishes to hear what the end of our warfare will be, we will reach the Ganges in a little distance, and the Eastern Ocean lies only a little beyond."

He outlined the shape of the eastern world as he thought it to be. On reaching Ocean, they could build a fleet and sail back past India, quickly indeed to Egypt, and thence perhaps coast south of Libya [Africa] to the Pillars of Heracles [Gibraltar].

Persuasively he summed up what they had gained by their labors—the Ionian coast, Asia Minor, the Phoenician coast, Egypt, Libya, parts of Arabia, the Syrian plain and the land of the Two Rivers, Babylon, the lands of Susa and Medea, Persia, the land beyond the Caspian Gates, and that of the Scythians as far as the steppes, and now India. They had endured and gained much. They need only endure a little more to make their gains secure.

"We have shared these labors. I have been with you in the suffering. And what we gain will be shared between us equally. You have no cause to lose spirit now. Who would want to go back now to sit in Macedon and beat off the attacks of Illyrian and Thracian tribesmen? If anyone does want to go back he may do so. But I swear to you that I will make those who remain objects of envy to those at home. Have I failed to do so, until now?"

He felt sure of their answer. So sure that he waited confidently, in spite of the officers' silence.

"If anyone does not agree," he said sharply, "let him speak up. You are free to speak your mind."

Coenus, who had been through the thick of the Jhelum battle, answered him—saying that he spoke for the bulk of the army. "And for you, our commander."

Alexander looked up, startled, hearing a murmur of agreement.

"I do not say this to please the men or you," Coenus went on stubbornly. "But the army believes that some end must be put now to its labor and danger, in order to hold what it has won. For this army is being decimated. You can see yourself how few are left of the Macedonians and Greeks who started with us. The rest have died in battle, or become invalided by wounds, or fallen in sickness, or have been left, unwilling, to settle in the cities you founded. Sickness has taken the greater part of us. Inspect the few of the long-service men who are left. They are in bad condition. A worse thing than that, they have lost spirit. You did well to send home the Thessalians, when they were not willing to go on———"

"In the name of the gods," Alexander broke in, "what do you *want?*"

Coenus faced him without moving, rubbing his hand over his head. "What?" he muttered. "Why, some of us ache to see our parents while they still live. Others yearn after their wives and youngsters, I think. Perhaps some of us only yearn to see home again. I can't say." He looked up suddenly. "Alexander, don't lead us now against our will, because we aren't the same as we were. If you would take us all home—then you can start out again, against Scythians or Carthaginians. You'll find plenty of young Greeks and Macedonians at home to follow you out, for reward. And warfare won't have terror for them, because they won't have any experience with it———"

His words ended in a shout of agreement from the listeners. The blunt Coenus had indeed spoken for the army. Alexander left the meeting in anger and secluded himself in his pavilion, seeing nobody except the servants who brought food. He knew by experience that if he did this, leaving the men to argue among themselves, they were apt to change their minds. But this time the soldiers only waited in silence, keeping away from his quarters. He sent one message out to the troops: that he himself was going on, and only those who wished to do so need go with him. The men made no response to this. The army was not prepared to divide itself. It wanted only one thing: to go home, taking Alexander with it.

For three days the test of wills went on. Then Alexander summoned the oldest Macedonian officers into his quarters, and a whisper went through the encampment, from tent to tent. He had called in the veterans, who had most at heart the welfare of the homeland. There is no record of what passed between them and Alexander; but they came out with his consent to take the omens for crossing the river. If the omens were unfavorable the army would turn back.

Officers routed out the aged Aristander, who had long ceased to care whether attention was paid his decisions and now found himself the center of the feverish interest of twenty thousand men. "Of all your auguries," Ptolemy reminded him, "this one should be the least favorable.'

And the liver of the sheep slaughtered showed that disaster would follow the crossing of the Beas. At the announcement masses of men ran to Alexander's tent, leaping and cheering. When they came near the entrance they chanted a prayer of thanksgiving. They thought they were going home, to Macedon. For Alexander ordered twelve pillars to be raised on the bank of the Beas, to mark the turning point of their journey. After that he agreed to return to the Jhelum and the ships, where Hephaestion was building the city of Victory.

XIX. RETURN TO THE WEST

When he turned his back to the east Alexander had given up more than his men realized. He had believed, and could not have thought otherwise, that he was close to the boundary of the habitable world, where the Eastern Ocean lay. No vision of grandeur or of further conquest had brought him this far. He had been following out his journey to the end, to discover the last secrets on earth.

More than that, he was giving up the splendor of his imagined world where stretched the heights of Parnassus, inhabited perhaps by beings who were above the beasts, who partook of the divine. He was putting an end to the years of dreaming over his books. What lay behind him he knew; what existed beyond the river he would never know now. All his tenacity and all the force of his tremendous will had been bound up in the quest to go himself as far as the last mystery. (He could never have reached the Pacific, which lay in reality much farther east than anyone of his time imagined; it was something of a miracle that he had got as far as the Beas—the legions of Rome did not penetrate within eighteen hundred miles of that point, and not for two thousand years would westerners voyage again in strength into northern India.)

For more than eight years he had been pushing toward the east, and the abandonment of his march brought about an almost physical change in him. Something of joyous confidence went out of him, to be replaced by moodiness and a concern for little things. He seemed anxious now to put his house in order.

Perhaps he felt a sense of betrayal; certainly he

314

drove the army that he had nursed eastward back the harder way, when fresh routes could be explored. Once he said that he would not force any Macedonian to follow him against his will. But he went himself where few Macedonians would have chosen to go.

Before the start down-river Coenus died of a fever and was buried in the new Nicaea, which had been damaged by the rains.

Rapidly Alexander provided for the government in northern India, leaving it in the hands of the native princes, except that Macedonian officers administered the towns west of the Indus. After settling invalids and not too willing volunteers in the new cities and dismissing the native troops with gifts, Alexander made the start down the Jhelum, toward the Indus and the southern sea.

From the prow of his ship he poured out of a golden goblet libations to Heracles, to Ammon, and to the other gods, and then he had the signal to start seaward given by a trumpet. After this signal, the ships forged ahead in order so as not to foul each other. Such a noise of rowing was never heard before; with it sounded the shouting of the boatswains who called the beat, and the chant of the rowers who kept the time. The banks of the river, being higher than the ships, and narrow, echoed the sounds; and the Indians who had submitted to Alexander became astonished at this, running along the high banks and singing also, because they were fond of singing.

This mood of feverish rejoicing did not last until the juncture with the Indus was reached. First the ships encountered rapids that did little harm to the potbellied cargo craft (hastily constructed by Nearchus and his Phoenician, Cypriote, and Egyptian shipwrights) but swamped some of the long, low galleys. Then Alexander scattered the army, to overrun the central plain of India.

He had divided it carefully to march with the wagon train on either side the Jhelum—keeping Hephaestion's command on one bank and Craterus's on the other, so his two lieutenants would have no cause to quarrel again. Now he sent out contingents to sweep the country, driving the warlike inhabitants back against the main forces along the river. They had reached the country of the *Malli* [Mahlova, or Aratta] near the edge of the great Thar Desert.

These were the bravest of the people, Arrian relates grimly, *so few of them surrendered.*

This unexpected resistance, in town after town, embittered the war-weary Macedonians. Their anger at the new hardships and delay hardened them to any suffering but their own. They drove the Mallians, hunted them through villages, out into the desert, killed them quickly in order to be finished with the task. For the first time the journals speak of massacres of all living humans within walls.

At this point it seemed to be an obsession with Alexander to leave no organized resistance behind him. Often he had to lead the troops himself to get them to attack. And one mishap to him sent a wave of fear through the army.

They had been trying to enter a citadel when Alexander, impatient with the delay, had a ladder raised to the wall and went up it himself, followed by Peucestas, and the bodyguard who carried the shield of Troy, and another front-line fighter. The four were atop the wall and under fire from surrounding towers when a press of soldiers tried to follow up the ladder, which broke with them.

Alexander, unwilling to remain a mark for missiles, jumped down inside the wall, the other three leaping after him. They backed against the wall, covered by their shields and were attacked by the defenders in a body—until the soldier was killed and Alexander hard hit by an arrow that entered his lung. When he collapsed Peucestas and the bodyguard, both wounded, covered him with their shields until the other Macedonians got over the wall and through the gate.

When Alexander was carried out, with air bubbling

316

from the wound in his body, the rumor spread that he had been killed.

At first, in the camp from which he had set out, the men raised a mighty grieving. Then they fell spiritless, bewildered in wondering who could become leader of the army now and how they were to get back to their own country, since the warlike nations around them would revolt as soon as they were freed of the dread of Alexander. Then, too, they were in the midst of strange rivers, and it did not seem possible to make a plan without Alexander.

When the word came to them that Alexander still lived they doubted it, even when a letter confirmed it. They feared among themselves that the letter had been made up by the bodyguards and generals.

When Alexander was in a condition to understand this, he thought the army might rebel. He had himself carried down to the river and put on a boat. Opposite the encampments he ordered the pavilion under which he lay to be raised so that the men along the banks could see him. Even then they doubted lest he be dead, until he lifted his hand to them.

At this indisputable proof that Alexander was alive, the men on shore marched along beside the ship, weaving flowers into garlands and throwing them out on the water, toward him.

When the vessel came in to land, Alexander ordered a horse brought down to it. In spite of the objection of his officers, he mounted the horse by a supreme effort. Mounted, he rode slowly to the tent prepared for him.

Nearchus, who was building more ships during the delay while Alexander lay critically weak, censured him sharply. "You are like a man mastered by drink—you can't hold back from throwing yourself into the danger of combat. You have no reason to risk yourself like a front-line soldier."

Alexander resented this criticism, and an old Macedonian who noticed his irritation answered in his native dialect that heroes had to pay the price of great

317

deeds in suffering. And Alexander was to pay a great price for the wound in his lung.

For a long time he lay without strength, keeping to the galley as it moved down the Indus. He was content to receive pledges of loyalty from the chieftains and princes along the river. At this point he seemed to be trying to build up alliances with the native rulers. After agreeing to return to the west, and particularly after his severe wound in the lungs, he lost interest in providing for the future government of India. But he showed increasing interest in the Indus as a water route. For the first time he was opening up a road by water.

When halts were made, the engineers dug wells and drainage channels, and built more shipyards at river junctions. Greek sculptors studied the Indian architecture and left specimens of their own handiwork behind them.

Their fine modeling of the human face and figure—even to the folds of the vestments—was imitated by Indian artists in succeeding generations, and by degrees shaped a style for the later Buddhist statuary that spread through central Asia and as far east as Angkor.

At the same time the scientists of the expedition were learning about new foods, sugar, saffron, rice; astronomers matched their observations with the Indian watchers of the stars. Physicians on both sides learned different methods of treating fever and plague.

Very gradually a change had taken place in the thought process of the younger westerners. They saw themselves, as it were, in perspective now. They talked less of Heracles and Dionysos—in fact it had become something of a joke to say that Heracles had been doing this sort of thing before them. Certainly that stalwart Argonaut had never ridden an elephant, nor had the good ship *Argos* ever set her prow into the greater seas. Evidently these heroes of antiquity had been no more than the patriarchs of folk memory, armed with clubs and swords, disporting themselves upon their own native shores.

As for that affluent monarch, Midas, they had by-passed his kingdom years ago, and his celebrated gold reserve seemed to be a small-change affair compared to the huge treasury now guarded by Harpalus at Ecbatana. And Artemis, that independent huntress of the Ephesians—was she not the weaker sister of the dreaded Lady of the Beasts who rode the night sky when doom impended?

As they floated down the Indus, now miles in width, they made sacrifice to the god of the river, to Ammon-Re, and to Ahura, the divinity of the sun. The water and the sun, and the desert, waterless and burned by the sun's heat, had been ever-present for years. The younger Macedonians had dealt with these natural powers. The Greeks had not seen the gilded statue of Athena for a long time; it seemed absurd, in the vastness of Asia with its teeming peoples, to remember that big stone woman of marble holding a spear above the stairway of the Parthenon. The living women who followed these men of Greece knew nothing about Athena.

Drifting down the Indus, watching the desert change to jungle, seeing vultures and pigeons pass across the sky as he lay on his cot, Alexander could hardly conceive of Zeus the God-Father as creator of this land and people. Ammon-Re of the Egyptian desert, Marduk of the towers of Babylon, and Ahura, tutelary of the tombs of Persepolis, belonged here, in the thoughts of the people. Out of these eastern deserts, out of everlasting fire and the sun's warmth, had come the mightiest of deities, whose sons, earth-bound, had been sacrificed yet had not died. Among them these gods of Asia shared the symbol of the eagle's wings, the pinions that could rise above the earth's surface to the empyrean.

Alexander had not found his Parnassus, nor had he come upon a visible sign of the invisible Mover of life. Yet in this journey he had set in motion something of which he could not have been aware. Before his coming the religions had been isolated. The shrines

319

of Zeus had extended no farther than the Greek colonies; the temples of Ammon-Re lay apart in the valley of the Nile; the fire altars of Ahura had rested isolated on the hilltops in the land of Kurush.

The incoming of the Macedonians had thrown these religions into juxtaposition, breaking down the isolation of temples and monasteries. As the boundaries of the nations had been broken, the thought barriers of the religions had been severed. Thought itself had not changed, but it had broadened to take in new concepts. The older concepts of the west had been derived, through almost forgotten channels, from the east; now western minds were in direct contact with the east, and thought itself had become to that extent world-wide.

On the vessels bound down the Indus there were fewer Greek philosophers—after the affair of Callisthenes—than before. There were mathematicians from Thebes, astronomers of Babylon, Magians, and now Indian ascetics.

At least one of these ascetics, Kalynas (as the Macedonians named him), had offered to go on with Alexander. Kalynas was an old man who appeared to have no possessions except a mat and food bowl. He would sit on the mat, waiting for food to be put in the bowl, when he desired to eat, which was not often. Otherwise he preferred to be left alone, although he would speak with Alexander, when the king came to him. At such times he had very little to say in praise of the Macedonians.

"You have taken much and destroyed much," he said. "Look at what you wear on your backs and be fearful for yourselves. It is not by such arms and wealth or captive beasts that you will live henceforth."

It seemed to the Macedonians that this Kalynas—this counselor—was an oracle of ill omen, a wizened Cassandra. True, he thought that he spoke from *bodhi*—illumination—and he said incredibly that men could pass through rebirth, back to life after death. The shades of the dead, he affirmed, did not linger in that shadowy mid-region between death and life.

"Why have you come with us?" Alexander asked him.

"Why have you come hither?" And he added fretfully, "You should have stayed in the center of your empire, and not gone robbing around its limits."

Kalynas fancied, then, that even Alexander of Macedon had not moved at his own will. The Greek philosophers pointed out that this was no more than the doctine of inexorable fate; yet it seemed to Alexander that Kalynas did not fear fate. The army in general accepted the Indian ascetic as a kind of talking mummy, a skeleton in their midst. But in the end Kalynas made them wonder.

The meeting with Ocean came before they expected it and gave even the journey-hardened Macedonians a taste of a new terror. They had lingered at the head of the delta of the Indus where the river branched to the sea, while Hephaestion started work on a permanent naval base at Patala [later Hyderabad]. Alexander, recuperating now, took some of the larger galleys to explore one of the branches. Apparently the bare delta lands were peopled only by barbaric tribes, and the fleet had neither experienced pilots nor warning of what was to come. Onesicritus, pilot in chief (who called himself Admiral of the Fleet in his journal), certainly had not anticipated the rush of the tidal bore, which nearly swamped the ships as they neared the river mouth.

It seemed to the westerners as if a giant wave had rushed at them, impelled by no natural agency. When they anchored the vessels to investigate the phenomenon the tide ebbed in due time, leaving their craft stranded in the mud.

Before the Macedonians could adjust themselves to this new situation—they had had no experience with tides in the Mediterranean—the tide flowed in, driving the anchored vessels violently inland against the higher shore. This appeared to be a manifestation of the anger of Ocean, until they learned from captured natives that

321

these tides moved ceaselessly without regard to human beings. Still, they observed fish at the river mouth larger in size than any they had known before.

When they sighted the blue-green of Ocean itself, pulsing with a slow swell, those versed in sea lore expected to meet with fetid water and the monsters of the encircling deep.

Nevertheless Alexander pushed far out upon the sea in his galley, perhaps to be able to say that he had sailed upon it, or perhaps to observe the coastline. In so doing he encountered only a fresh breeze and a clear sky, signs of benevolence. And he made sacrifice both to the tutelary spirit of Ocean and to Ammon-Re, flinging the gold vessels and bowl into the water as he did so, to insure success for the voyage of his fleet.

Before then he had determined to explore this unknown coast by sea, on the way back to Persepolis.

It was natural enough. He had arrived at Ocean in the south. No seamen of India could tell him what lay west of there, except that Arab ships had appeared from time to time at the Indus mouth, bringing the spice and ivory and pearls of Arabia. Evidently somewhere to the west the twin Tigris and Euphrates emptied into this sea. Beyond, apparently, stretched Arabia. And beyond that must lie the red coast of Egypt.

His fleet, then, would proceed along the coast, examining it as far as the mouth of the Tigris. But by all accounts this coast was desert. The Macedonian galleys could not carry water or food sufficient for more than three days; moreover if the fragile fleet were wrecked by a storm the surviving crews would be stranded on the barren coast.

The Macedonians had never ventured to sea before, and to the natural terrors of the voyage on blue water was added the suspense of navigating an unknown coast. Alexander had set his heart on the voyage. He *would* make certain of the shape of the habitable earth here at its southern edge. And he asked Nearchus the Cretan to name someone to take command of the ships.

Nearchus pondered the question. "There are others who know more about ships, and others who are more experienced leaders," he said. "But I would like well to command the fleet myself." Alexander, reluctant to part with Nearchus, finally agreed. "There is no one I trust so much as you, to accomplish what is hard to do."

It was a good choice, to send the unimaginative Cretan out to face the sea peopled with all the terrors of Greek imagination. Alexander had ceased to rely on the braggart Onesicritus.

And he had worked out a practical plan for the expedition. To supply the fleet along the desert coast the army must march beside it, inland. Since the heterogeneous host now following him could not be expected to get itself across an immense desert, Alexander sent Craterus with the main body, the wagon train, and the officers' families, to circle far back along easy roads to their old line of march by the Helmand lakes, which he should strike somewhere in the hills south of Bactria [Afghanistan]. Craterus could take his time, plant crops if necessary, and graze herds along the way, and rejoin the other two expeditions south of the Persian plateau. Actually Craterus wandered over much of the map, but he did escape the desert and he did effect a rendezvous.)

The column that was to strike along the coast, across the desert of Gedrosia [the Mekran], Alexander limited to twelve to fourteen thousand picked troops, including the ubiquitous Agrianians and valuable horse archers, as well as his own guards. Because he intended to lead the desert march himself.

It is hardly true that Alexander tried to cross the Mekran because he had heard that only the legendary Semiramis had been able to do so; nor did he plan it primarily as a punishment for the army that had mutinied. He had made up his mind to send the fleet on its mission, and he was prepared to march an army column across the desert to aid it. He seems to have learned something about the danger of the Mekran, but not enough.

"All the hardships of Asia, through which we had passed before," one soldier related, "were not equal to this."

Alexander had guides, and a wagon train with supplies. However, when the winds turned favorable for the ships after the setting of the Pleiades (November 325) and he marched away from the new port of Patala, he found that the inevitable following of women and newborn children, soothsayers, peddlers, and adventurers had swollen his column to unwieldy size. On this occasion he seems to have made no attempt to weed out the civilians.

Within a month they were all in trouble. Barbarian tribes raided them, and the scattered villages they entered contained no store of food. They managed to dig a few wells along the shore and leave several depots of corn and dried meat for Nearchus's seamen, as planned. They even founded another Alexandria at a river mouth. But the camp followers helped eat their reserve of food, and—although it was the season after the rains here—they entered an arid region, without grazing.

The gray waste of the Mekran, without road or city, was fragrant with unseen incense.

They beheld myrrh trees growing, and Phoenicians who had come along for trafficking gathered in sweet-smelling roots of nard. When this root was trampled by the passing ranks, a fragrant odor filled the air. Trees like the bay tree were in bloom with a flower like a huge white violet. A stalk grew out of the earth with thorns so strong that the thorns catching in the clothing of a rider would pull him from his horse.

From this baked plain the column entered sand dunes as difficult to climb as—the soldiers said—mounds of mud. And they found that marches had to be made at night to escape the heat of day. On such marches they could only hope that the morning would bring them to a supply of water.

324

Under this stress the silent antagonism of the army took shape once more against Alexander's driving. When he found that detachments sent down to the coast with jars of corn for the fleet were making off with the corn themselves, Alexander sealed the jars with his own seal; but still the men broke into them. They broke up the transport wagons at night, explaining that they had given way. Then the men ate the supplies in the wagons, using the wood for cooking fires. Later they ate the flesh of the transport animals. By doing so they deprived themselves of food and transport.

Alexander knew this but took no official notice of it. The desert march had become a test of will between the commander who would not turn back and the men who tried to force him to turn back.

He had failed to keep up the supply depots along the coast, and he had no tidings from Nearchus. Craterus was hundreds of miles distant by then, in the fertile northern region. Alexander kept stubbornly to the coast, until forced to turn inland by a mountain range that he had not known existed.

When they camped in a ravine hemmed in by bare slopes an unexpected storm, breaking over the hills, flooded the ravine, drowning most of the women and followers and washing away the remainder of the baggage. Most of the soldiers got safely to the slopes with their weapons; but some of these died the next day from drinking quantities of the muddied water after their long thirst. The sick could not be given transport because the bulk of the wagons had been lost.

So many were left behind along the track, being sick or worn out, or overcome by heat or thirst. There was no one to stay behind and tend them, because the column had to go on, regardless of the individuals who fell behind. Since they usually marched at night, many of them were overcome by sleep, and tried to follow the tracks when they waked, like ships getting out of their course at sea.

By now the guides had lost the way; they were out

of touch with the sea, and it would be useless to turn back to India. The officers took their bearings at night from the Great Bear. In this manner they could keep direction, but they could not know in which direction to head.

Alexander decided to keep to the left, to search for the coast. He worried constantly about the fleet. During the crossing of the Mekran he marched on foot with the men, drinking and eating no more than they did.

When they sighted the sea again they were able to dig shallow wells close to the shore. And he kept the camp, under guard, at a distance from the wells so that the men, half mad with thirst, could not drink themselves to death or churn the water into mud. Once on the coast, they were able to orient themselves. It was impossible to follow the sea further, and they struck inland to the city of Pura, where they found corn and meat and dates. Thence they were able to reach the rendezvous city in southern Persia, Gulaskird.

Legend relates that they entered the city waving garlands and drinking, as they reclined in wagons, in honor of Dionysos, the god who had shown them the way. What actually happened was that the army came in scarred and weakened, and feasted drunkenly on the wine they discovered in the city. Alexander got drunk with the rest.

But Craterus came in, impassive as always, with the elephant train and main body. They all waited in this fashion at the rendezvous, giving up hope of seeing Nearchus and the fleet again. Where the army had got through only by bare chance, they believed the fleet, without adequate supplies or depots, could not have survived. The loss of the fleet affected Alexander and he refused to leave Gulaskird. Months passed.

Once a rumor reached the Macedonians that the fleet had been sighted, but no one could be found who had actually seen the ships. The first tidings Alexander had of the fate of his vessels was when two chariots drove in to his quarters, bringing a half-dozen men.

The drivers of the chariots reported that they had picked up the strangers wandering on the road and had brought them in because they spoke Greek and asked for Alexander. The five wanderers were thin as skeletons, stained with brine, with matted hair covering their faces. They had only a remnant of clothing.

"We were looking for Nearchus and the fleet," said the chariot drivers, "and they said they were looking for Alexander, so here they are."

"Here," muttered one of the skeletons, "I am Nearchus, and I will give you an account of the fleet."

He pointed to the man beside him. "This is Archias."

It was a moment before Alexander believed them. Then he stepped aside and spoke with an effort. "I am grateful that you five survived, Nearchus. What happened to the ships and the others?"

"What happened?" Nearchus tried to understand. "Why, all the ships and crews are waiting down at the river, where we are making repairs. We couldn't find you."

That night Alexander sacrificed to all the gods and paraded the army by torchlight, with Nearchus garlanded in the lead, and flower girls dancing around him. They marched to flutes and the sound of laughter.

Alexander did not sleep that night until he had heard Nearchus's tale of the passage along the southern sea. Since the Cretan was no talker, the king had to question him about everything. And Nearchus answered the questions easily, because he had kept a daily record of stadia covered, the stars observed at full dark, and the length of the shadow at noon. Also he had noted down all promontories, islands, and harbors. . . .

Such details he gave readily. He had been ordered to make a survey of the coast and he had done so, as he hoped.

Had he found any food depots at all? He had found one, left by Alexander near the starting point, with ample corn and bread.

How had the men behaved—they who had never been at sea before? Well, those who became too terrified Nearchus had put ashore at that depot. After that, when he became afraid himself of the men deserting, he had kept the ships anchored well offshore until the crews were so weak from hunger that they thought of nothing but food.

How had he managed all those weeks, without food reserves? After the last of their corn was eaten they made trips inland and found some bread, dates, and fruit in villages of the hairy *Gedrosians*, and they carried off this food—not without fighting. After that along the coast of the Fish Eaters, which stretched for 1176 miles, they found that the savages made a kind of meal out of dried fish. To this fare they added sea mice, mussels, crabs, and oysters. They caught some fish in the pools left when the tide went out, and later on they ate a kind of cabbage which grew in the tops of palm trees. As for water, they often did not have any. But when they could not dig wells along the shore they explored inland and usually found water.

What dangers had they passed through? The hardest thing had been to repair the damaged ships, without good timber. Then, too, they had encountered the island of the Nereid. Natives on Nearchus's ship had sworn that the island was ruled by a Nereid who had such a disease that she enmeshed every human man who landed there in her arms and knew him physically and by so doing turned him into a fish, which she threw into the sea. When they passed the island of the Nereid one vessel had been missing, and Onesicritus, the pilot, the man of Astypalaea, had thought that the missing ship must have landed there and its crew had suffered a sea change from the arts of the Nereid. Nearchus, however, had taken a small boat and gone ashore on the island and searched it thoroughly, without finding a trace of the Nereid. Later the missing ship turned up.

Also, Nearchus related, they had encountered a fleet of leviathans—monsters of the sea. "At daybreak we saw the water of the sea blown violently upward in many places, as if by the action of bellows. But it was done by many monsters rushing under the surface of the water. This so startled the seamen that they began to let the oars drop from their hands. I went down among the rowers to encourage them, and took my ship past the others, ordering each to form in line as if for battle—to row together in time and raise a shout with the oar stroke. We went straight for the monsters, which were black and large in size as twelve-oared galleys. When we neared them we raised a loud shout and sounded trumpets, and so drove the monsters down under the surface. They vanished and did not come up again until they were behind us."

It was the Macedonians' first experience with whales. Later on they found houses of the Fish Eaters built out of the giant whalebones.

Just before landing to search for Alexander the fleet had sighted a promontory, rising out of the sea to the southwest. Onesicritus had wanted to cross over to it and land there, but Nearchus had decided it was desert and must be a headland of Arabia (it was actually Ras Masandam at the entrance to the Persian Gulf). So Nearchus judged that they had reached the end of the open sea and that a gulf lay ahead of them, extending on to the Tigris's mouth.

When Alexander wanted to relieve him of his command so that he could rest and recuperate, Nearchus begged to be allowed to take his fleet on to the Tigris, and the king granted his wish. And he gave his first admiral a chaplet of gold to wear in token of his victory over the sea.

This reported glimpse of the Arabian mainland fitted into the mental picture of the world shape which Alexander and the geographers were piecing together. (For the first and only time since crossing to Troy, his surveyors had failed to keep up their daily check of distances and direction during the terrible crossing of the Mekran. But the column had managed to keep itself fairly well oriented.)

He determined immediately—now that Nearchus had proved that a fleet could survive along these shores—to explore the perimeter of Arabia, to find a route by sea on to the coast of Ethiopia, whence he might reach the Nile or its headwaters. Beyond Ethiopia lay Libya [Africa], which had never, to his knowledge, been circumnavigated. If his ships could penetrate thither they would link up the far west to the east as far as the Indus mouth, and the shape of the southern Oikoumene would be established. Except for Nearchus's single encounter with sea monsters, there seemed to be no supernatural powers guarding this frontier of outer Ocean.

What were his plans, Arrian relates here, *I can only conjecture, but I can say with confidence that he planned nothing small or mean, for he would have gone on seeking for some unknown land, beyond those that he had mastered.*

His scheme of exploration had to be put aside. He had been away too long from the heart of his Eurasia. Twice in the last four years the report of his death had been carried west along the post and caravan routes. His reappearance in the hills near Persepolis with an army of many nations had been a surprise to most of the governors he had left behind him.

XX. CORROSION OF WEALTH

Under the circumstances what happened should have been no surprise to Alexander. Since leaving Ecbatana four years before, he had been out of personal touch with his government, which in any case he had thrown together most hurriedly.

Inevitably, much had gone wrong. Macedonians left in power had tried to increase that power. And, naturally, exact information as to the extent of the damage was slow in reaching the monarch's headquarters. Perhaps at first he tried to deceive himself as to the magnitude of the task of organization that faced him at Persepolis. Only the evidence of anxious Persians made it clear to him.

European military governors had failed to co-operate with Asiatic viceroys, in many cases and had started to amass their own treasury funds—something Alexander had tried to prevent. In Persia itself temples had been pillaged and native chieftains executed. Alexander appointed Peucestas—who had held a shield over him when he was cut down in India—satrap of Persia.

Elsewhere he punished savagely, hanging officers and officials, when guilty.

He was astonished at the multitude that came to besiege the royal stairway of Persepolis, where the columns of the ruined Hall of Xerxes towered like obelisks. This multitude pressed in from far places, bringing news, petitions, charges, and appeals from judgment. They brought from Ararat and Troy and Babylon the unfinished business of four years for him to attend to. For Alexander was the one supreme administrator and judge who could overrule other decisions, and the rigid purge of his European officers had given the Asiatics courage to appeal to this Great King.

They gave him a startling concept of the changes wrought in those four sweeping years. Scholars had graduated from the new academy in Alexandria-in-Egypt. Merchants in Alexandria-in-Laodicea complained that the Egyptian shipmasters banded together to prevent grain ships of the Euxine from landing there. (And the king had to think back, to recall that this particular Alexandria had been built within a march of the battlefield of Issus.) On their part, the following day, Egyptian dealers urged him to grant them a tariff to protect the price of grain in Memphis. They argued that the markets of Egypt had been secluded before his coming, but now, owing to the increased traffic through Alexandria, foreign grain was being imported by Athenian and Carthaginian convoys.

It seemed to the man now seated on the throne of Darius that, in spite of his effort to eliminate old frontiers, new blocs and centers were forming, struggling to protect their wealth. Within these growing mercantile centers individuals were scheming to secure their own gain.

It seemed as if a human tide was setting in, from Europe and the west, a flood of traders, adventurers, barbers, impoverished farmers, ex-soldiers, moving toward the new settlements in the east.

By penetrating Bactria and Soghd and India he had linked up the continental caravan routes with the coastal terminals; in consequence Sidon was loaded with luxury goods; caravan junctions like Petra, built upon red stone cliffs, levied new tolls to tap this current of wealth. They told him that the Nabateans had enlarged Petra, but he could not remember who the Nabateans were. Arabs, perhaps. The high priest of a city called Jerusalem sent to request his protection, saying that Kurush, the Great King before him, had granted that protection.

"Protection!" Alexander cried. "If there is peace,

have you not protection—all of you? Has there been a war or even a raid in seven years? You are protected."

Ionian slave dealers, who imported children from Delos and Lesbos, complained that the new minting of gold staters had reduced the value of the Athenian silver owls, in which they had taken payment for such slaves. Of course Alexander himself had fixed an exchange rate, but people—common folk—preferred gold to silver. Women, too, liked to bank money and have ornaments at the same time, by stringing the fine new gold coins into necklaces, instead of the silver ankle bangles of the old days. So slave traders had lost money by accepting silver.

Alexander had to force himself to sit in audience most of the day and go over petitions and accounts at night. The papers arrived in a babel of scripts, and even some odd stamped clay tablets. He had to work now with a staff of interpreters.

Greek, he came to understand, could be no more than the language of political intercourse; otherwise these people meant to keep their own speech. Their petitions came to him in Aramaic, Hebrew, Arabic, and Hittite. He wondered if they were actually mingling their trade and their schooling—or were growing together, in the throes of this meeting of east and west. Were they sharing ideas or fusing their ambitions?

He thought of moving masses of Asiatics into the Mediterranean, to quicken this process of cohesion, to balance the heavy immigration from the west.

In one record of payments Alexander noticed that a daily charge for one sheep, and flour and wine, to be supplied to the Magi who kept watch at the tomb of Kurush, had been stopped during his absence.

"Why?" he asked the secretaries.

The secretaries did not know. Hurriedly they sent for food accountants, who in turn found a courier who explained that the Magi in question were no longer given the food because they were not at their post in the watchhouse by the tomb. Why? The courier thought they were in prison now, and fed on prison fare.

"Well, what men *are* at the tomb?"

"Lord, there is no one. So the sheep—"

"I'm not thinking about the sheep. *Why were the guards taken from the tomb?*"

The courier did not know. When Alexander burst out at him in a rage, a revenue officer explained, fearfully. The tomb of the first Persian king had been brogen into and robbed of everything except a few strings of beads and purple- and hyacinth-colored cloaks, of no great value. So after the tomb had been robbed the Magi had been imprisoned.

Holding in his anger, Alexander left them and took a horse from the stables. He noticed it was a white charger, of the Nisaean herd. (Most of that famous horse herd he had discovered to be missing on his return.) Riding alone—although a troop of mounted Agema followed at a discreet distance—he climbed the hill road to Pasargadae, dismounting at daybreak by the stream where the great limestone sarcophagus of Kurush stood, exposed to the weather.

Climbing the pedestal steps, he saw that the aperture at one end had been broken through and was now blocked up by an empty keg. The coffin of hammered gold and the gifts laid on it had vanished, with what was left of the body of Kurush.

Running his hand along the side slab, Alexander felt under his fingers the lettering that he knew by heart. *O man, who passes by, I am Kurush who founded the empire of the Persians and formed the kingdom of Asia. So, do not begrudge me this resting place.*

The thieves had begrudged Kurush his tomb, because of the gold in it. Alexander did not think that the Magi had broken into the tomb they had guarded for centuries. A Macedonian had done it. Without a cloak he sat on the marble step, pondering, watching the hard gleam of the sun come over the bare hills, striking through the branches of the trees. He remembered that the trees had no leaves because it was winter.

Then he was aware of the old men. They stood waiting, just beneath him, wrapped in white garments bound with sashes the color of blood. They seemed to be awaiting permission to speak, and Alexander, recognizing them as Magi different from the watchers of the tomb, said to them, "Speak."

Then these three Magi spoke what was in their minds.

"O man, now that you are here, it is clear that you are and must be the successor to him who is gone. From the Niakan ancestors the succession descends, from king to king. But at times it descends upon no one, for it is the Hvareno, which is a Glory. And it cannot descend upon one unworthy. It cannot be seized by force. When it comes, it cannot be hid. Many kings the Glory has passed by, and their names will be forgotten. From Kurush it has come to you. But never ask whence the Glory cometh."

Alexander sat there, looking down into the aged, lined faces that made no salutation to him. When they had spoken they motioned to him to come down from his step. When he did so they sat around him on the cold ground and held out their hands. Their hands held figs wrapped in leaves, terebinth covered with linen, and sour milk in a silver cup.

This food, the Magi said, was for him, to break his fast. They shared it with him when he sat down by them. At the end of the unusual breakfast they brought him water from the stream to bathe his hands. It was very cold.

"He who is chosen the people's king," they said then, "can choose little for himself thereafter."

This time they bent their heads to him before going away, walking across the shafts of sunlight, not looking at the armed men of the Agema, who eyed them curiously. The soldiers thought it was a poor breakfast the beggars had brought to the king.

Alexander had eaten because the old men wanted him to. He wondered if they had been watching over the empty tomb, and he felt bewildered because he could not remember what language they had used. It had all seemed familiar, perhaps because he had watched himself at the sarcophagus of Kurush years before, perhaps because he had felt weak and confused like this when he drifted, wounded, down the Indus. Or was it when he strained to climb over the snow fields to the height of Indra? Or searched for the sea, in the passage of the desert?

Then he had been trying to find something that escaped him. And he wondered if he had found it here. He did not know, and his brain was too wearied to think about it. He wanted to sleep.

It was the hour when he usually drank himself into stupor, but he had no wine at the tomb. When he felt drowsy he stretched out on the steps, edging himself to the sunny side, and slept with his arm over his eyes.

He remembered the coming of the Magi, and thought of it again when Kalynas approached him, grumbling, soon after. "Yavana," said the ascetic, "you have troubled much of the earth, but you own no more of it than that which will cover your body when you die."

This was Kalynas's way of saying farewell. Because he announced that he was not well, and, being far from his land, he had no wish to go on living. He wanted to be burned.

At first Alexander did not believe him. But the ascetic was determined to lie upon a funeral pyre and burn. In the end Alexander gave orders to carry out his wish, and presented him with a fine horse and gold vessels for sacrifice with him.

Of these, however, Kalyna did not approve. He gave away the horse and gold objects to the Macedonians who crowded to see him burn. To their amazement, the fragile man lay motionless on the piled wood while the fire spread around him.

Alexander, watching, ordered the trumpets to sound and the elephants to give their roaring salute, because he thought that the Indian must be a very brave man.

The army felt as if it had lost a talisman and wished that Kalynas had not decided to burn himself.

The near chaos in the east had spread to the west. Hearing of Alexander's return and the punishment of other officials, Harpalus, the semi-invalid, whom Alexander had entrusted with the public treasure, fled from Babylon and Sardis. It appeared that he had built up a fortune for himself and with it bought a following of mercenaries. So with gold and a miniature army he sailed to Greece, landing at the port of Athens.

Harpalus—who had absconded for the second time—argued for a patriotic rebellion, overthrow of the Macedonian yoke by Athens, and a restoration of Athenian glory. The more hotheaded politicians fell in with him, and he bought others. But he could neither buy nor persuade Demosthenes, whom he needed most to inspire a rebellion.

Demosthenes, instead, spoke against Harpalus. "War with Alexander would be madness. It could only be the ruin of Athens."

Escaping from the city, Alexander's revenue collector sought greater safety elsewhere. But Demosthenes was accused of taking gold from him, when the funds Harpalus had abandoned in the Parthenon proved to be only half the amount expected. And Demosthenes was condemned by the war party for balking their plans, and by the Macedonian party for taking the stolen gold.

It was typical of the volatile Athenians that they should charge the one man of integrity among them of accepting a bribe. Had Demosthenes, at long last, changed his opinion of Alexander? Had Alexander ceased to dread the power of Demosthenes's oratory? Certainly the two who had been antagonists at Chaeronea shared the hope of peace under the Macedonian commonwealth.

The disturbance in Greece, the wrangle over Harpalus and his stolen treasure, and the quarreling of factions in Macedon caused Alexander to send Craterus, his ablest administrator, to replace Antipater. That aged general had carried out orders faithfully, but rather naturally he looked on the Greeks as rebels

337

against military authority, and Alexander felt the need of a younger man who could give orders at home—especially as his mother, Olympias, was forming a faction of her own. Besides, Craterus was weakened by fever, and Alexander feared for the life of his most brilliant lieutenant.

After Antipater's removal his son Cassander made the journey out to the east to protest to Alexander. "Those who accuse my father have framed charges against him from a great distance."

He phrased this carefully, making no mention of Alexander. Instantly the king caught the note of caution. "That sounds like one of Aristotle's sophisms," he sneered. "If you and your father are guilty you will be punished. I do not know, yet, if you are guilty."

The violence of this sunburned, emaciated man who moved painfully when he walked, who remained silent unless words poured out of him, affected Cassander strongly. He felt that this new Alexander no longer trusted his friends or placed hope in the gods to which he had sacrificed formerly. Cassander had not seen Alexander, or the surviving veterans, for ten years and he was not prepared for the change in them. Men said that he became so terrified that after Alexander's death he could not pass a statue of the king without trembling.

Before then Alexander had left the sanctuary of Persepolis, to journey over the ranges to Susa, where he could maintain closer contact with the west. The impact of his return was felt from the Danube to the Nile. And the incredible story of the Macedonian conquest was told in Memphis and Athens and Pella. Greek scholars found it difficult to grasp the entirety of such accomplishment. They heard the tale of seventy cities founded, of caravan trade arriving from twenty thousand stadia, of the navigation of the southern sea. This enlarged world perspective fascinated and disturbed them. It revealed resources that dwarfed the means of the Greek cities, and populations that reduced the

338

Greeks to a minority, at the western edge of the Oikoumene.

Wherever Alexander moved now the government moved with him. He was drawn, by the need of administration, toward the center of his dominion, as Kalynas had once suggested.

But what this government was to be remained uncertain. Contemporary records give no indication of Alexander's plan for the future. Some observers like Ptolemy seemed to think that Alexander had no plan. Certainly he announced none. As Aristotle had rejected the ideal city of Plato's *Republic,* Alexander appeared to have rejected Aristotle's reasoned concept of an educated oligarchy. For one thing, his dominion was so vast that no one city or privileged group could have controlled it.

Although Rushanak was pregnant now, Alexander made no public arrangement for a son who might succeed him. In fact he seemed to waste no thought at all on his close kinsmen in Macedon—or how they might act toward the child of an Asiatic woman.

It is said at this point that he was trying to restore the bounds of the Iranian Empire; and undoubtedly he was greatly influenced by the rule of Kurush and the peace that came out of it. But he said himself that the Macedonians had gone beyond the Persian rule. He hardly looked upon himself as a benevolent monarch, because he seemed to have the sense of a mission to be fulfilled. To the army he spoke of the new imperium as the Macedonian commonwealth.

The list of his titles that Ptolemy still kept out of curiosity had grown in strange fashion.

"Alexander, third of that name, king of the Macedonians, semidivine limited monarch of the Greek cities, wholly divine Pharaoh of Egypt, ally and master of the Ionian ports, full master of the Phoenician cities and fleets, protector of the high priest of Judea, overlord of the Magians of Persia, friend of the rajahs of the Punjab, and something unknown in the rest of India."

It was clear to Ptolemy that Alexander cared nothing for the titles as such. Yet Ptolemy was convinced that as long as Alexander lived he could maintain control over his embryo world state.

The Greeks seemed to have reached the same conclusion. When the Delphic oracle proclaimed that Alexander had departed from among men and had become divine even while living—so that sacrifices should be made to his image and games held in his honor—Ptolemy was not surprised, nor did Alexander seem either pleased or displeased. Probably the meticulous Greeks had taken this means of legalizing, to their satisfaction, Alexander's peculiar overlordship. It was no disgrace to give obedience or honor to a divine being.

Whatever plan he had in mind—and Alexander did not discuss the situation as he had done in earlier years with the military council—the lord of Eurasia seemed to be moved by a definite purpose. At Susa, where he might have rested, he faced his problems without respite. He demanded effort as unceasing from his subordinates.

The problem of famine and water throughout the lands of Asia dependent for crops on rainfall worried him, and he had work started on a canal system stemming out from the rivers.

His practice of pushing out settlements had borne fruit amazingly. Never had the ancient world seen so many cities arise in so short a time. Nor did later centuries repeat this phenomenon until settlements spread through inland America after two millenniums. Walls of sun-baked clay brick were raised in a few days, and open-air theaters and athletic fields could be scraped out of hillsides or laid out on the desert plain. For these community centers were modern in plan, with education and entertainment provided those who thronged in to them.

Mixed populations filled most of them, as traders sought the new *entrepôts* of supply and the folk of the countryside drifted in to the sources of money and goods. An older caravan city like Palmyra was peopled with Arabs, Armenians, Greeks, Jews, and Syrians when the first Romans ventured out to it. Both Palmyra and Petra levied taxes on the caravan trade that transshipped at their junctions. This rapid growth of trade took care of the growth of the new cities.

Many of the new settlements did not prosper in this way, and remnants of ex-soldiers and natives subsisted there as best they could. They became, in very fact, exiles.

For some reason Alexander recalled all bands of Greek mercenaries from the eastern posts and started them on the journey home. At the same time he discovered at Ecbatana full three thousand Greek actors, musicians, and artisans awaiting transport east. It seems clear that he began to break up military nuclei and encourage civilian settlers. Whether the soldiers proved troublesome of whether he felt the need for them had passed is not known.

At Susa he operated on the army itself. He had by no means forgotten the mutiny at the Beas. The test of will power between him and the Macedonian veterans—who now formed only a small proportion of the field army—was still undecided. Now he needed settlers, who could form a reserve of fighting men, more than a large field army. Moreover he could no longer keep Macedonian swords suspended over the heads of the Asiatic nations. At least he had no intention of doing so.

By now some thirty thousand Asiatic recruits had been fully trained in European drill, and Alexander began to sift them into the Macedonian commands, so that there was often only one Macedonian company to a regiment. And he disbanded the old phalanx, which had lost its spirit after the Jhelum. This hedgehog-like formation was useless in any case, as a unit, in the immense plains. Quietly he raised Iranian and Bactrian and Scythian officers to high rank, even among the Companions.

It was necessary, and he knew it, to have a Eurasian army in his new state, and not the troublesome Macedonian expeditionary force with which he had started.

The veterans, however, did not see it that way. Alexander called the new recruits the *Epigoni,* the Afterborn —borrowing the word from an old Greek legend. The veterans called them the Afterbirth.

Keenly aware of the situation, they felt that Alexander was working to free himself from the need of their services.

XXI. THE END OF THE ARMY

At Susa Alexander staged one of his immense celebrations, ostensibly to mark the end of their long march, actually to promote intermarriage among his people. For a long time he had treated with special favor officers like Peucestas who learned Persian and adapted to the customs of the east. Now he invited the officer corps as a whole to take Asiatic wives. He set the example himself by selecting the eldest daughter of Darius as a second bride.

Her sister he bestowed on Hephaestion, so that his friend's children should be first cousins to his own. For Craterus (who had not yet departed) he selected a younger sister of Rushanak. For Nearchus, absent at sea, the daughter of Barsine and Mentor was appointed. Seleucus took the daughter of the dead Spitama; Ptolemy, Perdiccas, and the other leaders had brides of the Iranian nobility. Eighty Companions followed their example.

This was the most popular measure Alexander ever enforced, Arrian testifies. *Alexander and the leaders put on the Persian and the Medic dress for the ceremony. This was carried out in the Asiatic fashion. After the feast, the brides came in for the first time, each seating herself by her husband-to-be, who took her by the hand and kissed her, Alexander being the first to do so. Then each man took his bride and led her away.*

To encourage the marriages, Alexander had remarked that now the Asiatics as well as Macedonian Companions would be his Kinsmen. And he gave dowries to all the brides. Perhaps ten thousand of the soldiers followed this example, thus gaining women and dowries and credit with Alexander. Because their names were listed in a special register.

Macedonian veterans made fun of the oriental dress and manners of these bridegrooms. But their real resentment lay in the growing conviction that, while they needed Alexander, he no longer needed the old army. They said he had become an oriental despot.

The final clash of wills occurred on the way to Babylon. Alexander had found that Susa lay too far up in the eastern ranges to serve as his capital. Babylon, on the King's Way, and the Euphrates water route, would be the real center of his dominion. Perhaps the river decided him, because his thoughts turned more and more toward exploration by sea.

Although suffering from sleeplessness and the ill-healed wound in his lung that caused intermittent fever, he seemed happy during the journey down—he insisted on making a detour through the marshes, to reach the coast where Nearchus was expected. And during the voyage up the Tigris he delayed to remove the weirs that the Iranians had set across the river (either to keep up the head of water or to prevent an enemy fleet from reaching Babylon). Alexander wanted the Tigris free for navigation.

"We have no enemy to fear," he said. "The ships will be our own."

On the way up the Tigris Alexander sent word to the Macedonians, whose grumbling had caught his attention, that all of them who were overage or incapicitated by wounds would be sent back to the west. They would go home with such rewards—he remembered his pledge at the time of the mutiny—that they would be objects of envy in Macedon. At the same time he would grant gold wreaths to those who had won honor in battle (such men were already drawing double pay).

This gilding of their discharge did not pacify the veterans. They reminded their officers that many of them had gone into debt to moneylenders or messmates, and a bonus in money might be confiscated to pay those debts.

344

Alexander's response was to offer to pay all their debts out of the public treasury, if each man would record his name and the amount of the debt.

This seemed too good to be true. The veterans felt there was a catch in it. They had been drawing extraordinary pay and had no excuse for borrowing more. Only the more property most of them had the more money they seemed to need. After discussing it they rejected the offer. Whereupon Alexander offered to pay the debts on the word of each man, without taking down the names.

All this was not the real grievance. The Macedonians had watched Parthians and Bactrians taken into the select guards. They had seen a regiment of these guards placed under command of Rushanak's brother. Jealous, and now afraid for themselves, they did not care about the money.

"He no longer cares whom he embraces as Kinsman now," they complained. "Why doesn't he dismiss us all and be done with it?"

It was hot along the lower Tigris, in the marshlands. The Macedonians saw themselves cut adrift, disowned, after the years of campaigning. They couldn't argue with Alexander now. There was no council to hear their grievance. They shouted at Alexander's messengers, "We will all go home, or none. Then he can wage war with his Asiatics, who bow down to his feet. Ay, his father Ammon can help him to wage war."

When he heard of that Alexander stormed into their camp with officers and Hypaspists following him. Climbing on a wagon, his nerves on edge, he waved to the veterans to close in around him.

"As far as I'm concerned," he shouted at them, "you men can go, all of you, whenever you wish."

There was a moment's silence. Then they shouted back at him, "We aren't men. You said so. We're casualties—we're ghosts. We won't take orders—"

Alexander jumped down among them. White with anger, he gripped the speakers and whirled them back toward the guards who pushed after him. Thirteen he

345

ordered executed. Then he stopped, because the mob of soldiers had fallen silent.

"Before you go I want you to know what kind of men you have been," he cried. "You wore hides, and hid in the heights when barbarian tribes attacked you. My father gave you cloaks and made you colonists of cities. He gave Greece to the commonwealth of the Macedonians. When we started forth from the country where you could not support yourselves I had only some gold and silver cups and sixty talents in money. I had a debt of five hundred talents, and I borrowed eight hundred more to equip you. I laid open to you the passage of the Hellespont, although the Asiatics then had command of the sea.

"In all the lands I won over for you I gave you the privilege of taking wealth for yourselves. The wealth of Lydia, the riches of Persia and India—and now control of the outer seas. I shared these things, and I shared your fatigue. I have fed on the same food you ate, and have gone with as little sleep. Who of you has endured more for me than I have for him? Where is he?

"Let him come forward and show his wounds, and I will show mine. You know there is no kind of weapon, whether for striking or throwing, that has not left its mark on me."

When he paused the silence remained unbroken. But the men were listening now, breathing deep. No one stepped forward.

"I am still leading you as conquerors. I have celebrated your weddings with mine. Your children in these lands are cared for. Your debts I have liquidated without caring to ask how you come to have them. Those of you who died have been honored as heroes. And not one of you was killed in flight under my leadership. I led you across the Indus, and I would have led you across the Hyphasis [Beas] if you had not turned back—you who now hold golden chaplets from my hand.

"Now, since you wish to leave me—depart, all of you. Go back, and report at home that you left your

346

king Alexander alone among subjected foreigners. Go!"

And he pushed his way out of the crowd, going direct to his quarters, saying that no one would be admitted to see him. The soldiers made no move to follow. Low-voiced, they discussed his decision, reminding each other that he had a magic tongue and had won them over like that before now.

The worst of it was that they knew he would carry out his word. He would stay, turn over the rewards to them, and let them march off. And what would be said of them in Macedon?

They were still arguing the next day, when they heard that Alexander had begun to appoint Persians to high command and to name Asiatic regiments as guards—even giving them silver shields like those of the Companions.

On the third day something like panic ran through the Macedonian ranks. The veterans pressed together in a crowd and pushed toward Alexander's tent. They threw their weapons down at the entrance, sending in word that they would stay there, day and night, until he heard them. Then they added a pledge that they would surrender the men who had been active in stirring them up against him.

When Alexander came out they took hold of his hands and touched his mantle, supplicating him. This time Alexander could not speak because he was close to tears himself. A captain of the Companions said, "What grieved us was that you took Persians for Kinsmen, when you have never accepted us so."

"You are my Kinsmen," Alexander said, "all of you."

The men caught up their weapons, shouting and running about him, until he promised that they would feast together. Before that he made sacrifice in the old way. And he seated the Macedonian officers nearest him at the banquet, the Persians below them. When the wine bowl was passed around the king drew a cup from it, with his men. Both the Greek soothsayers and the Magians presided at this thanksgiving. As Alexander drank he prayed for a commonwealth of the two peoples.

The long conflict between Alexander and his army came to its end here, at the love feast on the Tigris. Alexander got his way, as almost always happened, by persuasion. His oration to the mob at the river had operated on their minds as delicately as a surgeon's knife—for Alexander understood the mentality of his veterans.

Here in Asia he had been able to educate the Iranian and Syrian youth after a fashion; but he had had no control over the rude schooling of Macedonians at home. Their outlook had changed very little. The veterans of the India campaign had remained as they had been before Chaeronea, hardheaded peasants, stubborn, covetous of the feel of gold in their hands, craving the ownership of good soil, wagons, and animals. Beyond that, they had pride in their service records, and they felt satisfaction in their dominance over the more intelligent Asiatics, and in their fellowship with the almost worshiped Alexander.

Upon these traits Alexander had played—calling them conquerors and taking credit himself only for lands he had subjected without warfare, and for the battle ordeal he had shared with them. In this he had been honest. The thing closest to his heart had been the loyalty of the veterans. And for the last two years these Macedonian soldiers had been his greatest anxiety.

Some of the higher officers like Hephaestion and Peucestas had adapted themselves to the east and to Alexander's new viewpoint. Thousands of the rank and file must have done so also, and contented themselves with marrying eastern women and remaining as colonists in the new world. But the cleavage between Alexander and the homesick Macedonians could no longer be closed.

The choice was left to the men of all ranks and organizations. Some ten thousand elected to return to Macedon. They were given full pay, to include the time of their journey home. And Alexander gave a bonus of one talent (nominally about a thousand dollars, actually the equivalent of some fifteen thousand) to each man. The families of all soldiers who had died while on duty were freed from taxes and awarded privileges sufficient to support them. Alexander made one stipulation—that the children born to the demobilized soldiers by Asiatic women should be left behind. He promised that these children would receive a western education.

The returning veterans marched off with full honors, with no less a leader than Craterus.

Their dismissal made an end of the pahlanx and of the old units like the Agrianians. The paradox of Alexander's career is that he destroyed the army that his father Philip had created—which had been the first instrument of his own success. After the parting at the Tigris no such army of Macedon took the field again, unless as a shadow of its former greatness.

Philip had created a citizen army—of Thessalians and Agrianians as well as native Macedonians—imbued with a high spirit. Such a national army no longer fitted into the Eurasian scheme of things. What remained under Alexander's direction was an army of the nations.

Alexander had done something unprecedented in sharing his new wealth with the Macedonian veterans. In a literal sense he had carried out his promise to make them sharers in his enterprise.

His new armed forces were held together as yet only by the force of his personality. Whether volunteers or drafted contingents—such contingents had been drawn from the more unruly sections like the mountains of Turkestan or northern India—they had become obedient to the invincible Great King. Like Hannibal's mixed African forces in a later day, they admitted only the authority of their commander. Unlike Hannibal's command, these Eurasians had no mercenaries among them. Alexander had rid himself of the last of those.

Actually the new army had become a police force. From the Nile to the Indus there was no longer any sign of conflict.

XXII. THE WATERS
OF BABYLON

Paradoxically, of all the nations now subject to him Alexander found himself least able to control his homeland, Macedon.

The east was close to tranquillity. In the year since his return Alexander had forced himself to the limit of endurance, in restoring order. Egypt remained calm as usual under the rule of the new Pharaoh; the Magians had accepted Alexander as a true successor to the ancient Iranian kings; the priests of the temple at Jerusalem had appealed to him as to a second Kurush; the priests of Babylon were rebuilding the temple of their god Marduk and awaiting his coming.

Envoys had hurried across from the Greek cities. They had approached Alexander wearing garlands, doing reverence to him as to a divine being. (He had merely given them his right hand to clasp and had arranged for them to take back all the captured Greek statues found in Asia.) At Athens the party of Demosthenes had become neutral, if not friendly toward the former Macedonian. Defiant Sparta had lapsed into quietude after the subjection of Asia. The Aegean as well as the Red Sea was patrolled by friendly fleets.

But the Kinsen in Macedon cared for no fleet. The mountaineers of Pella could not become traffickers like the enterprising Carthaginians. Slaves and gold they might take from Asia, but what did Asia avail them if they, the chieftains of tribes, held no authority over it? And that authority Alexander would not give them, greatly as he rewarded them.

He cared for little himself, Arrian states, *yet he gave immense wealth to those connected with him.*

More than ten years of separation had estranged the wanderer from his people. To Alexander, Olympias's tempers, Antipater's rule-of-thumb discipline, the plotting of Cleopatra, and the thieving of sickly Harpalus had become dwarfed and distant. He no longer corresponded with Aristotle, who as master of the Peripatetic school seemed to have barricaded himself behind books. The Peripatetics, or Walking Philosophers, taught that Alexander, who had profited by fortune, was doomed to catastrophe by his own excess.

"Punishment will come to those who harbor conspirators against me," Alexander cried.

To this elder Greek-Macedonian world the master of Asia appeared as a madman. Voluntarily he had disappeared into the east, draining the young men from their homes, without regard for human life. Megalomania had seized him. He had challenged the gods—he had bowed down to strange deities. Lying on a gold couch among barbarians, with incense burning before him, he had made himself drunk with power. So reported Harpalus and Cassander in the spring of that year 323.

Alexander was journeying then from the heat of the Tigris up to the heights of Ecbatana. When he took to horseback, on the road, his mind became clearer. It satisfied him to be in motion again, even over familiar ground. And the cold air of the foothills held his fever in check. He had made no effort to go himself to Macedon. Instead he had sent Craterus, to do what might be done.

And he had shirked establishing his court in Babylon. He did not want to think of the lines of petitioners and officials waiting for him upon the pyramided towers of that city. The Hanging Gardens of Babylon were a poor imitation of the hills he loved.

Instead he busied himself with the project of exploring that inland sea, the Caspian. From the timber he had seen on its shore, a fleet could be built—he ordered the Phoenician and Cretan technicians to depart to start work on the shipyard—and by circling the inland sea they could settle the question whether it actually connected with the Euxine or drained north into the outer Ocean. If it did so, his ships could reach the northern edge of the habitable world. And he would know if both the River of Sands and the River of the Sea emptied into the Caspian. He could reach the dark homeland of the Scythian tribes.

For Alexander no longer expected to find his Parnassus. He had seen the snow line of the Himalayas and the last mighty barrier of earth. He had seen eagles flying over immeasurable chasms. His feet had measured the sands of the Mekran, and he had felt the surge of outer Ocean. Seated not upon the throne of Darius but in the splendors of his imagination, he traversed this kingdom of his, this kingdom of the natural earth. It had never been so clear in his mind, and he could not know his mind was failing him.

The news of Hephaestions's death struck him with terrible force. Hephaestion had been ill only seven days with fever, yet the physicians had not been able to cure him. There had been a celebration of games in Ecbatana while Hephaestion lay ill.

Hurrying to the scene, Alexander gave way to one of his neurotic spells of grieving, taking no food and speaking to no one for days. As with the killing of Cleitus, the loss of Hephaestion seemed to Alexander to take away something personal to him. In a passion of mourning, he commanded the games to go on at Ecbatana, in Hephaestion's name, and that all who took part should make sacrifice to his friend.

Among the Greek immigrants there Alexander found an imaginative architect, Stasicrates, who could design a fitting funeral pyre for Hephaestion. This was to be built of sandalwood and cedar, and sweetened with myrrh and nard. It was to be shaped like a temple, and ten thousand talents of the treasure of Ecbatana was to be spent in ornamenting it. Perhaps Alexander had not meant the memorial to burn, but it did burn.

Impressed with the immensity of Alexander's works, Stasicrates tried to win his favor. The architect drew up a plan for a memorial that would dwarf the pyramids, for Alexander himself. His idea was to make the stone face of Mount Athos into an effigy of the king, who would stand in this fashion for eternity, holding a city of ten thousand people in his left hand, while a river flowed from his right hand into the sea. Such a statue, Stasicrates swore, would be worthy even of Alexander.

But Alexander would not hear of it. He left Ecbatana on the pretext of leading a small expedition against the Kassite mountain tribes. Taking Ptolemy, his last surviving companion, he traversed the mountain range southward, following out an abandoned road close to the snows of the heights where brick watchtowers of Assyrian kings lined the way.

When he heard that Nearchus had arrived in Babylon he made his way down from the heights into the plain, where the post road was thronged, in greeting. Down this highway he had raced after Gaugamela a few years before.

There he found envoys from barbarian people, far off, who had taken long to reach him. They brought him salutations and gifts from the Libyans of Africa and a people called Etruscans from west of Greece.

When he was riding on, a deputation of priests from the temple of Marduk stood in his way. "Lord, do not enter the gate of Babylon," they urged him. "Evil will be thy fate, if that thou doest for the second time."

"A prophecy is no more than a guess," he said.

Among those with him, some said that the warning should be heeded, because the Chaldean watchers of the stars knew more about human fate than the Greeks; others, more cynical, remarked that these priests, who were custodians of Marduk's property, had become so rich during the rebuilding of the temple that they feared to have Alexander examine their accounts. Alexander remembered that the dead Aristander had warned him not to rebuild the temple.

353

He went on in, because Babylon was to be his capital city and Nearchus was waiting there.

On the roof of the palace where cool air stirred at night and the torches in the avenues beneath looked like fireflies he sat with Nearchus, discussing the expedition into Arabia, where frankincense and myrrh could be found.

"Archias came back from his trip," Alexander explained, "after coasting the west side as far as an island. The sea there is really a gulf, as you suspected. I named the island Icarus."

Nearchus had known this, but he knew also that Alexander liked to dwell on the exploration as if he had been there, ordering it. "Hieron reports," the captain of the sea added in his matter-of-fact way, "that he coasted on through the mouth of the gulf. After a while he turned back, meeting only desert when he touched shore."

"Why did he turn back?"

"He was afraid to go on."

Alexander laughed. It seemed strange to him to turn back for no other reason than fear.

"Hieron says that the land of Arabia must be as great in size as India."

This pleased Alexander, who began to long to set out to circumnavigate Arabia. A land expedition led by himself would work its way through the people of Arabia, while Nearchus, who turned back at nothing, would follow the coast, and together they would reach the land of the Nile and solve the mystery of what lay south of the great deserts.

Already the new shipyards in Babylon were launching ten-and-thirty-oared galleys. Alexander went out on one of the new ships for a test cruise downriver, and to examine the working of the canal system. He came back, entering Babylon through the water gate a second time. Peucestas had come in from Persia with a column of the new army, and Seleucus also had reported, with his elephant train. That night Alexander drank wine until daybreak, too restless to sleep.

When he could not sleep he went down to the river to swim and had himself ferried over—after laying the morning sacrifice on the altar—to the other side, to a pavilion by a pool where he could stretch out and be cool in the heat of the day. He felt fever rising in him, and bathed again in the pool, after which he tried to rest, ordering the officers to meet him at daybreak.

His fever now raged through the night, Arrian states. *He offered sacrifice and gave orders to Nearchus that the voyage should begin on the third day. When he offered sacrifice the next day, he could not keep quiet because of the fever. In spite of that he talked over with the officers how they should have everything in readiness for the start of the fleet.*

The next day, being very weak, he had to be carried out to make the sacrifice. In this condition he was carried over to the palace where the generals and officers waited outside the doors. When they entered the room he knew them but could not speak to them. For two days and two nights his fever mounted high.

Then the soldiers, hearing a report of this, fancied that he might be dead, and the fact kept from them by the confidential officers.

Some of them crowded the palace, grieving, and forced their way in to him. One by one they passed by him. Since he was still unable to speak, he greeted each with his right hand. He raised his head with difficulty to each one.

Soon after, Alexander died. He had lived for thirty-two years and eight months.

AFTERWORD

Alexander of Macedon had died unexpectedly there in the palace of Nebuchadnezzar over the gray Euphrates, probably of malaria. Any spearman of his army might have survived such an attack. But Alexander had worn out his body and his mind as well in those last years. Probably his death was due more to physical exhaustion and wounds than to the fever.

He died still young with his dream dominion only half completed. Would he ever had completed it? Some modern authorities hold that the task to which he had set himself was hopeless, and Alexander himself fortunate in that he did not survive to share in its collapse. There is no way of knowing the truth of that.

We do know that what he did—as Faure points out—was not so important as what he tried to do. Even as to that he had left no clear testimony. He had a way of taking people as he found them and meeting difficulties as they came. Obstacles seemed to cause him less anxiety than the doubts of his followers. In those last years he had driven whole peoples ahead upon a new path of civilization with such force that they could not return to the old ways. With almost inhuman energy he had shattered the norms of his time.

In so doing, he had set in motion forces too strong to be arrested. It is one of the many paradoxes that surround Alexander that the effect of his life was not really apparent until after his death. These forces released by him left their mark upon human history for a long time.

That mark can be seen clearly.

The first reaction against Alexander's embryo world kingdom came naturally enough from his neglected homeland of Macedon. He had died without assuming any definite title. To most of the highlanders at home he had become a despot in Asia, or a madman. Since Craterus had not arrived in the west, Antipater kept his authority and used his military strength to occupy Greece—which Alexander had always refused to do.

Demosthenes made a last effort for the liberty of Hellas and fled for safety to Aegina. When Macedonian patrols appeared there in search of him he took refuge within a temple sanctuary and committed suicide rather than be taken captive. Aristotle was accused of impiety and exiled himself in Chalcis, where he died within a year—thus ending the triumvirate of those dominant minds, Alexander's, Demosthenes's, and Aristotle's, each of which remained unequaled in its sphere throughout posterity.

In Greece itself Alexander was deified, and worshiped as a latter-day Heracles or Apollo, with sacrifices and images and supplication.

This was the beginning of the Alexander cult. Merely ceremonial, it did, however, give evidence of a change that had taken place. To Athenians, Alexander had ceased to be a Macedonian king. For a space he had taken from Athens the leadership of ideas. He had opened up new fields of conjecture that bewildered her academicians. So the Greeks settled the matter by proclaiming him a god and attending the discussions at the academies.

Macedon itself had had one half its manpower drained away to the east, or slain, and its feudal aristocracy had been thinned out. The enlightened peasantry refused to return to serfdom under the remaining Kinsmen or the surviving Olympias. This internal dissension was not helped by constant feuds with Asia Minor, which had come under the authority of Antigonus the One-Eyed. Greeks took over the tasks of skilled labor, and the army became an old-style professional affair, depending on an outmoded phalanx. Nothing in all this served to check the inroads of barbarian Gauls, later on, or the march of the scarcely less barbaric Roman legions two centuries afterward.

The Successors

When Alexander died in the palace at Babylon, Ptolemy, Seleucus, Perdiccas, Peucestas, and Nearchus had been there with him. Among these powerful lieutenants there seemed to be no question as to what to do. The Eurasian state was to be preserved for the descendants of Philip and Alexander—the two heirs being the feeble-minded Arrhidaeus, now a grown man, and the boy who was born to Rushanak in the months afterward. For the moment Perdiccas, a single-minded soldier, related to the royal family, was chosen regent. The politic Ptolemy elected to serve as satrap of Egypt, which he had always craved. Seleucus took upon himself the task of administering the real east, from Babylon.

Although Alexander's sarcophagus should have been sent back to Macedon, Ptolemy managed to take it with him to Egypt, thereby increasing his own prestige. Eventually he married Thais, who had attached her fortune to his. At Memphis and Alexandria Ptolemy established his new dynasty.

As might be expected, he played the monarch much more than the painstaking Seleucus, who looked on himself as the trustee of the dominion. Concerning these twain the prophecy of Daniel relates, *And the king of the south shall be strong, but one of his captains shall be stronger, and have dominion.*

While Ptolemy occupied himself with building the library at Alexandria, where his half brother had been interred, Thais played the role of empress at Memphis, becoming the mother of three children.

No one cared to, or dared, put on the imperial Iranian robes and tiara that Alexander had worn. The

Diadochi, Successors, as they came to be known, contented themselves with modified royal dress—with jeweled diadems, or headbands, purple cloaks and red riding boots, vestiges of the Macedonian garments, in Asiatic style, which became much later the costume of the Byzantine emperors. (Alexander had shaved smooth, and the Successors imitated him, so that in time beards ceased to be worn in the Greek-Roman world.)

Alexander had bequeathed to these Successors no clear plan of government; they had only his example and purpose to follow, and this they could not manage to do. They accomplished much, however, because, as Olympias had complained so often, they were the equals of kings. They could not manage to keep the military authority separate from the civilian administration and soon began to rely on the old-style tax collectors. Nor could Seleucus, that benevolent giant, hold intact the far eastern borders. Greek settlers in outer Bactria and Soghd rebelled on hearing of Alexander's death and started to march home. The fiefs in India Seleucus ceded soon after to Chandragupta, for a herd of his cherished elephants.

Greek became the language of the courts of the Successors, replacing the Macedonian dialect, as the *koiné* became the lingo of trade, so that as time went on the Successors tended to become monarchs of individual states, bound to Greek culture superimposed over the Asiatics. The Macedonian-Iranian fusion that Alexander had striven for changed imperceptibly into a Greek-Asiatic society, dominating what is known as the Hellenistic world.

The Companions, scattered throughout the new dominion, grew to power as nobles in their own right and called themselves Friends. They reverted to a professional soldiery, silver shields and all, and served the leader who could pay the best wages.

These changes had been unavoidable, perhaps, among men loyal to Alexander's memory. Real cleavage came out of civil war, caused by Macedon, and especially by the imperious Olympias, who had Arrhidaeus poisoned six years after Alexander's death—leaving Rushanak's son the only heir. (Apparently she had persuaded the eastern Successors to send the Bactrian princess and her boy to Pella.) Perdiccas had not survived, nor had Antipater. When the conflict between Asia Minor and Macedon grew into open war across the Dardanelles Cassander—who had trembled at his first sight of a statue of Alexander—joined the Antigonus family against the Macedonian royal family.

So Cassander, the son of Antipater, who had been Alexander's enemy, began his work of destruction of the Macedonian's kindred.

In 310 Cassander was able to capture Olympias, Rushanak, and the twelve-year-old boy, Alexander's son. Even Cassander could not persuade his soldiers to assassinate the now aged Olympias. The men would not use their weapons on the mother, the wife, and the son of the man who was now believed by many of them to have been a god. Cassander himself had Olympias bound and drowned with the two others.

This liquidated the last human ties to Philip and Alexander, leaving the Macedonian commanders free agents, without living heirs to the dream empire of Eurasia. Very quickly, four years later, Antigonus Gonatus (the Weak-Kneed)) proclaimed himself sole king, and his word law—subject to the agreement of the stubborn Macedonian soldiery.

Upon this the world state fragmented through civil war into four parts: Macedon, Asia Minor under the Antigonids, Egypt under the Ptolemies, and Syria to the Hind-i-Kuh under the Seleucids, with the borderlands fought over at intervals by their armies and a free Armenia rising in the mountains, with an independent kingdom of the Jews forming in Palestine—the whole joined by a common culture into the Hellenistic world.

But this political cleavage and the occasional campaigning of the now professional armies did not arrest an integration that was taking place outside the courts.

For in the Hellenistic world inpulses were at work which could not be controlled by a new king's law or by military force.

In the Greek cities, which remained free, although weak, there was growing a desire for kinship with the outer world, a horror of the old internecine wars. Philosophers had lifted their vision from the polis or small city to the greater universe of men. The limited refinement of the Epicureans, the enhancement of a selected society preached by the Plato-Aristotle groups, seemed no longer the greatest good. Neither Plato nor Aristotle had given thought to the human beings outside their select groups. Those beyond the limits of their refinement remained serfs or enemies. Men inbued with a new idea came forward and spoke of it from the *stoa*, the porches, and came to be called Stoics.

To them the individual city, the hearths and shrines of ancient Hellas, mattered not so much as the imagined Cosmopolis, or World City. What the Stoics put in words, especially their leader Zeno, was much in the thoughts of Greeks after Alexander's territorial expansion and imagined Eurasian state. The collapse of the older nations, the mingling of peoples, the use of a universal language, set men to groping for a new fellowship. Into the paths of this mingled humanity were to step the apostles of a new universal religion, Christianity.

The tide of migration to the east, started by Alexander, was running too strong to be checked. The discoveries in the east drew the more adventurous souls from the shores and islands of the Mediterranean toward the gold and the vast farmlands of Asia, as the discovery of the New World after Columbus drew the daring, the discontented, and the religious dissenters out of Europe in the sixteenth and seventeenth centuries.

Alexander's coinage—which now bore his head, with the lion's mane as designed by Lysippus—became the standard of the Hellenistic age. At his death no more than fifty thousand talents had remained in the treasury at Ecbatana. He had released the flood of gold that had been locked up by his predecessors of the Persian Empire. This, circulating freely among soldiers and traders, had put money into the hands of people as far as the frontier settlements.

At the same time the Asiatics had been losing their lines of racial grouping and had coalesced with the settlers from the west in new centers.

Imperceptibly centers of culture and activity were moving eastward. The flood of new coinage reduced the value of the Athenian drachma to half, and Athens ceased to be the commercial mistress of the Mediterranean—becoming less important than Rhodes, off the Asia coast. On that coast city building went on apace and became almost modern in character. Pergamum rose over paved streets, with marble façades of academies and public lounges, swimming pools and open-air theaters.

South of Pergamum the Successors raised mighty Antioch (founded by Antiochus) along the side of a valley where three caravan routes from the land of the Two Rivers came together. Antioch had a famous circus and gardens, especially in the grove called Delphi, named after the grotto of that famous oracle. In due time Antioch served as a resort for tired Roman businessmen, and as one of the earliest centers of the Nazarenes, followers of that strange faith of Christianity.

These new cities, like the now celebrated Alexandria on the Nile, departed sharply from the older European plan of a huddle of streets built around a defense citadel and a single temple—as Athens had grown up around the Acropolis. They were built for people to live in and learn, not simply for defense and the worship of a single god or of the pantheon. Rome itself, then growing up around its forum, or market place, and its Temple of Mars, sprawling over its seven hills, was not so modern in plan as these Hellenistic metropolitan centers of Pergamum and Antioch. But they served as models for Pompeii, with its villas and baths and parks. They had their Central Parks, their bowls and college stadiums, their International Houses and public theaters and medical dispensaries. Around them a new social cosmos had been created that endured throughout the Roman imperium and raised the dour, laboring, patriarchal Romans to its higher standard of living. This cultured nearer east, or Eurasia, invited westerners to a life in sunlight upon fertile soil, wherein music enlivened leisure hours and far-extending caravan roads tempted settlers to wander on.

The Hellenistic culture might stem from the Greeks, but the physical world of Eurasia had been opened up by Alexander, whose communications stretched as far as India. Before then, except on the narrow Ionian coast, westerners had entered the gates of Asia only as refugees or mercenaries. After Alexander, the westerners came as citizens, seeking land or opportunity. The human influx crowded shipping eastbound across the blue Aegean; it pressed through the new embarkation ports, seeking stages and animal transport—donkey, horse, or camel—to journey on toward Maracand, or Babylon, or one of the thirteen Alexandrias. It was not a case of the course of empire taking its way eastward; the road of humanity had opened up thither. Alexander, to whom nothing had seemed impossible, had drawn the west after him bodily into the east, and there it stayed.

Descendants of the Macedonian settlers left their physical characteristics among the white Kafirs of the Hind-i-Kuh, and until very recently the red banner of Samarkand was supposed by the natives there to be that of Iskander, or Alexander the Great.

The Caravan Cities

These caravan cities, seaports, and centers of learning were not founded by Alexander's caprice or the whims of the Successors. Antioch grew mightily because it stood at the juncture of trade routes; Seleucia, near by on the sea, was no pleasure resort of a Seleucid but was necessary as a port to serve the increasing trade of Antioch. (In following out the route of Alexander's journey, as this writer has done, one fact strikes the observer: of all the construction of his time and immediately after, nothing visible survives today. While in the case of the elder cities like Babylon and Athens much survives—or at least has been unearthed. Probably the Macedonian building was almost entirely in the prevalent clay-brick or timber and has succumbed to time and weather in sites that were abandoned after the Macedonian withdrawal. In some localities, as in the Taurus Range or the Afghan hills, granite and limestone are, and were, available and you would expect to find *some* remnants of construction there. But even the lighthouse at Alexandria on the Nile has vanished without a trace, and British archaeologists have not been able to identify with certainty the site of Alexander's twelve memorial pillars on the bank of the river Beas. The explanation of this disappearance of architectural remains may be the unusual but perfectly natural one—that where his cities flourished and grew[1] they were so overbuilt in more than two millenniums that all trace of earlier structures are buried under more modern work. Even the so-called sarcophagus of Alexander is probably later work. Almost alone among the greater monarchs of the ancient world, Alexander left no monument other than his intangible legacy of handiwork, of new opportunities and thoughts among those who lived after him.)

Not that the Hellenistic monarchs, the Successors, did not build on a huge scale and raise individual monuments of the modern skyscraper type. But they had a

---

[1]Authorities mention Alexandria [Egypt], Herat, Kabul, Kandahar, Ghazni [Afghanistan], Khojend [Turkestan], and Patala [India] as metropolitan centers founded by Alexander that have endured until today. There were unquestionably others. In contrast Aegae and Pella, the capitals of ancient Macedon, reveal only a few stone foundations today.

purpose. The giant Pharos (lighthouse) at Alexandria marked the narrow port entrance to shipping as far as the horizon could be seen, and the Colossus of the expanding seaport of Rhodes served the same purpose. At this time, so greatly had travel increased, men began to list such superstructures, calling them the seven wonders of the world. Those built before the Hellenistic age were mostly individual memorials or tombs—the statue of Zeus at Olympia in Greece, the tomb of Mausolus, Temple of Artemis at Ephesus, the pyramid tombs of the Nile, and the penthouse gardens of Babylon, which Semiramis may or may not have built for her comfort.

Shipping expanded sharply, to take care of the new traffic, especially in the more eastern points: Rhodes, Alexandria, Beirut. Some of the trans-Aegean liners could accommodate a thousand passengers. At least one of the sea lanes Alexander had meant to explore was opened up by the Ptolemies, who established ocean traffic around Arabia, transshipping to Indian vessels at the Yemen. They also ran a canal from the Nile to the Red Sea, and opened ports there, named after the first Ptolemy's mother, Arsinoë. (Macedonian women had shared rather fully the lives of their men, and the women of the Successors continued so to do, especially in Egypt where the name of Cleopatra became common in the reigning dynasty. This dynasty followed Egyptian custom in marrying brothers to sisters in the royal house. The women of the new Eurasia had emancipated themselves from the seclusion of the elder Greek homes, wherein wives had remained household objects with the sole privilege of bearing children.)

Some attempt was made to sail around Africa, as Alexander had planned, to reach Ocean in the west. But the Successors found, as Alexander had found, that such sallies out of the settled Eurasian zone brought them among more primitive people. They inferred, as his scientists had conjectured, that their sea captains had advanced close to the edges of the world.

365

(Actually Alexander's expeditions had not overrun the greater part of the *habitable* world, the Oikoumene as he must have known it toward the end of his short life; but he had penetrated almost all of the earth inhabited by people of any culture. China, of course, remained remote and unknown. He failed only to reach the people along the Ganges, and in Arabia, and the scattered cities of the western Mediterranean such as Carthage, Syracuse, or Gades. And he had been turned back in the effort to reach these peoples only by mutiny and his death. Perhaps he had discovered more about the far-distant populations than we realize, and had hoped to reach the limits not of the habitable earth but of that inhabited by intelligent humans. What he thought of the Latins who were then confined to the Italian peninsula is not known.)

Over sea routes and caravan tracks the rare products of the farther east—the spices, glass, silk, ivory, sugar, pearls, oil, and above all gold—gave comfort to the immigrants and trade to the new cities. These precious things worked their way into the hands of ordinary citizens, and the women especially never gave up wanting them. In Roman times and in the medieval world demand continued for the spices and luxuries of the east. This demand persisted and was one of the forces that pushed exploration by sea after a thousand years toward the Spice Isles and Cathay.

Naturally under these conditions Alexandria, situated where the Red Sea trade changed to Mediterranean shipping, became the focus of Hellenistic activity. Its marble gymnasiums, its ceramics and vessels of onyx and jasper gave a taste of new luxury to westerners. The first Ptolemy of Egypt had been a writer, or at least had kept journals at Alexander's bidding, and the library of Alexandria became the center of the new research. Geographers recorded new data there, with the natural history of Aristotle. Mathematicians were put to work to design novel *apparata*—Archimedes excelled at that—and to measure the earth itself, to chart the stars in their courses—Eratosthenes came very close to the exact measurement of the earth. Euclid worked out his geometry not as a theory but as a useful science. For nearly a century the *theoria* of the elder Greeks were harnessed to human needs. It was a period of vast experimentation.

They were not all Greeks at Alexandria; the librarians and students might come from Rhodes or Byzantium or Babylon. Artists tended to do the work of artisans, decorating buildings or wine vessels. Books were copied in great numbers, for a reading *public*, and not limited to a few copies for the study of the initiated.

Art itself became public property for a while—for Asiatics demanded that their dwellings be more than a square of stone walls. The influence of the cultured east penetrated farther into the west. (The works of Aristotle were to be preserved in the main through translation into Arabic, centuries later when they were neglected in Europe, after the decline of Rome.)

The cold concepts of earlier Greek philosophy were quickened and warmed by Asiatic mysticism. Iranian thought moved men to ponder the meaning of eternity. The influence of the Magi shaped Judaism and Christianity more than Greek concepts were able to do. Alexander's journey had made men familiar with other religions and had broken down the limitation of their thought. Henceforth—although superstition increased, and varied panaceas such as astrology were sought after—men were not so inclined to accept fate as inevitable. Except in the darkest west—among Celts, Teutons, and Gauls—a feeling grew that somehow human beings could escape the anger of the gods.

Although Greek was the first language of the Hellenistic revival, and Greek thought had spurred it, this spirit was not Greek but Eurasian. This art stemmed not from the sculptures of the Parthenon but from the designs of Asia. The splendors of Persepolis had indeed made the journey into the west, and men judged them by new standards. Iranian culture had shaped the Hellenistic world, and Hellenistic culture glorified the Roman world.

Upon this heritage the Romans entered by way of military conquest, building sound roads as they advanced, about two centuries after the death of Alexander. Before then a native dynasty, the Parthian, had swept over Iran [Persia]. In spite of all their attempts to do so the Romans never progressed much beyond the Euphrates—the frontier offered by Darius to Alexander—and the rest of Asia returned to the possession of the Asiatics. The frontier set up between Roman proconsuls and Parthian emperors was never cleared away. Growing difference in languages and religions made the demarcation sharper. Militant and materialistic Rome fed on the enlightenment of the Eurasian mid-region—when Rome collapsed in the west through internal deterioration she survived in this Eastern or Byzantine Empire for a millennium—but destroyed the incipient Hellenistic world culture.

Since then until very recent times there has been no mutual understanding of east and west. Only in the north, where the Macedonians barely penetrated, Russia has by slow and painful expansion formed a Eurasian state.

Emperors and Their Titles

Paradoxically the millions who held Alexander in their memory gave him no one clear title. But after a century or so they began spontaneously to call him Alexander the Great. Perhaps he was the first, if not the only, monarch to be so christened by many nations, and not by one alone. Certainly his personal name was borrowed by diverse lineages thereafter. For we find Alexanders appearing as Balkan kings, Scottish chieftains, tsars of Russia, and eight popes of Rome.

Alexander had set a pattern that the more powerful Europeans found it difficult to ignore after him. As they conceived it, he had for a few years been absolute ruler of a world state. He had been, in their minds, a conqueror. He had made the world one empire, as they phrased it. (A thing he never did.) So the man who never held a title—or at least no one title—set the style for the mightiest monarchs after him. Roman emperors (Imperator—Commander) claimed to be rulers of the world. Since Alexander had believed it possible to unite all peoples, they liked it to be assumed that they had done so. This concept of an emperor ruling mundane peoples by divine authority—later the phrase became "by God's will"—was not lost until modern times.

Augustus, first emperor of the Romans, ordered divine honors to be paid to Alexander.

The Basileus of Byzantium held to this shadowy sublimation over all humans; Charlemagne and the later monarchs of the Holy Roman Empire kept to the tradition of an eastern irredenta. Physically, in their hand, they gripped the golden orb or globe of the earth surmounted by a cross. This was the symbol of their authority. In title if not in fact they were successors of the earlier earth rulers.

Curiously enough, along with this concept of global rule, the myth bird of the Asiatics, the great winged eagle of the Magi—the bird that flew between mankind on earth and the seat of the gods in the sky—also traveled to Europe by devious ways. It is true that an eagle had been the favorite bird of Zeus and had found a perch in its natural form upon the standards of the Roman legions, which were a kind of regimental totem pole. But the mythical *Si-murg* of Asia, which resembled also a griffon or dragon, served later Iranians as symbol of divine power and was so adopted by Byzantine wearers of the purple. It appeared, still faintly resembling a dragon, on the banners and shields of monarchs of the Holy Roman Empire—and after that, twin, or two-headed, or single, it survived in the heraldry of German emperors, Polish kings, and tsars of Russia.

In a very different way Alexander's journey had affected the almost unknown India—the only first hand accounts of ancient India we have are those of his writers or the ambassadors of Seleucus—and after his passage India grew together as an empire of the whole. Among his followers for a time was an Indian adventurer, Chandragupta, who took advantage of the upheaval caused by the Macedonian passage to unite the peoples of northern India for the first time. In so doing Chandragupta paved the way for the empire of the enlightened Asoka. A strange empire, because after 267 B.C. the Buddhist Asoka ruled it by humanitarian measures rather than by military force—a method unknown to the western Romans of that age. Asoka gave away treasure, dug irrigation channels, planted medicinal herbs, and in general conducted himself as the agent and not the master of the authority he held.

So after Alexander, if not because of him, Asoka in the east and the Stoic Zeno in the west extended their vision to humanity as a whole. Cosmopolitan or Buddhist, they reached out toward the same thing. After Alexander such concepts had changed. After Alexander . . . Historians were to make that phrase a point in time.

The Legends

It was not strange that Asia should remember Alexander more than any other westerner; yet it was remarkable that she should remember him as she did, in legends that became the heritage of different peoples. For he endured in the memory of each land in a different way, and each land adopted him as belonging to it. But before the legends took shape, the writers with Alexander had finished their accounts.

His journey had been written up by many eyewitnesses. Callisthenes's story, the *Anabasis*, had been distorted flattery; Ptolemy, the son of Lagus and husband-king of Thais, had eulogized him for political reasons; so had the writer named Aristobulus. Nearchus had produced a factual record of the voyages; Onesicritus, an epitome of Amazons and marvels. Those diligent surveyors—and how they must have worked—

Baeton and Diognetes had turned in a topographical survey. There were other narratives.

But all of them, however colored by individual taste, seemed to be records of a journey rather than of a man. What Alexander thought, said, or planned is barely discernible from the fragments that survive today.

Most of these journals, written in Greek, were lost; only the later compilations of Roman writers have come down to us entire. For some reason, toward the end of the first century after Christ—perhaps because Roman power had then moved eastward to the threshold of the Orient—there was a vogue of Alexander books. Strabo, the first historical geographer and himself a man of the east, drew heavily upon Alexander's travels. He also followed out the Aristotle-Alexander method of defining the earth's shape through the course of rivers and mountain chains— which he said was the way to "geographize" a land. For a while Strabo worked at Alexandria, consulting Polybius and the other Alexandrian travel-tellers. A little after Strabo the celebrated Ptolemy the Geographer described the world and its climates. Neither Strabo nor this Ptolemy knew much about Asia farther east than the River of the Sands, where Alexander had made one of his about-faces.

Yet the geographies of Polybius, Strabo, and Ptolemy remained the standard of knowledge until the new age of exploration that began with the Portuguese and Spanish voyages across the Atlantic.

Of Alexander himself Quintus ("Red") Curtius wrote, and the Greek Plutarch added Alexander to his *Lives,* saying in his foreward, *My design is not to write histories but lives. . . . Exploits do not always reveal clearly the virtue of vice of men; sometimes a phrase or jest informs us better of their characters than the most famous sieges. I give most attention to these indications of the souls of men.*

Last of this group of biographers, Arrian (Flavius Arrianus), also a Greek by birth, and a governor in

Asia Minor, wrote the most complete account of the Macedonian's journey, calling it *The Anabasis of Alexander,* taking his material in the main from Ptolemy Lagus and Aristobulus. Arrian, the Stoic and soldier, pictured the Macedonian as an ideal leader, with few flaws, drawing the eulogy rather than the reality out of his sources, yet aware of the widely differing opinions that made Alexander appear as a god or madman. *More has been written about him than about any other man, yet with less agreement.*

Before then Asia had begun to have its say. Alexander had left his imprint for all time not upon its history but upon its imagination. Egyptians adopted him, by the simple expedient of explaining that he was a natural son of their last Pharaoh.

Human nature being what it is, the Egyptian fable—soon to be entitled *The Testament of Alexander*—found more favor with Europeans than the facts of Roman historians. Wonders were added by each later writer, until it appeared that Nectanebus, the last Pharaoh, had been a magician of great ability who had visited Olympias in the guise of an astrologer and had persuaded her that Zeus himself would visit her bed in the form of a dragon. Whereupon Nectanebus had doubled as the dragon, and Alexander had been born—a child small and limping, but great in courage and acumen. This child had apparently inherited Nectanebus's knack of magic, because he consorted with Amazons and explored the east as far as China, uncovering marvels as he went, after killing his father.

The Iranians also made Alexander a ruler in fable—and an Iranian. He had become in their legendry, the true son of the last of the royal line of Kurush the Achaemenian and not of Philip. True, he had stolen away many of their sacred books to make translations of them; but upon him the royal Glory had descended, as testified by the Magi.

Whereupon, as the story grew with time, Alexander had gone forth to accomplish miracles such as entering the Land of Darkness and engaging the Fagfur or Emperor of China in combat. This *Iskander nameh,* or Persian *Alexander Tale,* took its place in due course in Firdawsi's *Shah-nameh.* It has endured in the popular saga of a hero who overcame all monsters and dangers to bring illumination to his people. This classic has grown to nearly a thousand pages today and is a favorite of children and old folks in Iran who probably know nothing more about the real Iskander than that he burned Persepolis, if that.

In most curious fashion, and perhaps through the Iranian version, Alexander crept into the early tradition of Israel. This holds that Kurush was actually the servant not of Ahura or even Marduk but of Yahweh the God of Israel, who said to him, *"Be thou my shepherd."* So Alexander appears as a vague messiah-king, related to the House of David.

In their deserts the Arab tribes held his figure fast in their imagination, maintaining that *Iskander dhulcarnein,* Alexander of the Two Horns (like Moses), was a hero-saint of Islam, who shattered strange and antagonistic gods of infidel nations.

On their side of the Red Sea the Ethiopians, as might be expected, made a full-scale miracle out of the mysterious figure, who emerges as a Christian apostle, son of the martyred Philip. In this version also Alexander departs on a journey, healing people miraculously.

The Armenians and Syrians took over bits of the wonder tale which by that time had become something of a universal tradition. Even the sophisticated Byzantines adopted Alexander as a hero-king of their own, who had opened up the Silk Route to China. (The first vague description of the silkworm was written in the west by Aristotle, who probably learned of it from Alexander's reports.)

As might be anticipated, when the crusaders entered the nearer east they heard the legend from minstrels in the hall and storytellers in the bazaar. And it lost nothing in the retelling when the crusaders voyaged home. Alexander by then had become timeless and placeless. They interpreted him as a Christian

373

paladin who had gone before them in early days, only he had gone farther. He had built ships on the fetid inland sea and had built the gates of Gog and Magog of brass or iron—accounts differed as to that—to pen up the most savage pagans of the far northeast. On the way thither he had slept with the fascinating but destructive queen of the Amazons who lived in perpetual darkness. Perhaps he had found the Waters of Life. (Many would-be explorers who heard the legend carried salt fish with them, to wash in streams and fountains along the way. They believed that any water which could restore life to such salted fish would be indeed the Waters of Life.)

Perhaps these crusaders beyond the sea heard some Persian poet repeat Firdawsi's words: *He searched for more than anyone has sought. His story lies still on the horizon's rim.*

The imagination of medieval Europe fashioned him into a knight of romance, lavish in giving away the treasures of the earth. *Alisaundre,* it now seemed, searched for the road to Paradise. *Alixandre le Grant* caused the downfall of Rome and went his way through all nations—even, in one version, giving Scotland to England. Beyond the seas, in those regions which were more mysterious than when the real Alexander had traversed them, this knight of romance had lived with cannibals and dog-headed folk, and had plucked jewels in the way of fruit from trees with golden branches, having crossed the vast deserts to the court of Prester John of Asia. In a cage, borne by winged griffons, he explores the sky and receives the submission of all birds. Not content with that, he ventures down into the sea protected by a glass dome, and accepts the fish of all kinds as his subjects.

When books were printed, *Le Romans d' Alixandre* found a place as an international best seller.

After those seventeen centuries Alexander survived in the imagination of the world as the man without a country who had gone forth on the greatest of journeys, who had endured all the dangers that lay beyond the known familiar horizon, and had penetrated the last mysteries of the east. Upon him rested the hopes of human beings. Around him a dream world had taken shape.

The Verdict of Posterity

Twenty-three centuries are a long time, and we are far removed in thought, although not so far advanced as we might suppose, from the world of Alexander. Modern standards, whether better or worse, did not exist then; to try to appraise Alexander's character by modern concepts would be dangerous and probably useless. Was he a great conqueror, master of warfare, statesman, explorer, or scientific philosopher? The terminology will not fit the man.

Can he be compared to a man like Genghis Khan [Chingiz Khan] as a conqueror? The two worked from different motivation toward different ends; the purpose of Genghis Khan is clear, that of Alexander obscure. Plutarch compares him to Gaius Julius Caesar as a statesman; that, seemingly, is the best parallel the versatile author of the *Lives* could find. Did Alexander merely share Aristotle's knowledge of scientific philosophy? Midway in his short life the student turned to new spheres of thought.

He was one of the greatest explorers of this earth of ours—a circumstance that is often overlooked.

In another respect the verdict of posterity has been unjust to Alexander. It was long believed that Alexander the son lacked the administrative ability of Philip the father; that he abandoned Philip's well-ordered hegemony in Macedon-Greece to indulge in a mad attempt to subdue Asia.

On closer scrutiny, the father's national state in revealed as flimsy indeed. Philip had spent much of his youth in Thebes, yet he failed either to conciliate or to occupy that intractable city—it remained for Alexander to do so. Upon Philip's death his exchequer was found to be empty, and his tenancy as captain-general of Hellas most precarious. Aristotle evidently understood the true weakness of Philip's state-building, and warned Alexander against it. Philip could subdue but could not govern. It remained for Alexander to show supreme ability in governing the strange peoples of Asia by assimilating himself to them as if—as David Hogarth points out—he had lived among them during his younger years.

As to his attempt to traverse all Asia, it must be remembered that he had been taught that the habitable world was much smaller than we know it to be today. According to Greek notions, he had reached its northern and southern limits when he encountered the Celts beyond the river Danube and the Scythians in the steppes, and the Ethiopians and the Arabs of the southern deserts, and he was within a little distance of attaining its eastern limit, beyond the Indus.

Perhaps Alexander has been misunderstood in later histories because the Greek and Roman chroniclers who had access to the known facts after him concentrated their narratives on the early years in Macedonia and Greece—where he ruled only a year and a half and accomplished little. Of his infinitely greater accomplishment during the dozen years in Asia these Greeks and Romans knew less and cared not at all. Even the anecdotes given by Plutarch are drawn almost entirely from his boyhood and his reign until he started east from Egypt. There he departed from the horizon known to the Greeks. What happened after that remains obscured except for sparks of detail in Arrian and Quintus Curtius, in a haze of strange names and places.

As for comparison, two kings of the east resemble Alexander in many respects—Assur-bani-pal, the great Assyrian who built the library at Nineveh and tried to lift a militaristic empire into something more humane, and Kurush ["Cyrus the Great"] who first achieved world rule. But Assur-bani-pal came at the end of an epoch, Kurush established new norms upon that same civilization. Alexander tried to create an epoch.

In two respects Alexander can be judged by modern standards—his mastery of warfare and his sanity.

Was he without equal as a military commander, or was he no more than a figurehead of the veteran Macedonian army and its staff?

Against this last lies the fact that he dispensed with the older Macedonian staff (Parmenio, Antigonus, Antipater, Philotas, et cetera), after moving east from Ecbatana, without ill effects. He also reorganized the army itself, introducing horse archers, replacing lancers with javelin throwers, and adding more heavy mounted units as he went along. Practically speaking, he shifted the bulk of the army from foot to horseback. In Turkestan he had to face the new-style maneuvering of the horsemen of the steppes, and he was able to counter that effectively. Five Roman emperors and innumerable legions died or were taken captive later trying to do the same thing. Again in the mountains of Afghanistan, where the Macedonians had their grimmest years, Alexander seemed to be able to devise a new method of warfare. These campaigns in farther Asia have not been recognized by the Greek-Roman historians as the ordeals they were, because less was known about them than of the familiar affair at the Granicus and the surprising victory of Issus.

Arrian, a Roman soldier and governor of a province, said of him that *he was successful in every military operation he undertook.* That, of course, cannot be said of any other commander of men known to history.

The Macedonians revolutionized warfare, W. W. Tarn reminds us, *the great change they made was not this or that technical development, or even better generalship; it was the infusion of a new spirit.*

When Alexander after Gaugamela took steps to prevent his enemy ever fighting again as an organised force, he was doing exactly what Nelson afterwards meant when he said that a victory was not complete if one ship of the line got away. This new spirit is not quite expressed as a change from the amateur to the

377

professional—we almost feel as if we had passed from the ancient to the modern world.

It was rather the intense earnestness and thoroughness they brought to bear on the matter. They had no precedent, but they understood principles; if you had to fight, you fought for all you were worth, and with every sort of weapon except one. They did not, as a rule, practice the things we call atrocities; on balance, Macedonian warfare was distinctly more humane than either Greek or Roman. . . . But if unorthodox methods helped you, if it aided your military operations to start a revolution, to employ propaganda, to create a combination reaching from Epirus to India, you did just these things as part of the day's work. When somebody put to Antigonus Gonatus the question beloved of later text-book writers: "How should one attack the enemy?" his answer was, "Any way that seems useful."[1]

Before the Macedonians, armies had shut up shop during the winter seasons, and often during harvest time. The Macedonians rather favored working in winter. In the older Greek days sieges had been sit-down affairs in the main, with each side waiting to tire the other out. Under Philip's staff, and especially under Alexander, methods were devised for breaking into a fortified place quickly.

How much Alexander contributed to this new scientific warfare can only be inferred. Certainly he launched the Macedonians on the seas. They had been accustomed to rapid marching before him; under him they broke through the barriers of distance and natural obstacles. He was the first commander to drive his forces in headlong pursuit after an engagement, often for days at a time, as after Gaugamela. And he had an intuitive sense of the turn of a battle—the right moment to launch a final attack.

On the other hand, there was something lacking in Alexander as a master of the art of war. He could be drawn into accepting challenges, as at Thebes, or the

---

[1]*Hellenistic Military and Naval Development,* 1930.

Granicus, or the rock of Aornus, or at that last river crossing of the Jhelum. Repeatedly he gambled all his resources, winning every time. True, he had a very efficient intelligence service, and he gambled for great stakes; but the supreme masters of warfare do not gamble in that way. We cannot conceive of Hannibal—who led much the same type of mixed command, held together by loyalty to him—attempting what Alexander of Macedon accomplished.

Moreover it was the Macedonian staff, not he, which actually led the way from Pella and Thebes, as far as Tyre—if not to the turning point of the move from Egypt. Alexander's life was saved at least twice by the men of his command in that period of initiation. If we discount the recorded remark of Deiades that he—the engineer—captured Tyre with Alexander's assistance, we cannot pass over the fact that the Macedonian king-commander spent most of his time during the siege of Tyre exploring the back country, nearly losing his life again in the process. (Curtis affirms that Alexander went inland to protect Macedonian stone-cutting and wood-gathering parties from attacks by Arab tribes. But a commanding general does not usually act as guard for foragers unless he wants to be there.)

Then we are faced by Alexander's extraordinary silence on military affairs. He has left us no commentary on battle, or any ordered plan for battle. We would expect the Roman compilers, Arrian especially, to write down some maxim or opinion of this unequaled leader. Philip certainly made caustic comments after Chaeronea, and Parmenio apparently censored Alexander severely for his mistakes in tactics at the Granicus. Down the coast at Miletus it was Parmenio who argued the strategical advantage of a fleet. And again, before Gaugamela, it was Parmenio and the other officers who argued whether to make a night attack or to go on the defensive by fortifying the rear of the Macedonian position. Alexander went to sleep and overslept on the eve of his greatest engagement.

His orders, as they have survived, are of routes to be followed, bridges to be built, movement and medical care of troops, conduct of the officers in occupied territory, cases of individual soldiers or prisoners. Questions are of the characteristics of elephants, the force of river currents, rigging of ships. Only in talks to the men before an engagement does he reveal an intimate understanding of the military situation—as in pointing out before Issus that they were in contact with the main strength of the Iranians, and before Gaugamela that the units facing them were not the same as at Issus. But these talks were to encourage the men.

In the same way the monuments he ordered raised and the ceremonies held after an engagement were intended to honor the dead there rather than to exalt the memory of the Macedonian as a victor—the exception being the pillars he built to mark the final point of advance at the Beas, where no battle took place.

Unmistakably Alexander did not like to talk about military matters. Battle cunning he acquired in battle itself, and he learned the problems of command on the march as he had mastered the sciences and navigation while en route. His quick imagination dealt here as elsewhere with the most practical details—ropemaking, bits for the horses, cures for snakebite, the mood of war-weary men, the mental weakness of a Darius.

Only twice was he in trouble for supplies: in the crossing of the Hind-i-Kuh in winter and in the desert of the Mekran. Only once was he caught in ignorance of enemy movements: on the shore at Issus.

Alexander could be an inflexible as Genghis Khan in hunting down an enemy or destroying an enemy's power to resist. Yet he seemed to lack the Mongol's exultation in victory. By instinct, he was not a master of war; yet he could accomplish miracles with men when he chose to do so.

The Macedonian army served him as an instrument of exploration, of settlement, and of reaching the objectives of his dream world. The army, under him, became a moving nation, a creator of peoples, as manifold in its operation as a harvesting machine. Certainly he drove the veterans as he drove himself, beyond the point of human endurance. Strangely, in so doing, he won their unalterable devotion.

But as a leader of men he remains without equal. He was, in other matters, a genius.

The Successors knew his methods and applied them, without being able to get the results he obtained. With abundant gold they could hire soldiery, and they began to rely on heterogeneous elements like a camel corps and armored elephants. In the west, especially, individual monarchs paid lavishly for new war machines. Alexandrian scientists experimented with the "Greek" fire or "sea fire" that was produced from some combination of bitumen, pitch, sulphur, or petroleum, and could burn on water. Something like a steam engine was developed at Alexandria, along with novel siege engines, and Archimedes—who had little joy in the occupation—perfected a screw pump to bail out warships, and harnessed a fraction of the sun's heat by means of a giant concave mirror, or concentration of mirrors. For his master Heiro, tyrant of Syracuse, he worked out conveyor systems and gears for moving enormous weights—saying that he could move the earth if he had a place to stand on outside.

By such destructive war engines individual monarchs in the west could enhance their hold over serfdom and over their neighbors. Yet nothing of consequence came out of their small set-tos. Carthage, which had made itself a warehouse of eastern trade, could afford to hire an army entire. Hannibal's celebrated command was made up of these special forces, mercenaries, Numidian horse archers, an elephant corps.

The armies of the Roman Republic only with great difficulty disposed of Hannibal, and of the war engines at Syracuse, and then the elephants of Antiochus. By the time they had done so the legions had been altered into more flexible fighting teams, much like Alexander's Hypaspists, and the Romans had become masters of the new Hellenistic artillery and battle fleets. But they never mastered, as Alexander had done, the intractable soul of Asia.

The Romans built, as historians have pointed out, on foundations laid down by Alexander in the east, without being able to carry out his design.

The Manic Stages

Unquestionably Alexander had worn out his mind as well as his body in the last few years. The manic stages can be traced clearly, after his murder of Parmenio. Cassander gives evidence that toward the end *Alexander had lost his spirit, and his belief in the protection of the gods, and had grown suspicious of his old friends.* The massacre of the *Branchidae,* the spasmodic slaughter of prisoners and harrying of fugitives during the last phase in India, as well as the constant risking of his own life, showed that his mind was affected.

At that time he took to the nightly drinking spells which became constant thereafter, as well as the attacks of melancholia after the deaths of men like Cleitus and Hephaestion. At this stage he seemed to be driven by an uncontrollable force to journey on, dreading to return to a familiar scene or city, or to resume the routine of administration. Perhaps he routed his army across the Mekran with some idea of punishing it after its mutiny.

There is no evidence of sadism or megalomania, as in the case of the Romans, Caligula or Nero. According to the chroniclers who were with him, he seemed to be alarmed by unusual happenings and unfavorable omens after the return to the Tigris. Still, he remained reasonable when appealed to.

At Nysa, where the Macedonians discovered the ivy they cherished so much, Alexander levied upon the city a hundred of its most intelligent and respected men, to accompany the Macedonians. When he explained that, the headman of Nysa laughed.

"What amuses you?" Alexander asked.

"If you take a hundred of our best men, we won't have many left to run the city. Why not take two hundred of our worst men instead?"

Alexander would not do that, yet he agreed with the headman's viewpoint and took two hostages from that individual's family instead of the hundred leading citizens.

The military spectacles he ordered—the races, parades, and games—were intended to relax and amuse the troops. A gladiatorial contest would be the last thing one would expect from Alexander. The orgy of marriages at Susa was no more than an attempt to popularize intermarriage among his peoples.

Apparently he suffered from no illusions of grandeur—of which many Greek writers accused him. Instead he abandoned the custom of prostration in his presence; he contrived an agreement with the mutinous veterans on the Tigris, and refused to order the grandiose project of the architect Stasicrates for an everlasting memorial to himself to be carved out of Mount Athos—a project which would have delighted Nero—and did not allow his own head to be struck on the new coinage, in place of the image of Zeus. (Alexander's head, carved by Lysippus, was placed on the coinage of his immediate Successors, complete with lion's mane and paw.) In the last days on the Euphrates he occupied himself with clearing out the obstructions to navigation and testing the new shipping he hoped to use on the voyage to Arabia.

Arrian says that he may have started his last expedition against the Kassites in the mountains with the thought of making a holocaust, as sacrifice to the shade of Hephaestion. But in that month of spring Alexander was at Ecbatana, where the mountain foliage would have been fresh and the climate still cold as the mountains of Macedon. He had always liked to explore a new route, and he must have dreaded the return to the heat of the Tigris plain, and to the responsibilities awaiting him in Babylon.

He did go to Babylon, against the warning of the

priests of Marduk and his own desire. Nearchus and his commanders were waiting there for him. It was natural, in his near exhaustion, that he kept to the mountains as long as possible, on the pretext of punishing the tribes. In this effort there is no trace of megalomania, but rather clear evidence of an invincible determination to go through with what must be done. The wreck of a man forced itself on, toward the royal palace.

Even in Babylon he tried desperately to start out again on his ships.

If Alexander had abandoned his dominion before then, at Ecbatana, and had gone on wandering through new lands and strange people, he might have lived.

NOTES

The greater part of this book was written in Asia during the war. It so happened that I followed out for more than two years the course of Alexander's journeying, except within northern India. Macedonia, Greece, and most of the Aegean islands had been visited after the last war. So as far as the journey itself is concerned, I had seen almost all of the land over which the Macedonians passed, during wartime.

For any mistakes in the Greek names, in personalities and facts, I offer my apology. The identity of "Barsine," for instance, is uncertain; and there seem to have been more than two Ptolemys and two officers of the name of Coenus with the Macedonian army, and these may have been confused in some of the happenings.

The pages of an English translation of Arrian's long chronicle were taken along; a Latin edition of Quintus Curtius was picked up on the way; a French edition of Strabo, and Plutarch's *Lives* were found in the Archeological Museum in Teheran. Aristotle's works, both in Arabic and English, were found in Baghdad. A worried Greek minister lent a copy of Demosthenes's orations, in French. An American archaeologist, Dr. Joseph Upton, then in Iran, lent a copy of Sir Aurel Stein's commentary on Alexander's route across the Mekran.

More help was gleaned from the fine library of the American University in Beirut. Along the route oriental scholars aided in giving data on the eastern peoples and culture of that time, as well as in restoring the cities as Alexander must have found them. Archeological details were pieced together to form a rather full picture of all that the Macedonians must have found in their venture into the east.

This book is an endeavor to re-create for the reader today that journey of the Macedonians, under Alexander.

So this book is a re-creation from imagination only in the sense that details were pieced together from different sources on the scene itself, in an attempt to form a whole. It is an attempt to visualize Alexander as he was at that time, to see what he might well have seen in his long journey, and to consider the people and the problems with which he had to deal.

After twenty-two hundred years details cannot easily be verified. But it is possible to make certain of the knowledge *then* possessed by the Greeks, Egyptians, Iranians, Syrians, and other peoples. For that would have been shared by Alexander.

Ideology that came after Alexander has no place in this book.

Index

388

389

392

393

SHERLOCK HOLMES FANS! REJOICE—HERE IS SOLAR PONS, MASTER DETECTIVE IN SIX BRILLIANT DETECTIVE STORIES.

"Only August Derleth perceived the obvious truth—that the vacuum had to be filled. And how admirably Solar Pons fills it."

—*The New York Times*

"None is more worthy than Pons to wear the deerstalker."

—*San Francisco Chronicle*

"These stories recall, as nothing else has done, those delicious days and nights on Baker Street."

—*Louisville Journal*

"A *tour de force* . . . avowedly an imitation . . . it is more; it is an excellent series in detection in its own right."

—*Chicago Tribune*